G000256790

mily Tree

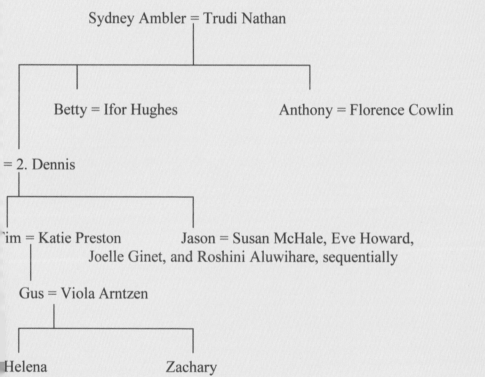

Sydney Ambler = Trudi Nathan

Betty = Ifor Hughes                    Anthony = Florence Cowlin

= 2. Dennis

'im = Katie Preston          Jason = Susan McHale, Eve Howard,
                 Joelle Ginet, and Roshini Aluwihare, sequentially

Gus = Viola Arntzen

Helena                    Zachary

# The Lucky Marketeer

# The Lucky
# Marketeer

## Tim Ambler

For Helena and Zachary

ISBN 978-1-870948-02-9
Copyright © 2014 Tim Ambler
First published 2014
No part of this work may be reproduced in any form and by any
means without prior written permission of the author or publisher.
Published by:
JJG Publishing
Sparrow Hall
Hindringham
Norfolk NR21 0DP
Designed by Graham Hiles
Printed in China through Colorcraft Ltd, Hong Kong

# Contents

# Foreword

My not-to-be-denied but otherwise lovely wife, Katie, has been pressing me, for some time now, to write these memoirs. My resistance has been due to their likely similarity to those dreadful Christmas letters only, being longer, worse. They are intended for our grandchildren but I hope they will entertain anyone else into whose hands they fall.

My editor and publisher, Quill Greenwood, to whom I am extremely grateful, demanded to know who the non-family readers might be and why they should read this personal story. To some extent the booze business has been central but I think the thread is thicker than that. I became a convert to marketing at MIT in 1969 and every private and public venture since then has been as a marketeer, first as a practitioner in the UK and then internationally, then with London Business School as a researcher, teacher and writer and finally with the Adam Smith Institute, trying to persuade government to use less red tape and better marketing to achieve its goals.

The memoirs chronicle the times of a lucky person in a lucky generation. From evading the Japanese invasion of Malaya and U-Boats on the way back, an attempt to burn the house down when Oxford was being bombed, joyful schooling and national service when no serious warfare was afoot, to a career in that happiest in all businesses, the wine trade, semi-retirement in academia and full retirement with music and the best of company. Luck has been plentiful and disasters even more so but I will spare you those. Best of all was finding a spouse, who has put up with aggravation for almost 50 years and added joy to all of them. She read and commented on the first draft of these memoirs.

Especial thanks go also to family and colleagues who were good enough to read and comment on individual chapters: Paddy Barwise (especially), John Brackenbury, George Bull, Marah Dickson-Wright, Christopher Pearman, Dudley Plunkett, William Swabey and Nader Tavassoli. Thanks also go to all those others, mostly chronicled in these memoirs who provided help, fun and friendship over the years.

# Foreword

*Disclaimers*:

Occasions are frequently recounted as conversations. I have no diaries and although the episodes are as accurate as I can make them, the words chosen are not exact and should be regarded as fiction. Indeed, these chapters are all memories, not necessarily realities, and maybe it is all fiction.

I have only named the names of those I like, admire and approve. The unnamed may or may not recognise themselves but if they are offended, they must be wrong. No hurt is intended.

I have written enough academic papers and this is not one of them. A few footnotes are included but by no means all references and acknowledgements.

And finally thanks to Graham Hiles for design and Gill Jarrett for pulling the typescript together.

# The Lucky Generation

We are the lucky generation. Consider just these matters:

- We did not have to fight in the big wars.
- We caught the end of National Service which set so many of us up for life. It was, mostly, good fun and I have yet to regain the standard of living I had then in Singapore.
- University was funded wholly by government and little work was required.
- Jobs were easy to get.
- We saw the rise and fall of Communism without, in this country, a drop of blood being shed.
- The UK government picked up the tab for us to attend US business schools as there were none in the UK.
- We hit the dark economic days of the 1970s early enough in our careers for the ensuing economic march to be, for us, all upward.
- 20 years at London Business School showed just how unfettered UK academics have been.
- We were the last generation to receive generous company pensions.
- Better still we rode the property escalator from 1965 onwards and upwards. With a decent house one accumulated significant capital whilst just lying in bed.

Marketeers are supposed to spread pleasure, make more enjoyable a world that takes itself too seriously. My generation of marketeers has been lucky indeed.

# Chapter 1

# What we did in the War

*The two signature events of May 1937 were crowning George VI on the 12th and my arrival, late, on the 30th. One should not interrupt a good coronation. After a lengthy stay in the Buckinghamshire nursing home and then with her parents in Lyme Regis, my mother returned to Kuala Kangsar with infant in tow. This chapter describes my wartime and in particular:*
- *A timely escape from Malaya*
- *Walmington-on-Sea, a.k.a. Lyme Regis*
- *Loch Fyne with the Nobles*
- *Dennis's and Peter's wars*

As a young woman, my mother Patricia was beautiful but wild. She was brilliant with horses but not with Society. As her father's military salary did not stretch to her doing the Season, her rich aunt Amy provided the wherewithal. It proved unsuccessful and Amy broke the rules in doing it again the following year. None of the debs' delights took the bait and the family was relieved when Godfrey Wilkinson, a Forestry Commission Officer on leave from Malaya, proposed. His social credentials passed muster and his brother was a director of Shell.

Colin was born in Ipoh in 1928 but the marriage was never going to work. Even so, it was 10 years before Patricia teamed up with a new partner. Dennis was from Yorkshire stock. After a classics scholarship from Shrewsbury to St John's Oxford, where he partied long and hard, his lowly degree was deemed a disgrace, at least by him and his mother Trudi. Trudi's brother Jen was a District Officer in Malaya and they shipped him out to teach at the Malay College, Kuala Kangsar, the traditional royal capital of Malaya. The Malay College was modelled on the British public school and Dennis took to it like a goose to roast potatoes.

Some might think it careless to make illicit love in the centre of the world's rubber plantations without the use of one of its products but my parents always insisted that my arrival was a deliberate and public manifestation of their blissful union. Whether the bliss extended to Godfrey, I know not, but the imminence of war delayed the formalities.

Britain finally declared war on Germany on 1st September 1939 and Patricia's father, Wilfred, died of a stroke 12 days later. He had served very bravely throughout WWI. According to Patricia's account: 'An old soldier, he saw no place for himself in this conflict. This, and the possibility of both his sons being killed, distressed him deeply.' He was only 68 and it was a shock for the family. Patricia was ordered to take the next ship home.

Shipping movements became classified information. Patricia was lucky to find a ship at all and was delighted it was the *Viceroy of India*, one of P&O's finest. She did not wish to abandon our black cat. On arrival in Penang she bought a hamper, attached a posy of what looked very like white heather and a message: 'Good luck'. She hired a rowing boat to take it straight to the Captain. Seamen are superstitious folk, she figured, and no Captain would refuse luck.

On the voyage the cat learnt where to find our cabin (and food) but, according to Patricia: 'The cat continually misbehaved itself on the Chinese embroidered cushions of the Chief Officer, whom the Captain disliked.' The cat became a valued and beloved pet so far as the Captain was concerned.

She wrote that 'the daily bulletins of war news sounded most unrealistic in those, still halcyon, days of blue seas and skies on the way to Colombo' – and then Bombay. The Admiralty instructed that passenger ships were now to be painted the same grey as warships. Whilst this took place, the passengers stayed at the Taj Mahal hotel in Bombay.

As we were about to re-board the newly-painted ships, the Admiralty changed what passes for its mind: passenger ships would be in more danger if they looked like warships than if they didn't. P&O passenger ships were to be repainted back in their original beige and black. Of course we now know that U Boats regarded all British shipping, civilian or military as fair game, but they didn't then. The Admiralty then decided to place a few small guns about the deck. Also not a good idea as they were too small to be effective but large enough to give a military appearance. All they did was to shatter the glass on the upper decks when they were fired. After testing, they weren't used again.

Patricia much enjoyed her two weeks in Bombay. She rode race-horses at the Turf Club in the cool of the morning. I had an ayah and we spent most of our days at the Breach Candy swimming club, south of Bombay. Money restrictions in Malaya meant that she had little cash but with her looks she was not short of partners and danced all night, every night.

Unaccountably we were transferred to the *Stratheden* whose Captain was the brother of our Captain French on the *Viceroy*. Sibling rivalry promoted a race home but they sailed into Gibraltar side by side.

In Gibraltar the brothers French were summoned to Admiralty House. The two naval officers on board each ship were ordered to take command. Navigational directions were to be implemented to the exact letter and involved complicated zigzags across the Bay of Biscay. The brothers French were not impressed. Full speed on a direct course seemed to them much safer. One said 'he was damned if he was going to be treated like the Captain of a tramp steamer'. Once at sea they told the naval officers to stand down or be locked in their cabins. As it turned out, we were lucky: there really had been a lurking submarine, but the brothers French were right: in those days, a passenger liner at full speed was faster than a U Boat. The submarine was later sunk as were both the *Viceroy* and the *Stratheden*.

Coincidentally, one of my best friends, 60 years later at London Business School, was John Stopford who had come back from Singapore with his mother and brother a few months later. John was also born in 1937. Their ship was torpedoed by a submarine in the Bay of Biscay with huge loss of life including his mother. The two boys were rescued from the sea by strangers and it was quite a while before they were reunited. A dreadful experience.

We rejoined my grandmother, Maud, in Lyme Regis which could have been the model for the Walmington-on-Sea of *Dad's Army*. 120 years earlier it had been a fashionable place to visit – as Jane Austen did in 1818. By WWII it was, so far as Patricia was concerned, down-right dull. Patricia became a volunteer for the ARP (Air Raid Precautions – the Warden in *Dad's Army*) and I dimly recall spending time with her in a cellar up the hill a bit, amid tin helmets, cigarette smoke and endless cups of tea. We were waiting for something to happen. It never did.

In autumn 1941, Patricia decided to make house again with ex-husband-to-be Godfrey, now a Lieutenant in the Royal Navy. I have no idea why a Malayan forestry expert would suddenly become an RN Lieutenant. His 'ship', HMS *Royal Arthur*, had been the Butlin's Skegness Holiday Camp before being requisitioned and converted to the UK reception depot for all naval recruits. The parade ground was, at least to the eye of a four-year-old, immense. I was brought to watch the recruits endlessly marching up and down. It didn't seem like 'life on the ocean wave' to me and I never did understand why those about to be tightly packed into metal warships had to be so drilled in marching.

We, thank goodness, were installed in a b&b in town and not in one of Billy Butlin's freezing cabins as the recruits were. 1941/2 was bitterly cold. One winter in wartime Skegness was enough and Patricia was determined to make a more personal contribution to the war effort. Military Intelligence seemed just the thing.

Spring 1942 saw us transported to a small flat which made up the first floor of a north Oxford house. Patricia, like many other colonials, was employed to sift through holiday snaps and other photographic records of territory now in enemy hands, in her case Malaya. All the photos were black and white and most of them were less than two inches square. The idea was to help the RAF pinpoint drop zones for supply to guerrillas and insurgents but the effort cannot have been worthwhile. From above, one piece of jungle looks exactly like another. Indeed it looks that way from below too.

Patricia may have taken up painting again in Lyme Regis and she had more formal tuition by taking a year or so – it cannot have been the full three year course – at the Slade School, transferred from London to Ruskin College Oxford 1939-46 to escape the bombing. In the event, Oxford did not escape the bombing (Cowley, I think, copped it) and I do remember bombs raining down and lighting up the night sky as we made our way to the bomb shelter. They looked like fireworks to me.

During the day I was left alone in the flat, although Patricia must have come home for lunch. The authorities today would be shocked by leaving a five-year-old without supervision for hours on end. I recall being bored but not otherwise bothered. The upside was that I spent most of the time learning to read. There were only adult books in the flat so I never did catch up with Enid Blyton or other books for young children.

There was only one drama but it was quite a big one. The heating was a gas fire and I decided to investigate the flammability of cotton wool. Do not bother to look for reasons for five-year-olds doing daft things; it all looked quite sensible to me at the time.

Glueing some cotton wool onto one of the tapers used to light the fire, and holding it to the flame produced indifferent results. The cotton wool caught but no more than that – even with the spirit-based glue. Time to upgrade the experiment. I arranged the full pack of cotton wool on the window sill and lit it with a taper. This was far more satisfactory. It went up with a whoosh and so did the curtains. That was frightening. I will always remember the upturned, horrified face of a woman on the street seeing me in the burning window. Luckily a phone box was nearby and so were other people. The door was knocked down and I was ushered out.

It was extremely pleasing to attract no fewer than five fire engines. A very large, he seemed to me, policeman arrived to ask what had happened and was very sympathetic. He indicated this could have happened to anyone. By the time Patricia got back, the fire was out but the flat was black and very wet. The policeman was still there and a great deal less nice to Patricia than he had been to me. Quite hurtful, in fact.

By now, Patricia was bored with her Oxford job. Maybe she had done all she could. She reasoned that racehorse stable lads had been called up and her best contribution would be taking one of their places in Newmarket. The problem was that I could not be expected, still less allowed, to entertain myself. She must have telephoned her cousin, and my godmother, Anastasia Noble (1911-2000)* who lived with other Nobles in a huge Edwardian pile, Ardkinglas, on the edge of Loch Fyne, north of Glasgow. 'Send him up' and I was promptly on the train headed north.

The Nobles made a fortune through their control of the Armstrong Whitworth company in north-east England. John Noble decided to spend some of his wealth, as was the fashion of the day, in building a Scottish baronial mansion on the southern shore of Loch Fyne, near Cairndow. This was Ardkinglas: completed in 1905, it had every possible con that was then mod. Across the water was Inveraray, the seat

---

* Two of my grandmother Maud's sisters, Amy and Mary Ethel, married Sir John and Sir George Noble respectively. Anastasia was Amy's daughter.

of the Duke of Argyll and head of the Campbells with whom they soon became involved. John became the Baronet of Ardkinglas in 1923.

According to niece Veronica, Sir John became, by WWI, one of the richest men in Britain and the owner of the largest private yacht on the Mediterranean. He married my grandmother Maud's sister Amy (later also spelt Amie and sometimes Aimée). Veronica's memoirs are a charming description of decreasing finances but increasing happiness beginning with sailing in her uncle's yacht and concluding with her just having finished mucking out the pigs on Christmas day so that her farmer son could enjoy the day with his family.

Sir John was reserved but Great Aunt Amy was anything but. She was beautiful, flighty and fun. I only knew her in her 70s, but she was still all of those things. At a lunch party at the English Speaking Union in the 1950s she was a joy to sit beside: amusing, interesting and interested. She would descend to stay with relations at a moment's notice. Dennis and Patricia got one telegram on a Friday in Singapore in the late 1940s saying something like 'Darlings – I'm now in Hong Kong so I thought it would be fun briefly to stay with you. Only a week. I'll see you Monday. No need to meet my flight. Much love Amy'.

She then wafted in trailing (and losing) diamonds. She never took 'no' for an answer and, in any case, my mother owed her for two Seasons.

Anastasia, my godmother, was the only Noble not to marry. She became one of the two top breeders of Scottish deerhounds, an animal that would otherwise have become extinct. As the name implies, they were large and fast, rather like an overgrown greyhound with long hair. With Patricia's enthusiasm for greyhounds, coursing and country pursuits, it was no surprise that they got on well.

When Johnnie inherited Ardkinglas about 35 years later, it was saddled with hefty estate duties, a large work force and losing money. After land sales and various schemes, 'Loch Fyne Oysters' proved very successful.

There is not much to say about my time there. It was a beautiful place to be and the family was kind, especially Elizabeth, the chatelaine, and the governess. It was my first schooling of any kind and she did a good job. The house was simply huge with great long corridors and plenty of space for playing. Being wartime, few of the rooms were warm but the summer months were fine. As the youngest of the four, I was, understandably, looked down upon by the others. We all wore kilts in Campbell tartan. I remember being unconvinced that we were entitled to do so, certainly I wasn't, but they are extremely sensible children's clothing to pass on down the line.

Godfrey paid a visit once and he must have made a major effort to do so. The roads were empty but poor and it was a great distance. So it was a big kindness to the little boy but he must have felt a bit out of place. We didn't have a lot to say to each other.

When the idyll was over, Patricia came up to collect me if only to spend time catching up with Anastasia and the deerhounds. South we went by bus and then train and I was back in the war.

Patricia had set up home in East Ilsley, just north of Newbury on the main road to Oxford. The Kennet House racing stables, the oldest in Berkshire, established by the Duke of Cumberland in the early 19th C, were just across the road, and provided Patricia with some employment.

One surprise was that while I was in Scotland and she was in Newmarket, she had become a Roman Catholic. The priest in Newmarket was clearly amusing and charming and not too doctrinal. Patricia was never likely to learn the Catechism. She had Catholic friends but most of all she was a rebel and did not like to conform. She was spiritual but not religious. Later in life she explored all kinds of spirituality both eastern and western and her catholicism was, to put it mildly, liberal. However much she wavered, and she did, she ended her days in close contact with a wonderful Catholic priest in Christ Church who conducted her funeral.

Her conversion was probably to annoy her mother who was the blackest of black Northern Irish protestants. Maud mellowed with age but to her dying day she was convinced that the Pope was an agent of Satan. When, after the war, she came to live near us on Harrow-on-the-Hill, she was convinced that the papists were digging a tunnel from the Vatican so they could pop up by her door and whisk her back to Rome. I used to ask, in the annoying way small boys do, why they would tunnel up to the top of the hill, when it would be much easier to come out at the bottom.

My step-brother Colin was with us now, having been chucked out of at least two schools. The term 'learning difficulties' had not been invented, still less catered for. As he was all his life, he was fascinated by stamps and traded in them by post. He certainly never made money from them but he cannot have lost much either as he didn't have any and nor did Patricia beyond the essentials for housing and food. At 16 Colin was available for employment but there wasn't much around East Ilsley even in wartime. He was completely uninterested in sport or exercise. Me too. Apart from stamps, we passed the time, for a while, with cards and Monopoly. Colin was clever in his way, and cunning certainly, but he also cheated. After some huge rows, Patricia decreed that we should no longer attempt to play together.

Not far away in West Ilsley lived Patricia's best friend of those days, Mike [sic] Edwards, the wife of probably the most famous Oxford rowing coach, Hugh but always known as Jumbo. Here is an extract from Wikipedia: 'After rowing in the 1930 Oxford Blue Boat, in the 1932 Olympics he won the gold medal in the coxless pairs event with Lewis Clive, and a second gold in the Great Britain coxless four.

'During the Second World War Edwards served in the RAF, once saving his own life by rowing four miles through a minefield in a dinghy after his plane crashed in the Atlantic Ocean. He was invited back to be a member of the Oxford coaching team in 1949, although resigned in 1957 after a disagreement with the Australian-born President, Roderick Carnegie. He was brought back in 1959 by OUBC President Ronnie Howard, but provoked a rebellion by certain members of the crew over his demands on them. Despite the resignation of certain members of the squad, Oxford beat Cambridge, and his subsequent coaching efforts made him an Oxford legend. In 1962, he coached the Wales four containing his two sons that won silver at the Commonwealth Games in Perth, Australia.'

His sons John and David were roughly my contemporaries and we got on well enough. Jumbo was mostly away but a large and amiable presence when he was around. The war was now my major interest, reading the daily press (propaganda, much of it) and lying on the downs watching the planes circling above. Of course they were British or American by then but I liked to imagine some might be German and I would see a dogfight or, better, nuns descending on parachutes. We were all convinced that German paratroopers would dress up as nuns to fool us. There was a Royal Observer Corps observation post up on the downs and I often used to drop in to see them. It was a measure of how bored they must have been, in early 1944, that they seemed quite pleased to see me.

The unique skill of ROC personnel, believe it or not, was that they could distinguish between Allied and German warplanes and they had silhouettes to help them do so. Their finest hour was, as part of the D-Day landings, when they were allocated to US Navy and armed merchant shipping and put in charge of the ships' anti-aircraft guns. Surprising that the US Navy permitted that but it seems they did. The objective, of course, was to avoid 'friendly fire' at Allied warplanes. It worked splendidly and the RAF later reported that the only friendly fire was from Royal Navy vessels.

After D-Day – big excitement that – the daily maps of progress with the arrows as in the introduction to episodes of *Dad's Army* were the highlight of each day.

Although photographs make the A34 through East Ilsley seem wide, it really was not. It was quiet enough when we arrived but as D-Day approached one unending line of traffic passed by, and occasionally into, our house. Almost all of them were American and their boys had not got the hang of driving large trucks through narrow winding English villages.

School was a problem. The most suitable, I gathered, was Gorselands – about as far south of Newbury as we were north. Public transport, i.e. the bus, was dire. Although a private day school, they also accepted weekly boarders including me. We spent much time on music which was jolly enough but I never managed to beat my assigned tambourine on time.

A year or so later, it was up sticks again and off to Pewsey, further down the Kennet valley in the middle of Wiltshire, i.e. the middle of nowhere. It was more of a small town than a village so that was an improvement.

Patricia and Dennis, still in the Far East, must have been in communication and the pretty little cottage up a lane from Pewsey centre would have seemed, as indeed it was, far more romantic than the East Ilsley house on the main road. The cottage was called Black Mikes and it was owned by Jumbo and Mike Edwards who rented it to us on friendly terms. The name may have been given by Jumbo; it would certainly have amused them both.

Colin had gone off to his father, Godfrey, and Patricia and I experienced country life at its most primitive. Milk, cheese, junket and puddings were from the long suffering goat. Transport was by pony and trap, most agreeable when things went well but they didn't always. After helping harness the pony, my job was to hold its head while Patricia clambered into the trap. A well-schooled pony knows all about that and waits patiently. Our ponies, however, were usually bought from farmers who had good reasons for getting rid of them.

Sometimes I could persuade an irritated pony (horses were better – as a rule of thumb, the smaller the animal the worse behaved it is) to hang around for the embarkation process; sometimes I couldn't. I lost count of the number of occasions I was left standing beside the road as the pony and trap disappeared into the middle distance. They always returned but not necessarily soon. Maybe we were giving them too many oats.

Another clear memory is our efforts to supplement rations which officially were:

---

**Rations for 1 Week for 1 Person**
- 1oz cheese (Roughly about 2 inch by 1 inch by half inch cube, barely enough to fill 1 sandwich)
- 2oz tea (Equivalent to about 20 teabags today)
- 2oz jam spread
- 4oz bacon or ham
- 8oz sugar
- 1 shilling's worth of meat
- 8oz fats of which only 2oz could be butter

---

Later sweets and tinned goods could be had on a points system. Bread was not rationed until after the war in 1946. For many rationing was harder after the war in the late 40s and early 50s than during the war.

Having not so much as boiled an egg before the war, Patricia was by now quite a decent cook – but rations for one-and-a-half did not go far. Milk was plentiful and that took care of puddings (custard and junket) and eggs were always available in the country. Meat was the problem. The theory was that the greyhound would catch hares but that did not work because it requires two dogs and enough space to work in. The fields round Pewsey were too small and the open spaces too far away for our transport. So it had to be rabbits, then much bigger and better.

We acquired a couple of ferrets. The trouble with ferreting is that you are always one net short. Having found a likely warren and spent ages covering every hole, the ferret is inserted under one net and off it goes joyfully into the tunnels. After a few minutes a rabbit whistles out of the one hole you did not see and failed to net. Followed by the others and a rather rueful ferret.

It wasn't always like that and we did get a decent supply, sometimes due to the greyhound standing at third man and catching one of the rabbits flying out of the unnetted hole. We only had one seriously disagreeable day when the farmer wielding a shot gun caught us unawares and demanded to know why we were poaching on his land. I'm not sure now what the law is but rabbits are surely vermin and open to all takers – but the farmer wasn't much interested in the law. He marched us back to his farm at the point of his 12 bore which he said was loaded. Patricia made out she wasn't frightened but I certainly was. He ushered us into an outhouse and locked the door. Now that certainly was illegal but who was arguing? After what seemed an eternity to me but was probably only an hour, he returned, ushered us out and made threatening noises about not doing it again. We didn't. There were plenty of other warrens.

A Catholic boarding prep school was now deemed the thing for me, not least because my Catholic education to-date had been precisely nil. St Richard's, Little Malvern, was selected. They claimed to send boys on to Downside which Patricia, with or without input from Dennis, had decided would be my public school. We even drove, with Mike Edwards, to Downside for Midnight Mass at Christmas.

St Richard's is still going. From its website: 'St Richard's was founded in 1921 by John Keble, an Oxford MA and published poet, and his wife Audrey. The school opened at Aucott House, Malvern, with six boys, and moved after ten years to the old presbytery at St Wulstan's, Little Malvern, where it remained until 1968.' The Kebles were still in charge when I arrived 23 or 24 years later.

It was a jolly enough place. The food was dreadful but it was wartime. The standard evening meal was bread and dripping washed down with cocoa without much milk. The academic work was dictated by the endgame: common entrance. I came top in maths and bottom in handicraft. I seem to recall that my woodwork contribution – and admittedly I had done little on it – was pronounced the worst contribution the master had ever seen. But most of the teachers were elderly and grumpy.

There were some games (cricket and rugby) but most often we trailed up the road to the Malvern Hills and cast our eyes over Housman country which seemed as bleak as most of his poetry. I was there certainly a year and maybe two before Dennis decided it was insufficiently stretching and, as they had moved to Harrow-on-the-Hill, I was then sent to Harrow's main feeder prep school, Orley Farm, an excellent choice. Before considering that, it is time to relate as much as I know of Dennis's and of Uncle Peter's wars.

Japanese soldiers walked ashore in north-east Malaya just after midnight on 8th December 1941, 90 minutes before they attacked Pearl Harbour. Japanese war planning was nothing if not precise. As at Pearl Harbour it was a complete surprise. Nevertheless British forces, largely Indian Army and the Australians, fought a rearguard action until the whole of Malaya, bar Singapore, was in Japanese hands by the end of January.

As is famously known, Lt General Arthur Percival, arguably the worst general in British history, had six weeks to prepare the defence of Singapore, their key target, but insisted on pointing his guns and defences toward the south when the Japanese were advancing from the north. For a wonderful analysis of Percival's mindset, see *On the Psychology of Military Incompetence* by Norman F Dixon.

Thanks to his stupidity, all 2000 men of the Royal Norfolk Regiment were handed over to the Japanese within two weeks of arrival, thence to Changi and, for many of them, death on the Siam Burma railway construction. Their ships could, and should, have been sent back to India.

Percival retired from the army in 1948 and although he was denied the customary knighthood he was loaded with other honours and died in 1966, aged 79. An extraordinary life.

When Japan invaded, Dennis was happily teaching at the Malay College on the other side of the peninsula. I do not know what part, if any, he played in the fall back to Singapore but he was definitely on one of the last sampans (small fishing boats) to leave Singapore in mid February. With huge difficulty they crossed Sumatra and were picked up by an Australian submarine.

The military had spotted Dennis's Malayan connections and signed him up for Force 136, as the Special Operations Executive (SOE or special forces) were known. He was on the submarines sent to Malaya to arm and equip the guerrillas who were supposed to attack the Japanese. Unfortunately they did not. Their supplies came in useful when the British returned after the war. The 'Emergency' started, and Dennis returned to get his guns back.

When war broke out, my mother's younger brother, Peter, not

being keen on walking, was commissioned into the cavalry, the 3rd Hussars, with a troop of four tanks. Thanks to his father and some bullying from Patricia, he was a reasonable horseman which his brother John never was. That may have helped his choice of regiment, the cavalry having only just moved from horses to armoured vehicles.

On 28th November 1942 he wrote a truly historic 14 page, typed account of El Alamein to his mother Maud, who had been complaining about too little information. His unit, the 9th Armoured Brigade, led the attack and other histories conclude that it played the key role in the final victory. You would not have gathered that from Peter's modest account of the chaos and cock-ups they encountered.

Its commanding officer, Brigadier Petrie, was an outstanding leader both by the official war record and Peter's account. He led from the front and gave every appearance of being unafraid even though he knew that, in their final assault which clinched Alamein, his brigade faced almost total annihilation from Rommel's anti-tank guns. In the event it was not quite that bad. According to the records of the 9th Queen's Royal Lancers following up behind, Peter's 3rd Hussars lost 14 officers, about 60 other ranks and 48 of its 52 tanks.*

Peter put it thus: 'All this time the Brigadier has been standing or sitting on top of his tank with his red-banded hat on the side of his head, looking as untroubled as if he was on the top deck of a London bus. I don't know if he believes he's invulnerable but the rest of the Brigade are quite certain nothing will ever hit him.' Peter recounts that at one point in the lull before the battle Petrie went off into the dunes to relieve himself 'with a shovel in one hand and a pistol in the other. He returned with the 27 German prisoners he had captured and was as bucked as a cat with 27 tails'.

Peter's account of the battle is very similar to the official record but seen through the other end of the telescope. The main difference is the extent to which it rained (bad luck in the desert) which turned the soft sand into mud. Rain or dust the vehicles were constantly getting stuck. While Montgomery had been waiting for reinforcements, Rommel had been laying out half a million mines. The official record was that the Allies had so increased their mine clearance skills that they could do double the number per hour. There is no mention of that in Peter's account which is full of stories of the mines he had run

---

\* *9th Queen's Royal Lancers 1936-45*, Edited by Joan Bright, OBE, Gale & Polden, 1951, p.118.

over failing to explode and their untrained hands digging the others out.

Peter was on Montgomery's staff, back in Norfolk House, London, when the Normandy campaign was planned and he also invented a much improved tank gun sight. I cannot do justice to Dennis's and Peter's wars*. Peter always claimed that it was the happiest time of his life and Dennis certainly enjoyed it too, but they were lucky.

---

* Anyone wishing a fuller account can email me on tambler@london.edu.

# Chapter 2

# Never let your school interfere with your education*

L ife at Pewsey brightened up quite a bit when Dennis returned in 1946. There was money, no more poaching and I was given a bicycle for downtown errands. One errand I still feel guilty about.

Patricia and Dennis's first priority was to sort out their matrimonial situation. As soon as the divorce from Godfrey went through, they married on 10th September 1946 (presumably in the Marlborough registry office but I have never seen the certificate). My surname changed from Wilkinson to Ambler. One of my daily missions was to collect *The Times* from the village and I did notice that, on returning, they grabbed it with interest increasing day by day. They were about to phone the Hatch, Match and Dispatch editor when they checked with me that I really had posted the wedding announcement the previous week. Ah no – it was still in my pocket. To say that Dennis was

---

* Mark Twain.

vexed is an understatement but luckily he was still in his 'be nice to the boy' phase.

With his polio leg, he was none too enthusiastic about climbing into the pony cart but at least he was able to do it while it was stable. But the leg was mending and he had to return to work. It was only later I discovered it was MI6 rather than the Foreign Office but it made no difference.

Given my cockeyed start in life, I was unsurprised that Godfrey, who after all had helped bring me up, wanted to maintain some sort of parental role. Presumably the divorce judge, not being too clued up on the background, awarded him two weeks a year. Godfrey was now a farmer near Ramsey in the Isle of Man, so just getting there at the age of nine or ten was a problem. I have always loved the sea, especially in rough weather, and the open foredeck of the ferry to Douglas was a truly bracing experience. The second visit involved a biplane from Liverpool. Fun again but the best was next.

In those days, BEA (British European Airways merged with BOAC in 1974 to create BA) had its London Terminal just west of Victoria Station. The building is now used by the National Audit Office. Flying was gracious in those days (rather as portrayed in the Poirot episodes). After checking in, with proper grovelling by the reception staff, one was ushered into a Daimler limousine which purred sedately down to Croydon airport. The facilities there were not much more than a garage and forecourt but with more charm oozing from all parts, one boarded a plane about the size of a Dakota. A small boy travelling alone must have been under some kind of surveillance but it was far from obvious.

Godfrey did not really have enough capital to set up as even a subsistence farmer but, as his skills lay only in forestry, what else was he to do? The farm, smallholding really, had water and electricity but that was a limit to the mod cons. Eggs came from the hens and the other non-rationed food came from illegal trading. Godfrey was kind and did his best to entertain me. One year we had the practice laps for the Manx TT but, and I expect I was an ungrateful child, watching smelly machines whizz by at 160mph gets a bit tedious. Stuck on a B road at some point of a godforsaken Manx moor with no idea of what is happening, who is leading, or who is losing, doesn't get the adrenaline going. One's best hope was to wait by a bend and hope someone would fall off – except they didn't, even when it rained.

Sensibly he gave up farming and moved to a civil service job, living in Essex where his family had come from. Before long he was married, happily, and lived comfortably until the 1970s. Not a lot of scope for striding around though. Looking back, it is astonishing that Godfrey and Patricia should ever have married or even spent 10 minutes in each other's company.

After a brief spell in an elegant maisonette in Harrington Gardens, SW7, funds decreed the suburbs and Dennis and Patricia decided that Harrow-on-the-Hill – that's up on the hill where the school itself is – was the least nasty suburb accessible to St James's Park. A cousin of Patricia's was a housemaster at the school and he may have found our large ground floor flat at 'The Butts' at the top of Roxeth Hill.

Dennis had polio at the end of the war so the commute into St James's Park, involving the steep hill from South Harrow, was dreadful for him. MI6's office, by Queen Anne's Gate in those days, was both small and secret. John Le Carré (David Cornwell), so far as I could gather (I never got further than the front door), captured it just right in his Smiley books.

Cornwell became an MI5 officer in 1958; he ran agents, conducted interrogations, tapped telephone lines, and effected break-ins. Lord Clanmorris (who wrote crime novels as 'John Bingham' whilst an active MI5 officer), encouraged Cornwell to write. Clanmorris, the father of my Downside friend Simon Bingham (more later), was the model for George Smiley, although most of Dennis's friends and I thought that's who he was. From 1960-64, Cornwell worked for MI6, under Foreign Office cover in Bonn and Hamburg.

A few strange people came to the door, but Dennis made Patricia and me swear never to reveal his work or anything about his visitors. As an 11-year-old, I was impressed by that but the amazing thing was that a woman as indiscreet as Patricia never said a word out of place.

I had a similar to Dennis's, but more agreeable, walk down to Orley Farm prep school where I joined Miss Holmes's class. She had been teaching there for 40 years and, with her hair in a tight bun and a steely look, terrified everyone, especially the other grown ups. Discipline was not a problem in her class and, looking back, she was a great teacher. There were two routes to the school: the shorter was a leafy lane (a road now presumably) followed by a cut across the school playing fields. This had the further advantage that I might meet up with one of my best friends at that time, Robin Butler, who lived on the lane. The longer route was by the main road but that had the advantage that if Miss Holmes was being driven to school at that time in her huge black limousine and if she spotted me, she would give me a lift. That had the further advantage that I got to know her quite well. She was a charming old thing. The disadvantage of course was that if the lift did not materialise one would be late for school. Leaving home earlier by main road would have been really dumb because then she would certainly have missed me.

Orley Farm was a feeder school for Harrow where about a quarter of the boys went on. Robin Butler was the star – good at games, academically gifted and nice with it. No surprise he went on to be head boy at Harrow, double first in Mods and Greats (with blues in rugger) at Oxford, Treasury and long-serving head of the civil service and finally, by now Lord Butler, head of his old college, University College. All I had to do with all this was to help him carry his cricket gear when he went to Lord's for coaching.

In later life our paths rarely crossed but he was invariably his charming self when they did, with one exception. Bear in mind that Robin is tall, blond, patrician and, at the time of this story, one of the best known men in the country, routinely appearing in the media. The date is about 2000, the Northern Ireland troubles are about to be settled (for the time being) and I'm in one of the posh seats near the front of the plane en route to Dublin to give some lectures. Across the aisle is Robin deep in his papers so I leave him in peace. When we land and are taking our bags out of the rags, I say perhaps too loudly something like 'Butler, dear boy, how *is* you?' This is greeted with 'Shut up you fool, I'm travelling incognito.' I'm sure that must have fooled the IRA.

Patricia's housemaster relation meant that we had access so Harrow's sporting facilities, notably the huge open air pool. 1947 was a hot summer and picnicking by the pool was wonderful. Other locals had similar privileges, notably the Spencer family. Tom Spencer ran the family engineering business which kept him out of the war and provided a respectable income and, by the standards of those days, a posh car. Tom's wife Joan had a couple of horses near by and, unsurprisingly, became Patricia's best friend. They lived in a large house, with a very large garden, on my leafy lane route to school. At one of the parties, I was introduced to an elderly (he seemed to me) man who lived opposite known locally as Jetsy Whittle. Actually he was a year younger than Patricia.

What does the inventor of the jet engine and legendary adversary of the Air Ministry, who had just become Sir Frank Whittle, have to say to an 11-year-old schoolboy? Obviously not a lot but he was very courteous and having ascertained that I passed his house on the way home every evening, he said, 'Do pop in for tea sometime.' At that age, I had not yet twigged that an invitation without a date is not an invitation. I wanted to know more about jet engines, so the next week I did.

Answering the door he did look a bit surprised. He lived alone but soon rustled up a pot of tea and some biscuits. I cannot recall how long I stayed but I do recall that it was a pleasant enough time. His knighthood was small recognition of the Air Ministry's rejection of the jet engine, allowing the Germans to build them first. We should have had them throughout WWII. When I got back, rather late, there was a demand to know where I had been. Patricia, and Dennis too when he got home, were shocked that I had been so impudent.

In 1947, Patricia decided we should have a family holiday in a house she had rented at the top of the cliff immediately east of Cadgwith Cove in Cornwall. Unbeknownst to Dennis, she then decided we needed a car. By far the most glamorous affordable model was a 1934 Talbot Tourer. It had an eight-foot bonnet secured with a stout leather strap, followed by two comfortable seats and then two rather less comfortable ones. The salesman gave us a test run and chose the dual carriageway A40 past Northolt airport. The salesman had the car up to 85mph with no trouble and Patricia announced that she was convinced. She handed him a cheque and when he drove us back to the Butts, he arranged insurance and took a taxi back to his office.

The car had the 'pre-selectric' gear, that is to say you decided which gear should be next and it changed automatically when you next hit the clutch pedal. That does require the driver to remember which gear will be next and which it is in now. It is hardly surprising the system fell out of favour for the ordinary car driver. That did not bother Patricia: she did not drive. Nor did Dennis: much of his post-polio pension depended on his not being able to. He was not pleased: 'Who,' he demanded, 'is going to drive this thing?'

'It just so happens,' she replied, 'that I met a delightful young man on the underground this afternoon and he said he would be happy to join us on holiday and do the driving. He will be joining us for supper so you can see if you like him.'

I was agog. How many mothers would do something like that?

When the bell rang, I rushed to open the door to a tall, dark and very handsome young American. Surprisingly enough, it all worked out very well. The American took a while to figure out the gear system – American drivers have never been good with gears – and Patricia and I squeezed in the back. There was little room for luggage but enough. Fortunately the American was as good an engineer as the car was temperamental. The AA would not have advised purchase and we spent quite a while exploring the 12 cylinders under the bonnet. Luckily petrol and oil then were cheap.

The house was spacious and well-appointed with wonderful views over Cadgwith and the channel. Cornish ice cream was a revelation, swimming in the cove a total joy and the only downside was walking back up another bloody hill to the house.

Norman Lewis, the travel writer, came to stay for a few days. A friend and contemporary of Dennis, he was working on his first two post-war books: *A Dragon Apparent – Travels in Indo-China* (1951) and *Golden Earth – Travels in Burma* (1952). He tended to dominate the conversation but he was interesting and good company. I wanted to know how a complete stranger could rock up in a country like Burma, stay a few weeks and then write the definitive guide to the place. He was not much pleased by the question but, of course, if you are beating the best trodden path for people who will only be there for two weeks themselves, it seemed to be enough. In that pre-Google age, it did also require a fair bit of library research back home.

Our week was up too soon. We said goodbye to our driver and the rather surprised salesman said hello again to the Talbot. We heard that he sold it again quite quickly.

The big event in our family in 1948 was the arrival of Jason in August. Dennis had been deprived of watching a child grow up and, come to that, Patricia had had little sight of me during the war. For that and doubtless other reasons, they decided to adopt. In those days, at least among the middle classes, adoption agencies played little part; the doctors worked solutions through their networks. In this case Aunt Florence, a paediatric doctor, located an imminent baby. Our flat at the Butts was spacious and on the ground floor and included the garden for the old mansion. Jason was subjected to at least six hours a day outside in his pram.

The garden was also a good run around for Patricia's assorted dogs and ferrets. Ferrets make delightful pets and will play games for hours running through tunnels made of rolled up newspaper, play-fighting and generally taking an interest in everything around. And that includes next door. Much as we liked the ferrets, Dennis did not and the neighbours still less. However friendly one moment, they are likely to bite the next. One got my finger and in trying to shake it off, I stood up. Three feet in the air it was still hanging on. I still have the scar.

This did not put Patricia off and ferrets used to appear in her life from time to time thereafter. Twenty-five years later I took Katie, then my fiancée, to Sunday lunch with Dennis and Patricia in the London suburb of Richmond. We had drinks in hand when Patricia came fly-ing into the room saying, 'I have a treat for you. We have a brand new litter of ferrets!' She was followed by the proud parents and 12 little biting things. I am not sure Katie had even seen a ferret before but she knew enough to get clear of them, in this case by standing on a chair. Scenting fear, the litter and parents immediately surrounded the chair trying to climb the legs which were rocking ominously. Patricia was demanding to know what the problem was. Maybe I should have done something but I was laughing too much. One would not really expect ferrets in Richmond and it did not do much for the prospective mother-in-law relationship.

Harrow did one major thing for Jason, namely creating a relation-ship with the Spencer family, Tom and Joan and their two children: Petronel and Francis. As noted above, they were old school, old money. They were the only family we knew with two servants, Kerry and Edith, both of whom by then were quite elderly and by the time they moved to Kintbury, Berkshire, ten years later were positively geriatric. The cook was delightful but possibly the worst professional cook in the kingdom. Maybe rationing had dimmed her skills but I suspect that thought to be generous. In any case, any guest's grumble about the food was quickly shushed by Tom with the words 'she might leave'. So far as they were concerned, they had never cooked for themselves and anything was better than that.

Jason, like Dennis, caught polio. Despite that he passed all the medical and other requirements for Sandhurst but the M.O. there turned him down on arrival. It was a bitter blow and there was no appeal. Left in the career wilderness, Jason thought he might as well be in the real wilderness and went off to Australia to be a Jackaroo.

Jason liked the outback, with its horses to ride and reality farming, for a while but it did have the big disadvantage, for an uxorious chap like Jason, of a lack of nubile companionship. So it was off to Adelaide where he and Susan married. When that broke up, he caught another wife, Eve, in Sydney, though they married in some grandeur at the Raffles Hotel in Singapore. The glamorous Brooke was the daughter from the first marriage and Felicity and Nicholas were Eve's progeny.

By 1949 Dennis was judged fit enough to return to Singapore as part of the 'diplomatic'. I think he was a Second Secretary officially but everyone soon found out what he was about, namely helping the police and the military track down the terrorists.

Dennis met the ship in Singapore and took us to our new home. The department that ordains these things had allocated us rather a nice, I thought, open and spacious semi-detached house in the Katong district near the Singapore [European] Swimming Club. Nothing then was air-conditioned in Singapore except the Elizabeth Restaurant. The fans in the ceilings were hardly necessary as the balmy breezes wafted through.

Dennis made excellent decisions about my education. He reckoned that I was tough enough not to attend the conventional International School but Raffles Institution, then and now the best English speaking secondary school on the island. It had 1500 pupils of whom precisely two, an American and myself, were Caucasian. A parallel Chinese speaking school system existed, then as now also, and the quality was similar.

Dennis's syce (driver) dropped me off in the mornings and I came home with the other students on the buses. They were almost all Chinese with a few Malays and Indians and all quite a bit older than me. The oldest was 19. With hindsight I should have taken the opportunity to learn Chinese but it would have been 50 years before I needed it.

The academic side was fine being based pretty much on the UK syllabus and the classes were well taught. At the end of year exams, I came in the middle of the pack except for English in which I came top – unsurprisingly you may think but my co-pupils did not. The English teacher was himself English and they put it down to favouritism and racism. Raffles was a competitive place.

In fact the only time race discrimination did become an issue was at the school's annual swimming gala which was held at the Chinese Swimming Club. One of the reasons that the Brits and the Chinese have mostly rubbed along so well, opium wars apart, is that each race knows that it is superior to all others. The Chinese for China means the 'Centre of the World' and the rest of us are barbarians.

The European clubs excluded Asians and, more embarrassingly, Anglo-Asians. The Chinese clubs did exactly the same in reverse and I was duly banned from the Gala. To their credit, my fellow students thought this was unfair and their parents appealed to the Club Committee who made me an honorary Chinese for the day. Not that it did me any good: I came nowhere in the races.

The school facilities were good enough albeit fairly basic. I think it was still on the same site adopted by Sir Stamford Raffles when he established the school four years after Singapore itself, in 1823. But the buildings were newer than that, probably 1930s. There was a large playground but no sporting facilities. As a result we spent a great deal of time at our Swimming Club which was wonderful for me and for Jason, by now in the care of an amah, and deadly boring for Patricia who disliked swimming, sunbathing and especially having to talk to wives she considered tedious. It was her considered opinion that the social class of British expatriates in Malaya had seriously declined compared with the pre-war years. The fact that the antagonism was mutual mattered not a jot.

One solution was to go to the Tanglin Club which had always been a haven for those who considered themselves at the posher end of the scale – and so it remained until independence. But the Tanglin facilities were less good.

The best social engagement of the week for Dennis and Patricia, and the worst for me, was Sunday Tiffin. The curry, with all the trimmings, lunch was delicious but the 1pm on the invitation invariably turned into 5pm before anyone was drunk enough to need to sit down. For a hungry 12-year-old those four hours were purgatory.

Our main host on these occasions was Denis Murphy, a most delightful lawyer, who was a lifelong friend of Dennis and Patricia (and Jason), and popped up again as 'boyfriend' of Carmen Molony, mother of a Downside friend, after she was widowed in the 1970s. I don't recall ever meeting him sober but, according to Dennis, he was an outstandingly successful lawyer and, indeed, must have been so to have afforded his lifestyle. They had a large house and garden running out to the sea, some way off the main road to Changi (eastern tip of the island). One diversion to while away the time was water-skiing which I never successfully achieved but I did manage the one level down, namely standing on a tray being tugged by the motorboat. The sea round Singapore is not very attractive; it is grey and murky, but it is warm and flat and ideal for flopping around. Later the place was demolished and now the Airport Highway runs through the garden.

Of course the waters are great for sailing too. Some of Dennis's friends had sailing boats and the best outing was to one of the nearest Indonesian islands. Neither D nor P nor their wives liked sailing so they opted out. We set out in the morning on a compass bearing and made it by late afternoon. I was impressed by that as a compass bearing is fine if you are sailing in a straight line but not so easy if you are tacking to and fro. But then I'm no sailor.

It was a pretty small island populated by just one village with fishing as its main industry. No problem, except one could not fail to notice that passing Indonesians would turn away and spit onto the ground. My companions explained that they thought we were Dutch. Indonesia had only received its independence the year before (1949) and the Dutch were much hated. We tried to explain that we were English but their grasp of our language was about as good as our grasp of theirs.

The guesthouse was comfortable enough and the bathhouse was a revelation. It contained just a huge tub of water, stool, bar of soap and a scoop (a wok with a handle). Stupidly as I subsequently realised, I soaped up and climbed into the tub which felt much colder than the 80° that it must have been. Fortunately nobody else discovered my transgression. One is supposed to use the scoop to chuck the water over oneself, like a shower. If they had known I had got straight into the tub, it would have been emptied and refilled. No mean task.

As mentioned above, Dennis's cloak-and-dagger role was widely known but he still had to pretend to be a diplomat. Every diplomat of Dennis's rank and above, from every embassy or other diplomatic mission, was given an allowance to cover the cost of an annual drinks party. Add to that the Queen's Birthday and a few other events requiring celebration and there must have been at least one a week. This endless round of cocktail parties, for reasons that made little sense to me then or later, included me. I do not recall any other children being there although there may have been. I did get to know the participants a bit as they were always the same people. The food was excellent and, in a Moslem country, good provision was made for teetotallers. Chatting with me, I suppose, was no more boring than having the same conversations with diplomatic colleagues that they had had in the previous weeks.

This experience has coloured my view of our diplomatic missions ever since and it has been confirmed by visiting them in later life. To a large extent, diplomats are cut off from the real world and just exchange gossip, however hush-hush they think it is. That includes those overseas intelligence services operating under diplomatic cover. So it was absolutely no surprise that the intelligence services failed to predict the demise of the Shah of Iran or that of the Berlin Wall or the Velvet Revolution or most other seismic international events. They are lucky that their cloak of secrecy prevents the failures being more widely known.

An attempt was made to brush up my religious education, before Downside found me out, by sending me to some well meaning but dreary nuns on Saturday mornings. They did their best to teach me the catechism but that was of no interest to Downside. In similar vein, Dennis took me for a walk to explain the 'facts of life', as sex instruction was called. He was even more embarrassed than me and I returned none the wiser. The boys at Orley Farm had been far more informative.

In all, Raffles Institution was a happy experience and I have been known to wear the alumnus tie. Many if not most of the senior members of Singapore governments over the years were there, including Lee Kuan Yew, Prime Minister 1959–1990 and then effectively President until 2011 when he retired, aged only 88, and left the Cabinet. Lee was succeeded by Goh Chok Thong, also a Raffles alumnus.

Raffles Institution has become immensely wealthy, no doubt due to these connections. It moved from downtown to a large site in the middle of the island and the campus now resembles a well endowed US university, rather than a secondary school.

Sadly, after four terms, it was time to move on and in January 1951 I was on the boat back to England.

After failing the spring scholarship exams – no surprise there – I arrived at Downside for the summer term. Dom Simon was the housemaster for the Junior house. Tall, lean and from the immensely grand Van Zeller family, he was, to all our amusement, a snob, not just a minor one but a grade A, full size SNOB – albeit both holy* and charming with it. Parents received his time pro rata to their social

---

* His brother Fr Hubert, also a Benedictine monk, was positively ascetic.

standing. Luckily he never met mine. Despite all this we had many happy hours playing bridge and mah jong in his office. His bridge was just about good enough to hold its own with 13-year-olds.

The Benedictines are a flexible lot. Dom Bruno Scott James also came from a grand family and resisted the vow of poverty. It wasn't the money so much as his wine cellar that he would have missed, shades of Monsignor Val Elwes the Oxford chaplain. Accordingly he had to live in the village, not the monastery. But he too was a holy man and later went to Naples to work with Fr. Borelli, the 'Master of the House of Urchins', i.e. the street-children.

July found me back at Heathrow, this time catching the plane myself. The Argonaut had only been in service with BOAC for about a year and was wide and more spacious than the DC3 it replaced, comparable with all the flying boats BOAC was then, reluctantly, phasing out. The flying boat was good for the South African run, given the chain of lakes all the way down that continent, but not for anywhere it had to come down on sea – quite often too rough for landing or taking off. And they carried too few passengers given the weight and size of the plane. The US never much bothered with them and, with hindsight, it is hard to see why we did.

The Argonaut was acknowledged to be noisy and lumbered along at 300mph, but that may have been later models as I recall mine being slower than that and with a lower cruising altitude than the claimed 11K metres. Unlike a modern Jumbo, it resembled travel on a country bus, slow and low enough to enjoy the countryside. The range was 4K miles (again possibly for later models) so it should have been able to make Singapore (6732 miles as the crow flies) with just one stop. We stopped en route at Rome, Cairo, Basra, Karachi, Calcutta, Rangoon and Bangkok. The 52 all first class passengers were provided with overnight accommodation in grand hotels certainly in Rangoon and, perhaps, in Basra too. In any case, the view in those days was that those wealthy enough to fly (it was twice the price of the ship) should not have to endure the rigours of sitting up all night. We dined and breakfasted in the hotel and then flew for eight hours with one or two stops. I had been put in the charge of one of the flight crew and she determined that I dined and retired to bed earlier than I would have chosen. In Rangoon therefore I dined alone, apart from a couple of dozen staff, in a vast and magnificent dining room otherwise filled with palms. Entertaining in its way to raise a finger and have half a dozen waiters rush over.

Dennis, Patricia and Jason had moved to a new and, in my view, far less attractive house just off the Bukit Timah Road – the main road from downtown north to Johore. The big appeal for Patricia was that it was just across the road from the racecourse and training stables. She had acquired a horse and a syce (stable lad) to look after it and also the one she had bought for me, Naiad, the sweetest little horse that ever walked and the only one I ever owned. The back of the racecourse was good riding country. The paths were odd as I never saw anyone else on them either on foot or horseback.

Usually I rode out in the early mornings with Patricia but occasionally Naiad and I went by ourselves. Hacking round lightly wooded countryside was very agreeable. One morning something spooked the horse and she bolted. Nothing would stop her so I just hung on like grim death, crashing through the branches and, frankly, terrified. If I came off, I didn't know how I would get back or recapture her. It was a wild ride and, in retrospect, exciting. Eventually she calmed down and we trotted home. Thereafter, if Patricia could not go out, the syce did. Of course, she never bolted again.

Dennis was no longer part of the diplomatic service but was pretending to be the South East Asia rep for Methuen Books, with an office in Collyer Quay. It was, still is, a very busy part of town and visitors of any kind would not be noticed. The 'cover' fooled no-one but it did not matter. Until January 1952, when Winston Churchill appointed Gerald Templer as British High Commissioner in Malaya, we had been making a right mess of countering the communist insurgency. In five years, little had changed. In 1951 that was about all I knew. The story returns to Malaya in the next chapter.

My first term at Downside was in the fourth form but I was treated as if I had won a scholarship, put in all the A streams and promoted to the fifth form for the autumn term. The newly arriving scholarship winners, mostly from Worth and many of them also in Barlow, were placed immediately into the fifth form. I found kindred spirits both amongst them and also in their friends following on.

Fr. Wilfrid Passmore was headmaster and devoted to achieving the highest academic grades. Only one offence was punished by expulsion. If the first beating for 'failing to profit from the school' i.e. slacking, was not heeded, you were out. It was not how bright you were or what the results were, it was how hard you were working and Dom Wilfrid was the sole judge of that. There was no appeal. With 450 boys to watch, he did make mistakes but beating a boy who had just come top of his class for slacking made a point no one could misunderstand.

Physics and chemistry were completely new to me and I ended up with just one year in the science wing. The physics master was boring and the chemistry master barking so it was just as well I was not eligible for O Level (the GCSE of its day). The government had decided in a supposedly egalitarian measure that everyone should take the exam at the same age. Most schools complied by holding brighter children back so the fifth form was the same age group. Passmore was far more interested in top university places and therefore giving his brighter boys three years in the sixth even at the expense of missing O Levels.

The one year of chemistry did give me access to the smells and bangs the Health and Safety people would now prevent. A chemicals supply business allowed me to have a large jar of sodium, provided I collected it. It was too dangerous to despatch but not, apparently, too dangerous for a small boy to carry home on the underground. As the jar was about a foot tall and four inches wide, it was a good quantity, ample for many experiments. The lumps of metal were slightly smaller than centimetre cubes held in a non-interactive oil of some sort. Sodium goes off with a big bang, flying bits of metal and smoke when it meets water.

Water closets provided an ideal laboratory. As the cubicle dividers, of what is known at Downside as the 'yard' for some reason, only reached six feet, standing on the lavatory gave access to the one next door. Dropping the sodium at the precise moment that the neighbour's unclothed derrière was above, but not covering, the pan required skilful timing. I was fully successful just once and the trousers round his ankles prohibited pursuit.

Passmore, to a small boy, had a terrifying aspect. Large in all dimensions, his black habit was spattered with badly aimed food and his head was crowned with little spikes. On closer inspection it was just hair cut to a regulation one centimetre. Relative to the size of his head he had tiny wire framed spectacles with lenses an inch thick, magnifying the eyes boring down upon one.

Our housemaster was the much loved Fr Oliver Brayden, a man of considerable tolerance and understanding. Relaxed himself, a few minutes in his company would ensure you were equally relaxed.

Calmness and wisdom prevailed. The school disapproved strongly of smoking, a caning offence, and drugs had yet to surface. Alcohol however was not deemed to be an issue. The nearest pub was barred but only because the lay masters objected to being the subject of our attention. In summer bicycling out to country pubs and locally brewed rough cider was a joy. If one could bicycle, one was deemed sober. My parents' dinner parties in Singapore had taught me a thing or two about wines and spirits and my friends' parents had been similarly progressive. When the funds were in place, we allowed ourselves to be taxied to Wells or Bath or Colerne (the furthest and most expensive but also the best). Bath's Hole in the Wall restaurant was the best value as the food was excellent and, as it had no licence, we had to visit a wine merchant en route. No one ever questioned our age – we started at 14 – or our excessive consumption. The ensuing rowdy behaviour did provoke the occasional complaint but never any retribution by the school.

Of course we were spoilt brats and complete yobs and if our own children had behaved like that we would have been furious. But maybe they did and our parents too.

Another characteristic of Fr Oliver's benevolence was his attitude to afternoon exercise. While pretty hopeless at all games, I enjoyed them all except football. Cricket in summer, rugby in autumn, and hockey in the second half of the spring term were all fine by me – but soccer was not. The balls were leather then, heavier than now but tolerable when new as the wax kept the water out. The balls that got passed on to us in the lower orders, however, had seen more seasons than we had. Kicking them felt as if one's tibia would fracture.

As bad as soccer were the days when games were not scheduled or one wasn't picked for any team (so often true) or the weather was too bad. Then one was supposed to go for a run of two miles or more or at least a walk. The solution was a visit to Fr Oliver's study. A bridge player himself, he quickly understood that, due to the bad and deteriorating weather, a game of cards would be better for us than risking our health outdoors. It did not take long to discover that he was amenable to this argument even if there was barely a cloud in the sky. I never did a single run anyway but even the walks became a thing of the past.

The usual four was drawn from Nick Sibley, Denis Cross, Michael Wakeford, Simon Bingham and myself. We christened ourselves the Lotos Eaters in reference to our restaurant indulgences on whole holidays and, with help from Sibley's uncle then managing director at *The Times* and Dennis's friend, Malcolm Muggeridge, then editor of *Punch*, we produced a not wholly scurrilous *Independent* newspaper for our last speech day. A not unprofitable venture.

The slightly younger Auberon Waugh referred in one of his memoirs to the Lotos Eaters as being a gang of the most deplorable sort. He disapproved of gangs of any sort but was, of course, the leader of one himself. Whether his father Evelyn was to blame or not, Auberon was a pain and probably holds the record for the most strokes of Passmore's cane. They were entirely merited. He was invalided out of his ensuing Royal Horse Guards national service after being riddled with machine gun bullets in Cyprus. The EOKA insurgents were not to blame. The official account tells of Auberon bravely unjamming the gun – and that is doubtless correct. The scuttlebutt alternative was that his own soldiers were so fed up with him that they shot him from behind, exactly as had happened to Evelyn in his time. Auberon was always talented but his classics scholarship to Oxford did not manage to keep him there long.

Remarkably, the brat of the 1950s became the most charming, civilised and courteous man in middle age. Not just a funny, percipient and elegant writer, he came to stand for British values at their best.

Graduating from the fifth form required us to choose our A Level subjects. Nowadays bright pupils have to do huge numbers but then, as now for most, the norm was three. I had no real idea what I wanted until Major Page ('Major' because he ran the Combined Cadet Force [CCF]) suggested I do maths with him. I liked maths so that was fine by me and it had the merit of counting as two subjects. I have never understood why. He also reeled in Denis Cross and John Clifford (Barlow again). Downside had never had any success with maths and Page reckoned that with the three of us, he might crack the problem. Part of his difficulty was that he was not much good at sums himself, although that turned out later to be an advantage.

We became 'Crombleford', jointly solving the maths problems we were set and then explaining how we did it in terms simple enough for even the Major to grasp. Of course that may have been a cunning ruse but it worked and we all landed up at Oxford with scholarships or exhibitions.

I had a slight advantage in that the Headmaster forgot to put me down for A Level Physics (the standard link with double maths).

Having found it pretty tedious in the fifth form, I decided not to tell him (or my parents) and occupied the swathes of free class time by working my way through most of the famous Victorian novels: Scott, Stevenson, George Eliot, Hardy and so on. I was a little nervous of his reaction when he did eventually find out but I need not have been. Only two A Levels were needed and we had to go back and sweep up a couple of O Levels, in my case Latin (also required for Oxford entry), French and Religious Knowledge. I do not recall uttering a word of French beyond 'oui' in the oral but that seemed to be enough. Our son Gus, thirty years on, was not so lucky.

One could recount vignettes of Downside life for many more pages and perhaps there are too many already. There seemed masses of time for everything, squash, tennis, two Gilbert and Sullivans and three other plays, snooker and bridge. Accommodation was tolerable but the food was barely so:

> **A Wasted Bullet** (written Summer 1955)
> His ear to prayer being deaf,
> Eventually we shot the chef.
> That really was an awful shame:
> The food we're served is still the same.

All in all, schooldays were happy, partly because I got on so well with Passmore (I have no idea why he was always known as 'Passmore' whilst all other monks were interchangeably Dom or Fr. Christian name). Some pupils did and some did not. Favourites would face Gestapo type interrogations when invited to pop in for a chat around bedtime. Passmore had terrible eyesight and the reading light on his desk would be shone full face on the victim, more or less blinding him. All one could see of Passmore was an outline of his vast habit (he was a big man) and glinting from his glasses. Not the most relaxing basis for a chat. It would always begin 'Now tell me ....' and would progressively try to extract information on boys, masters, other monks or parents that he could use to his advantage. What he already knew was used as bait, indicating that one shouldn't worry. He knew it all already. Unsurprisingly, he was a very successful criminal barrister before taking the habit.

The bribe was a case of beer beside one's armchair with a bottle opener and encouragement to drink as much as one liked. From his point of view, the more the better. As may be apparent, I rather enjoyed these sessions. It was a game and playing involved giving him enough information, expressed in an amusing enough way, to keep him interested. He had a very good sense of humour so that was not too difficult. At the same time one had to steer around anything damaging. Again not too difficult as I didn't know anything damaging. And as the beer was the dire 'George's Bottled Piss', there was little incentive to drink much of it or chance of inebriation.

He was a lovely, intelligent, holy man and became, inevitably, rather a controversial Abbot. Such an outstanding man could not be denied the top job but abbots are not supposed to be controllists. We kept in touch and he married Katie and me in 1966. The last time we saw him, he pronounced that Gus was a very pretty little boy as indeed he was. If it was a hint to keep him away from Downside, we missed it.

Passmore was a keen flogger. No prefects or other masters were allowed to do it and it was his only form of exercise. I may have been one of his favourites but he never spared the rod. In my last term, now 18, loaded with honours and, in my opinion, rather grand, I received more strokes of the cane than in my entire Downside career to that point.

One of these last occasions was when all Barlow house prefects were flogged for being beastly to our incoming housemaster, Dom John Roberts. Passmore was quite right, we were. As one of the chief troublemakers, I still feel guilty about it. Dom John replaced the retiring (ill health probably as age means nothing to monks) and beloved Dom Oliver. Passmore briefed the house that we should be nice to Dom John not least because he was still recovering from the war. He had been caught at Dunkirk and spent the war as a POW. He was nervous and self effacing.

We set out with the best of intentions but after a while his indecisions, uncertainties and lack of conversation began to grate. It was the custom for house prefects, after ensuring that the dormitories were quiet and with lights out, to repair to the housemaster's study for coffee or tea or whatever and a chat about whatever young men chat about. Dom John always managed to bring conversation to silence. Eventually we cracked, relationships – such as they were – fell apart and we were rewarded with sore bottoms.

Passmore and Dom John were opposite ends of the spectrum. Passmore was a great headmaster but perhaps not a great abbot. Dom John was initially (he improved after our time) a hopeless housemaster but a very successful, much loved and long serving abbot. I guess if you loved one of them you were unlikely to love the other. Whenever Abbot John met me in later years, polite and pleasant as he always was, I could see the pain return to his eyes.

The other monks occupied the spaces between the Passmore and Dom John extremes. Passmore's successor Dom Aelred, Caverel housemaster and my history teacher, was too academic to be a success as headmaster but one should not be judgmental. All the monks we met were priests first and school teachers second, if not third. Today few if any teach. I used to grumble at the folly of appointing headmasters from the ranks of the community without giving them any professional training whatever. The headmastership of a major public school is, amongst other things, a managerial job requiring managerial training. Passmore was at least a trained barrister and that was better than nothing.

Whilst other schools were already suffering from paedophilia, notably Ealing, I am certain that was not a problem for us. One housemaster was rumoured as not being safe to be with on one's own and some older boys fancied some younger. The one who did amazingly realistic impressions of Marilyn Monroe received particular attention, including from me, but I do not know if anything came to anything.

At the Dom John end of the scale was Tusky Russell, so called because of his improbable dentures. He was lovely, with a large shiny pate, but dotty. Remarkably, or so it was alleged, he made more converts to Catholicism than anyone else in the monastery. Next along the scale was Dom Cyprian Stockford who played the organ and taught lower level maths. With charm and persistence he created a chess club which played other schools and hosted a top ranked player to give simultaneous exhibitions in which the visitor played all six or ten of us at the same time and at lightning speed. He waited for us, not us for him. Dom Cyprian died in 2012 aged 90.

Dom Illtyd Trethowen had a withered arm which he used to hold pages down in a breeze. Easily the most intellectual of the then community, he taught religious studies and ran the debating society. I had expected the teaching of religion at Downside to be dogmatic, like the nuns and their catechism, yet it was anything but. We were encouraged to take as communist, atheist or any other viewpoint as we wished, provided we could argue that view. He was terrific.

Then there was Dom Denis Agius who represented the legion of

Maltese boys. He was editor of the *Raven*, the school magazine then produced termly. In the school I had avidly read the news from Oxford and Cambridge which recounted the moral deprivation of the OGs[3] there. The accounts contributed to my wish to go to Oxford. So when I arrived and was appointed Correspondent, I set about discovering and then recounting a *News of the World* version of our life there. Dom Denis summoned me for interview to say that much as he enjoyed my column, and so did the boys, I was hereby sacked. Those possibly libelled had not complained and may even have enjoyed their infamy but their parents did not. Parents paid Downside's fees and their views rather outweighed anyone else's.

The chastisement from Passmore in my final term may have been good preparation for National Service. If life is a game of snakes and ladders, the transition from the top of a boarding school to the very bottom of the army hierarchy is a very big snake indeed.

# Chapter 3

# For Queen and Country

*This chapter covers national service and in particular:*
- *The 1950s transition from austerity and rationing to 'never having had it so good'.*
- *Berkshire*
- *National Service*
  - *Basic training*
  - *Mons*
  - *The rest of officer training*
- *Back to Singapore*
  - *The 'emergency'*
  - *The Empire Orwell troopship*
  - *HMS Simbang*
  - *Singapore riots*
  - *SEATO Conference*
  - *Criminal soldiers*
  - *The Tanglin Club required personal transport*
  - *Mess dances*
  - *My last military assignment*

My school years saw a steady improvement in living standards. Winston Churchill was voted out and then voted back in again when austerity was blamed on Labour. Served them right, of course, as by the end of the war they had been promising all manner of impossible dreams.

Sweets were the last to come off ration and many would say they never should have done. Buying coupons at the beginning of term when they were plentiful and selling them at the end afforded a modest increase in my pocket money.

The government's first effort to cheer us up was the Festival of Britain in 1951. New architectural and fabric designs, new science, new music and a whole new experience including the Skylon, the Shot Tower and the Festival Hall for Londoners and visitors. Battersea Park hosted a funfair which, to a 14-year-old, was far more fun especially the Rotor which spun round as the floor was lowered and you were left sticking to the rubberised wall. For me it was an early explanation of the non-existence of centrifugal forces. Nick Sibley's glamorous mother took us both to the Festival itself. I am glad I went if only because I did not have to go again. Just like the Millennium Dome fifty years later it was designed by civil servants and an in-crowd of designers on the basis of what would be good and educational for 'the people'. Both had the same results, a far cry from the Great Exhibition of 1851 which they were seeking to emulate. Many of us have hated the 1951 designs ever since, and that includes Katie.

At the beginning of the 1950s, customers queued outside corner shops and paid cash (or had weekly accounts if they were a little grander). In 1951 the first supermarket opened in Streatham ('Premier') with a turnover of £59,000 a year. By 2011, 8000 of them made £107 billion. Barclaycard arrived in 1966.

The accession of Queen Elizabeth, by contrast to the Festival of Britain, was a big fillip (sorry!) to the national cheerfulness along with the carefully stage managed announcement of Hillary's (NZ but seen as an honorary Brit) ascent of Everest. Downside gave us a whole holiday which saw us crowded round a tiny black-and-white TV screen in a Bath hotel before repairing to the Hole in the Wall for a celebratory lunch. This was the first time most of us had seen a TV set, although Dennis had organised for me to have a tour of Alexandra Palace, the birthplace of TV, when we were living in Harrow. It was replaced as the BBC's TV centre around the time of the Coronation.

The international scene was less placid. The Korean War, which had taken a turn for the worse with the entry of China, rumbled on until the armistice a month after the Coronation. Sixty years on, that agreement is still no more than a ceasefire with no peace treaty. North Korean and US troops still patrol each side of the 38th parallel, although the cross-fire has been no more than verbal in recent years.

Europe was still riven by the Cold War. It was at its coldest, apart from the 1962 Cuban crisis, during the 1950s. 1953 was also brightened by Stalin's death. Over the same period, Europe was united by the Schuman Declaration in 1950 which in turn led to the creation of the EEC in 1957. With hindsight, the UK made a major error in failing to join when it was created. We participated in the preparatory talks and Guy Mollet, the French Prime Minister who was to become the architect of the EEC, suggested that France and Britain first form a joint economic union, as Churchill had suggested in 1940. Anthony Eden, probably the worst British Prime Minister of the 20th century, shied away. Astonishingly the then alternative was that France would join the [British] Commonwealth – more likely you may think than snow in Hades.

Our rather pathetic attempts to join in 1963 and 1967 were rejected and only Edward Heath grovelled enough in 1972 to be accepted. One of the ironies of WWII was that our enemy, Adolf Hitler, actually rather liked and admired the British whereas the supposed ally that we had nurtured all through the war and allowed to 'recapture' Paris, hated us with extraordinary venom. De Gaulle's speech vetoing British entry in 1963 was worthy of Shakespeare's Iago. Amongst other derogatory observations, he claimed that the UK had not only declined to join the EEC but attempted to sabotage it. He must have made that up as Mollet's France and Eden's UK were exceedingly pally at the time.


Dennis and Patricia had sold the Harrow flat when we went to Singapore and Patricia returned to a cottage in Inkpen, a village west of Newbury and not far from Kintbury where the Spencers now lived. It was isolated but, *mirabile dictu*, she passed her driving test at only the second attempt and bought a pre-war Singer, more like a sewing machine than a car. It (or she) had troubles with hills but otherwise buzzed along pretty well. The impatient back seat driver would remonstrate whenever the car slowed down on entering a 30mph zone, as 30 was all it managed.

Dennis returned and Inkpen was replaced by Midgham, two stations east of Newbury so he could commute to Queen Anne's Gate. It was a long day for him but often got off to a bright start as Patricia tended to leave a little late. The A4 runs beside the railway line. If, as one was about to turn off the main road, the train was already in the station, the foot hit the floor and the new car would get to the next station before the train did. Apparently, on these occasions, Dennis was less than his usual courteous self.

The Midgham place was a small farmhouse on its own down a half mile lane. Water had to be pumped up to the tank as it had no mains electricity. A diesel turbine worked well enough until the electricity company relented. Heating was only the cooker in the kitchen and a coal fire in the living room. Sprinting up the stairs to bed was necessary to maintain body heat but we did have hot water bottles. It was a reminder of holidays in the Isle of Man.

The farmhouse, its outbuildings and paddock were ideal for Patricia and the menagerie included a horse for her (and occasionally me), a pony for Jason (but oh the tedium of gymkhanas), a goat (for the milk), a bird of some sort and a whippet or greyhound or both. When the post stopped arriving, Patricia phoned the sorting office to be told that the greyhound was threatening the postman. She explained that, when this particular dog bared its teeth, it was a welcoming smile. It was the gentlest of animals. Postal deliveries were resumed.

One of my less favourite chores was to take the goat for its daily walk. Apparently it needed proper exercise, and the thought that I did too may have crossed her mind. The trouble was that a large goat is extremely strong and had its own ideas on where we should go. I was dragged along as it chose the most unsuitable things to eat. There may not be anything a goat will not eat. Sooner or later it turned for home and the so-called leading rein slackened.

## Next stop NATIONAL SERVICE

In 1955, those intending to go to university were given a choice of doing national service first or after. We had no idea that choosing to do it after would in reality have meant not doing it at all (almost all of us would have made that choice) because it was abolished in 1957. For me it would have been the wrong choice. Two years not doing sums ruined any Oxford studies, which might well have not amounted to much in any case, and it was a good deal in all other respects. Along with all contemporaries who did national service, we were glad we did.

It didn't look quite such a good choice on the 1st October when I rocked up at Buller Barracks with one very small suitcase. The Royal Army Service Corps had assured us they would take care of all our needs.

Luckily warned that, when we paraded for the first time, the sergeant would ask who had been in the CCF, my arm remained firmly by my side when he did. The volunteers were marched off to peel potatoes and do whatever other menial tasks the cooks could devise. Even the parade ground was better than that.

This had a certain justice as I had escaped almost all the parade ground stuff at Downside. One afternoon a week we changed into battledress and were drilled by the older boys masquerading as NCOs and under-officers. This was no fun so when Paul Focke and I elicited from Major Page that the signals platoon had emptied itself and he needed volunteers, we signed up sharpish. As, initially, the only members, we appointed ourselves Under-Officer, that being Focke as the more elegant, and myself as sergeant, on the grounds I had the louder voice. Focke has brown curly hair and an innocent demeanour. No doubt his mother considered him pretty but that concealed trouble of the highest order. As we were mere fifth formers, our ranks were two years ahead of where they should have been.

Not only was being drilled a thing of the past, we inherited a signals room full of the wonders of the then communications age. There was a transmitter powerful enough to interrupt the local BBC and a receiver that could pick up anything. We had half a dozen walkie talkies which then took the form of quite heavy rucksacks and a tape recorder/playback. The latter was a new invention. We wondered how to smuggle it into a physics class and play the tape back to show the master just how boring he was. Fortunately, we never made it.

There was no point in being in charge of the platoon if there was no one to be in charge of so we recruited fourth formers with various inducements. And being the sergeant, I also set about doing some drilling of my own until the lads pointed out that they had joined the signals platoon precisely to avoid that. Nicky Reynolds, one of the fourth formers we recruited and later a Guards officer and lifelong friend, still rarely fails to mention what a formative experience he found this to be.

The annual CCF field day was where we really came into our own. Some grey haired general would arrive with an entourage of regulars and watch as half Downside's CCF attacked the other half encamped on some hillside. 50% of our walkie talkies and their operators were deployed to each side, supposedly on different wavelengths. Then as now the technology dipped in and out and chaos ensued until the general pronounced that he was well pleased with the whole affair and that Major Page and his troops should be congratulated on a fine display of military readiness.

National service turned out to be much the same: a continuing hope that one's inadequacies would be overlooked. One inadequacy was ending up in the RASC in the first place. Not being too keen on walking, I had put myself down for Uncle Peter's regiment, the 3rd Hussars. At the pre-call-up medical, the doctor, as others have since, pronounced unkindly on my girth. His view was that I would not be able to escape the tank's turret fast enough in an emergency and that would be rather unfair on those trapped below. Passing second class precluded any respectable regiment without being bad enough to be precluded altogether. Flat feet would have been better.

Anyway, if the RASC was good enough for Grandfather Wilfred, it was good enough for me. As things turned out it was both an ideal training for my future career and the gateway to a wonderful time back in Singapore.

Marching round the parade ground at Buller Barracks was not that bad. Winter cold meant keeping one's pyjamas on day and night. First thing after breakfast was the inspection to ensure we were properly turned out, boots bulled, brasses shining and all that. The sergeant would pass along the line with his nose about four inches from ours, staring intently. Sample humour: 'Ambler, did you shave this morning?' 'Yes, sergeant.' 'Did you use a mirror?' 'Yes, sergeant.' 'Well next time use a f*cking razor.'

Unfortunately we were the last intake before a lively House of Commons debate, doubtless including MPs with squaddie sons, persuaded the army to do away with 'bull' or at least some aspects of it. The silliest example was whitewashing the piles of coal waiting to go into the barrack room solid fuel heater. Another was polishing the underneath, the soles, of our boots. Every morning we had to strip our beds and fold the sheets, blankets and pillow case to form a neat 'box' at the end of the bed. If it was not neat enough the NCO would use his swagger cane to scatter it across the room. A more pointless activity is hard to imagine. Be that as it may, bull was for us part of basic training.

The public schoolboys were the only ones who had been away from their families and therefore did not suffer from homesickness. Many of the others could barely read or write and we helped them with their correspondence. They helped us with cunning ways of undermining the NCOs. I won't say a good time was had by all but it could have been much worse.

Guard duty goes with the job but it has to be about the most tedious inactivity known. My two hour shift seemed always to be at the coldest darkest point in the night, and it was very cold. The IRA were taking up arms again although their 'Border Campaign'

(December 1956 – February 1962) proved to be modest by later standards – only about 11 IRA and 6 RUC were killed in the five years, with 32 RUC officers wounded and 400 IRA suspects interned. With remarkable prescience by Aldershot RASC NCOs a year earlier, they told us that the IRA were expected to raid our barracks, as soft targets, for our rifles and we should be all the more alert.

This sounded pretty unlikely so the priority was to find a relatively cosy shelter and wake up in time for the relief. Nothing happened apart from a few practical jokers who had found midnight supplies of booze:

'Halt! Who goes there?'

'Murphy.'

'Murphy who?'

'Murphy O'Kelly.'

'Advance friend and give me a beer.'

Bull and guard duty apart, life was good. The system had not quite caught up with the fact that we were not volunteers. When we failed to run a mile in full kit – and of course I couldn't run a mile in any kit – the irate Sergeant Major pronounced we would be discharged unless we completed the task the next day. A great cheer rang out and, strangely, no more was said.

The pay was 28/6 (£1.42) a week but that was enough for beer and choc bars from the NAAFI and I think the army paid for our travel home on free weekends, 36 or 48 hour passes. A friend living near us in Berkshire had an MG which was wonderful except in the pea souper fogs we had that winter. It was so thick in places that I had to walk in front waving him on with a torch.

Life brightened, for some of us, with the news of WOSB (War Office Selection Board). The tests involved planks, barrels, ropes and getting squads from one side of the river to the other. Each of us took turns to be in command. This posed an interesting dilemma: did one mess things up to make the temporary commander look foolish, with the risks of reprisals and being marked down for unsporting behaviour, or did one cover up the commander's mistakes? Competition (they seemed to have fixed pass/fail ratios) meant that successes had to be balanced by failures. In the event it was almost all catastrophic yet our invigilators maintained their enthusiasm for our efforts, just like a Field Day at Downside.

Later it turned out that I passed only because I gave a moderately coherent lecture. On our return we consoled the unlucky ones and said goodbye to the rest of our colleagues. We were sorry to part as we had all got along remarkably well. It was all 'Strictly Come Dancing'.

At Mons, also in the Aldershot army-land, we became officer cadets with white flashes on our shoulders. We were met with Regimental Sergeant Major Brittain's traditional greeting: 'I call you Sir and you call me Sir but only one of us means it.' Brittain was famous and 40,000 officer cadets passed through his care at Mons. He retired the year before we got there but such was his presence that we thought it was him.

Our Company Sergeant Major also did a lot of shouting. He rapidly became a figure of fun partly because his rifle tended to knock his hat off when he demonstrated how to shoulder arms. Other things tended also to go wrong for him but laughter in the ranks was not tolerated. How he had percolated up through the Welsh Guards to be a CSM at Mons was a matter of some conjecture.

Our new colleagues were mostly cavalry and very congenial. Nothing was taken too seriously.

Mons was partly basic training all over again. We were better at square bashing by now but the military wit was much the same. Those who sloped up to London's West End in the evenings suffered most. Kit still had to be bulled and sleep deprivation was the norm.

The course was eight weeks, much of it in the classroom, with an exam and a field exercise at the end. The exercise part – shades of Field Days – involved half the company attacking the other half entrenched at the top of some Surrey hill. The invigilators accidentally or on purpose picked the less fit as the attacking force. I think the roles were supposed to be reversed in the afternoon but we never got that far.

It was a blissful spring day. The birds were singing, the flowers were out and the sun was shining down from a blue sky. We lay there in the grass in our battledress and full kit waiting for the order to advance. Some people claimed they never heard it and others hoped that their camouflage would render them invisible. Be that as it may, when the chief instructor shouted 'charge', nobody did. The sight of the instructors running up and down, shouting and enpurpling gave us all much satisfaction. We had had enough of them by then. And, as I said, it was a lovely day.

We were matched back to barracks and then, as you might imagine, there was hell to pay. The main penalty at Mons (and Eaton Hall, the infantry officer school) for idleness or incompetence or misbehaviour was relegation, i.e. you had to do the eight weeks all over again. Usually about five to ten percent had that pleasure.

When we got back we were fell in and addressed by the Officer Commanding. (The military go in for quaint titles. The Officer Commanding is a Major whereas a Commanding Officer is a Colonel.) I do not know if you have ever seen an old-fashioned, enraged Major. The neck throbs and the voice becomes a hoarse shout. The drift of his peroration went like this:

'The performance this afternoon was a disgrace for you, your regiments and Mons. I have never seen a worse display, or perhaps lack of it. I cannot say it was a surprise as your performance as a company has been useless throughout the eight weeks you have been here. The entire company will now be relegated and, if things do not improve, you will be reassigned from your present regiments to the Pioneer Corps.' I do not know how often an entire intake had been relegated within the Mons system and maybe we were the first. It was certainly rare.

Nor did I find out what the Pioneer Corps did apart from digging latrines. It was clearly a serious threat. After a brief silence, we were fallen out. One of the more civilised captains who had been enjoying the show, pulled two or three of us out of the ranks and ushered us into his office. Worse, I thought, was to come. Not a bit of it: 'You lot should consider yourselves very lucky. You deserve relegation as much as the others but, in the light of your exam results, we cannot really do it. Passing or failing here at Mons is based on a combination of the exam and the practical exercise marks. You got zero for the exercise but with almost 100% for the exam you have passed. You would be wise to keep this to yourselves and not tell the others.'

And so it was that our small band left Mons as fast as possible and returned to our units.

The final ten weeks of training were all downhill. Much of the time was learning to drive 3 ton Bedford trucks on and off the road. I had failed my driving test before joining up so this was both good fun and useful. We learned how to take the engine to pieces and correct basic faults like dirty petrol.

Although we were all proficient by the end, we were not given driving licences, so it was not until later, when the army rather conveniently put me in charge of issuing licences, that I was able to issue one to myself, or rather, have my sergeant do so. I still drive on it to this day. Motor bikes had proved such a disaster that I failed myself on them, probably why I am still alive.

It was a boy scout existence: nice weather, picnics, cooking with bonfires and mess tins and camping under camouflage. If it did rain, my truck provided plenty of cover and comfort.

Soon enough we had our marching orders. The War Office chose and we did not. The captain was astonished to discover that I was given a choice: Bulford Barracks on the Salisbury Plain and Cyprus where the emergency was in full swing.

'Not lucky at all,' said I in response, 'they are equally disagreeable. The first is boring and the second involves being shot at. I did not join the army to be shot at.'

'So what are you going to do?'

'I will write to the War Office to suggest they use my invaluable experience in Singapore. The RASC has a platoon of small boats there and that would suit me nicely.'

'You must be mad. If they get a letter like that, they will find some complete hell hole for you.'

Life is not predictable and, by return, I had a posting to Singapore – albeit not the boat platoon. I was off to save Malaya from the communist bandits. Pity about the boat platoon, though, as its only function seemed to be taking the daughters, and occasionally wives, of senior officers out for picnics on the surrounding islands.

One painful interview remained. Although it was unusual, it was possible to fail this last ten week module. On presenting myself for assessment, the officers' faces were full of gloom. 'You've done some good things, Ambler, but you are not really officer material. We have not been able to discern any leadership skills (was this influenced by my views on Cyprus?). You are bright but if we did pass you, we don't know how you could possibly be useful to the army. Luckily you will be joining a new unit in Singapore. We have suggested you are not put in charge of any of the transport platoons but of the company headquarters.' The blow to my self-esteem apart, that seemed just fine.

Training was finally over and it was up to the London shops to buy a hat to go with the new shiny brass pips and some tropical uniform.

The Malayan 'emergency' (they couldn't call it a 'war' because the insurance companies would not then pay up) lasted from 1948 until 1957 so far as Britain was concerned. It started up again after independence in the 1960s but that was nothing substantial.

Despite the Permanent Secretary for Malaya, Sir Robert Grainger Ker Thompson, having served with the Chindits in the war and supposedly knowing all about jungle warfare, the army did not fare well until General Gerald Templer arrived in 1952 and implemented his predecessor's 'Briggs Plan'* with more vigour.

According to Wikipedia: 'During the conflict, security forces killed 6710 MRLA guerrillas and captured 1287, while 2702 guerrillas surrendered during the conflict, and approximately 500 more did so at its conclusion. 1345 Malayan troops and police were killed during the fighting, as well as 519 Commonwealth personnel (mostly British). 2478 civilians were killed, with another 810 recorded as missing.' Southern Rhodesia contributed soldiers but the Australians only arrived in 1955 when it was nearly over. The terrorists killed all of our troops they captured.

The communists had support from the Malays in kampongs that fringed the jungle either because they were sympathisers or, more often, because of coercion – the alternative being vicious. By and large the terrorists were Chinese who normally lived in the towns whereas the countryside was populated by Malays. The two ethnic groups have never liked each other. For the security forces it had the advantage that if you met a Chinese on a jungle trail, the odds were that he was a terrorist. You could shoot him and ask questions later.

The conventional wisdom in my time was that Templer devised the right strategy of moving (where necessary) kampongs and certainly fortified them with enough guards to eliminate contact with the terrorists and cut off that source of food and information. Spotter planes looked for jungle clearings where the terrorists grew their food.

Then Templer cleared areas in a methodical manner, adding each new 'white' area to adjacent white areas so that the whole frontier could be guarded against infiltration. Previously the army cleared areas and the terrorists moved back in when they left. Lastly we fought the terrorists at their own game, namely using highly trained troops (albeit national servicemen) following jungle trails in platoons and not using large numbers in sweeps.

Much of the writing about this period has been biased by left-wing guilt about colonisation and the application of contemporary values to 50-year-old situations. A particular example of this genre is Calder

---

* The strategy was actually devised by General Sir Harold Briggs, the British Army's Director of Operations in Malaya, a few years earlier.

Walton* who expects readers to be horrified that our soldiers, when engaging the guerrillas in the jungle, operated a 'shoot to kill' policy. Killing the enemy has long proved an effective means of stopping him killing you. Yes, some things should not have happened and the Foreign and Colonial Office was daft to file those records. Pay up or shut up. Only FCO civil servants could have failed to grasp either nettle. On the other side, the motivation of writers who delve selectively into these records, distort history and heap excessive guilt and odium on their fellow countrymen is obscure. Even Calder Walton grudgingly admits that we were successful in Malaya. Perhaps more importantly (but not mentioned by Walton and his ilk), the locals were extremely grateful for what we did. Long after independence, Dennis was twice invited back to be feted by the Malaysian government for his role. And the British government gave him an OBE, followed by a CBE.

Wikipedia has an interesting comparison of the Malayan and Vietnam campaign 20 years later. Vietnam was more difficult in some ways but there is little doubt that if the Americans had learned more from the British experience in Malaya they would have been more successful.

Dennis and Patricia drove me down to the Southampton dockside just like old times except I was going, not them. The troopship, the *Empire Orwell*, was mostly occupied by the 1st Battalion, Royal Sussex, destined for Korea. Fighting had officially stopped three years earlier but it was still modestly dangerous with about 5000 ceasefire violations a year. There were 50 casualties but, disgracefully, no medals.† The Royal Sussex was the last British regiment to keep the peace in Korea.

Accommodation and shipboard routines were more or less exactly as I recalled from the P&O liners. First class was allocated to officers and the wives of officers important enough to have been flown out.

We subalterns soon spotted the opportunity – a ready supply of lonely women for three weeks sailing under the tropical moon. Better still, the best looking girl on the ship was in the cabin next door. Things did not work out quite as we hoped. When the glamour girl

---

* *Empire of Secrets*, Harper Press, 2013.

† By contrast, we in Singapore each got a General Service Medal after 48 hours and without ever coming within miles of a hostile bullet. No distinction was made between the soldiers fighting up-country and those, like me, partying safely in Singapore. No doubt GHQ wanted to ensure they got them.

made it plain she wanted nothing to do with any of us, we came up with a cunning plan. We would chat up her cabin-mate, an older blonde, bring her into our social group and she would, in turn, involve her cabin-mate. Of course this ruse soon exploded in our faces but friendly relations developed, alas not more than that.

Strange as it may seem, when I later came across them in Singapore, shopping with their husbands, neither recognised me at all.

Three Sussex national service subalterns and I were billeted in a small, inside cabin. A bit smelly from time to time, it worked well enough. One, the son of a vicar, disapproved of the other three of us returning late at night and the worse for wear. He disapproved of bad language, chasing women and especially the two in the next cabin. Most of all he had absolutely no sense of humour. He came across as a prig and a bore and we probably made our opinion clear. I doubt he enjoyed the voyage.

All of which shows just how little one can learn of a cellmate if he is not a soulmate. The man was John Wells who went on to Oxford and became, perhaps, the funniest man in British showbiz. His impersonation of Denis Thatcher was wonderful. Not all those who are funny on stage are funny in private life but Wells later was, and he made many good friends. When our paths crossed at Oxford, though, he showed no wish to include me in that circle.

At the other extreme another Sussex subaltern immediately became a good friend, later my flatmate and then best man: James Wiltshire. James's undoing, if that is what it was, was the price of spirits once we were at sea. A good tot ('large' in a modern pub) was 6d, or 2.5p and a subaltern's salary added up to quite a few tots. James was funny and great company sober but even better when not. One tot invariably led to another and he was sozzled for virtually the entire journey.

This proved advantageous. He was appointed orderly officer on the first or second day out. The idea was that each subaltern would do one day. We weren't sure what it involved and none of us ever found out, especially not James. An orderly officer is supposed to be on duty, sober, alert and ready to draw the attention of the Commanding Officer, the Colonel of the Sussex in this case, to any imminent danger. Staggering from bar to mess deck in an inebriated condition, as Wiltshire did, is not good form. At the end of his first day, he was punished by being appointed orderly officer for the next day. And so it continued throughout the voyage. None of the rest us ever thereafter had that duty.

His CO was Colonel George de Stacpoole, an Irish aristocrat who left Downside in 1935 and fought through WWII. He was a tolerant man. Today's anxiety about binge drinking would have locked Wiltshire up and probably his CO for failing to put a stop to it. He did get Wiltshire to slow things down a bit when they got to Korea but not before he had had a few more extra orderly officer days.

When not propping Wiltshire up on his bar stool, we played bridge by day and danced with the military wives by night. The Colonel enjoyed bridge and was not in the least rank conscious – maybe that was the Downside connection. There are worse ways of spending three weeks.

Someone kindly met me off the ship and we drove up to my unit which was based on an airfield shared by the Fleet Air Arm and the Army Air Corps. The navy thought it was a ship, even though it was four miles from the nearest water, and called it HMS Simbang, a corruption of the village name. Sembawang is just south of the huge naval base at the north of the island and beside the causeway to Johore. The much larger army barracks at Nee Soon must have been full and/or insecure for our future role.

No. 6 Company had just been created by asking the five or six nearest RASC units each to send 20 men. You can guess which 20 they sent. Most had criminal tendencies and all were trouble. I was to command the HQ platoon, i.e. everyone who was not in the transport (lorry) platoons. HQ included cooks, clerks, mechanics and other specialists who were deemed not to need leadership. It was formed, I learned later, as part of preparing for the expected riots and insurrection in Singapore itself.

Looking back I cannot believe the opulence of our life-style. The common mess areas were many and spacious, flags flew in front, and the two-floor cabin wing accommodated perhaps eight of us but could have managed two dozen more, all in rooms 20' by 20' or so. We had two tennis courts, an olympic standard swimming pool and a cinema for all ranks – but the film only started when we rolled in after dinner. Besides cooks, cleaners and waitstaff, we had our own drivers, Landrovers, and batmen.

Three kinds of missions were flown up-country from HMS Simbang: reconnaissance by Austers flown by the Army Air Corps, air to ground strikes by RN Buccaneers and jungle support by RN helicopters.

The Austers were little use for seeing what was going on under the tree canopies. They left soon after I arrived and they may have been withdrawn altogether. The Buccaneers were pulled in to attack map references so it mattered little whether they could see anything or not. We had a few accidents but the missions were not, in themselves, dangerous.

The helicopter missions were another matter and the pilots who flew them were incredibly brave. The usual form was for enough jungle to be cleared to give space to land and take off either bringing in fresh men and supplies and/or taking the wounded out. The first problem was that the soldiers on the ground often failed to make the clearings big enough. Even if the pilots were exact, and they were pretty good, you have to add to the width of the rotors enough space for the downdraught to escape without causing the helicopter to wobble. And if the space was not quite enough, the pilot couldn't hang there while they chopped some more trees down. Nor did they like returning home with the mission aborted just for a few inches of space. It was something the army should have sorted out. We lost only a few pilots but that was still too many.

The next problem was that the helicopters, being very noisy, showed the terrorists exactly where they could attack and they did.

Attending the funerals was far the saddest thing I did in my time there. The pilots were in their 30s, married and with children. Often as not we had been drinking with them in the bar the day before.

My OC was Major Boyldue who could have been a model for Captain Mainwaring of TV's *Dads' Army*. Generally amiable, he bristled when provoked. He was supported by three regular army captains, and two of us national service 2nd lieutenants. Company Sergeant Major James really ran the unit. The senior Captain needed to start each day with a large horse's neck (brandy, angostura and ginger ale) without which he would not make breakfast, never mind lunch. Then there was one with a bristly moustache who was, I think, second in command and reasonably sane. Four of us quartered in the mess. Boyldue lived with his wife in married quarters nearby and the other, exceedingly stuffy but more of that later, captain was also in married quarters.

With the end of national service two years later, most of these middle ranking officers and senior NCOs became redundant. That was sad.

The naval and army flyers were great fun. Most were married and living out but we held the parties and they all came. Visiting army chiefs looked confused when we asked them when they were going ashore and whether their cabins were satisfactory. And when we referred to our Commanding Officer we meant the Royal Naval Captain (to whom Boyldue officially reported) and not Major Boyldue himself or some RASC Colonel downtown (the main town and GHQ was about 12 miles south).

Being a ship proved handy on one occasion. The Captain announced a party at his quarters about a mile or so 'ashore'. Very regretfully I had to refuse as I was orderly officer than evening. Not only should I have been in camp but also in uniform. 'Nonsense,' says the Captain, 'whatever I instruct you to wear is your uniform.' I was easily persuaded and a very good party it was.

Next morning I was summoned by Boyldue in one of many such confrontations.

'Where were you last night? You were supposed to be orderly officer.'

'With the Captain, sir.'

'Well I looked for you all over the camp and the guard sergeant told me you had left.'

'Well that is true, sir, but I was on the ship. The Captain's cabin is part of the ship and our base is HMS Simbang, sir, as I am sure the Captain will confirm.' And, of course, he did.

Singapore was building up its own communist insurgency based around the Chinese middle school students (and presumably their parents). By 1956 Singapore had achieved self government but not full independence. The cry was for Merdeka (freedom). David Marshall, a socialist lawyer and friend of Dennis, was the first Chief Minister and trying, but failing, to keep order. Britain offered troops to help but Marshall argued that the sight of British troops on the streets would only inflame matters.

A big pow-wow was held in London in May 1956 with Marshall explaining his plan, more power for him, and the FCO expressing doubts about his ability to control the situation with or without more power. Marshall had threatened to resign if he did not get his way and now did so, being succeeded by Lim Yew Hock.

Maybe Dennis played a part in this as the Brits, for once, were clever. They knew Marshall could not deliver and therefore the talks would fail. A plan was laid before the talks began and called 'PHOTO', an anagram of sorts for 'Failure Of Talks Operation'. The operational units in Singapore were made up of locals and although professional and British officered, they could not wholly be relied on, and certainly not if it came to firing on their own kith and kin. Various RAF and cavalry units were cobbled together but they were not the sort of steady line troops needed to confront rioters. The government brought the 6th battalion of Queen Elizabeth's Own Gurkha Rifles down 470 miles from the Cameron Highlands but only at the last moment.

The riots began on 25th October and I was summoned by Major Boyldue. The conversation went something like this:

'Ambler, we have a job for you.'

'Yessir, what do you have in mind?'

'You know about these riots that have just started.'

'Yessir.'

'Well we want you to put a stop to them.'

'Just me sir?'

'No you idiot, not just you. We cannot rely on the native troops so we are bringing a battalion of Gurkhas down to stand behind the local troops and make sure they do what they are supposed to do. Otherwise they can chop a few heads off.'

'Local troops or rioters?'

'Doesn't matter. The point is that you can never tell about foreigners in a foreign land so we are sending you with 30 men to stand behind the Gurkhas and make sure they do their job. Realistically there is no chance the Gurkhas will not do so but apparently it will comfort High Command if British troops are backing up. Here's a revolver with six rounds of ammunition. I want them all back after the riots. Make sure your men's rifles have full magazines but no more.'

Boyldue failed to mention the RAF or cavalry or other sundry army units already in place, nor the busloads of police under the command of Commissioner N G Morris, also a friend of Dennis. It was a far bigger operation than I was told at the time. Morris was a first-class senior police officer and the two worked closely together over the years but, at this juncture, Dennis was in England.

Anyway, all very exciting for me. Apart from leading truck convoys up into Malaya itself, it was as close as I got to combat. Tooled up, we piled into our lorry and headed for town where they were indeed rioting. We observed from a safe distance. Our troops, locals, Gurkhas and others were visibly there but did not seem to be doing anything. Disappointingly, there were no heads on poles. In a few days it was all over. 13 rioters were killed, 12 by the police and none by the military. 761 rounds were fired by the security forces on 114 occasions, but the military fired only 14 rounds and none of them was mine. It was a textbook case for handling civil disorder. Apart, perhaps, from the psychological influence of seeing that the troops were there, the police had wrapped it all up by themselves.

A couple of months later David Marshall, now ex-Chief Minister, invited me for Christmas. He was larger than life, great fun and a genial host. He had a lovely house by the sea, with all mod cons and hot and cold, leggy, Australian blondes. I don't know how many lived there but certainly more than one. The modern prurient press would have loved it. So did I. Lounging in the warm water in the dark with a whisky in one hand and a blonde in the other made for a memorable Christmas. Berlusconi might have called it a bunga bunga party but we did not get that far.

The epilogue was amusing. Some 45 years later, I was having lunch with friends in Norfolk. One of the other guests was a retired Gurkha officer even older than me. In the course of chatting it emerged that he had been one of the majors involved in the 1956 Singapore riots. I complimented him on the part they had played and told him that he need not have worried, if he had, because he had the security of our platoon standing behind him. His response was unprintable.

Another day, another summons from Boyldue:

'Ambler, I have a job for you.'

'What is that sir?'

'You know there is a major SEATO* Conference in Singapore next month?'

'No sir, I had no idea.'

'Well there is. A fleet of 30 staff cars are being delivered here today.

---

* The south-east Asia version of NATO but without assets. It was created by the Americans in 1954 to liaise anti-communist planning and served as a cover for the US invasion of Vietnam. If the US had accepted the unification of Vietnam when it was proposed in the first place instead of having SEATO reject it, many US lives would have been saved and we would have been where we finished anyway. SEATO was rightly seen by independent Asian nations as neo-colonialist and did not survive long.

It is your job to pick 30 of our drivers and turn them into chauffeurs. You have two weeks to do it.'

With which he returned to the papers on his desk, brooking no further questions.

The men thought this a thoroughly good skive and it was difficult to get them to take it seriously. On a 3 Tonner you double declutch and gear changing is far from smooth for the passengers, not that they usually have passengers. And the idea of getting out of one's own seat to walk round the back, not the front mind you, to open the door for the passenger in the back who could perfectly well open it for himself was considered laughable.

The 30 Austin 90s, then a popular large family car, were painted khaki, but the prize was a Daimler, long, black and shiny. The bonnet started going round a corner a long time before the rest of the car and you could have fitted a rugby team in the passenger space.

All went amazingly well with no accidents or mishaps bar one. The Daimler had a flagpole on the front and we had been given a little Union Jack, presumably because the most senior person at the conference would be a British general. My driver and I agreed that it would be quite fun to test the reflexes of the Singapore GHQ when an unexpected VIP arrived. We rolled up at the guardhouse, with me lolling in the back, and panic ensued. The guard was turned out and presented arms and I could hear phones being madly rung inside. In those days you didn't press buttons, you wound the handle.

I lowered the window and said to the guard commander as languidly as I could manage: 'We are not staying in fact but I'd be glad if you would tell the General that we will be back tomorrow.' With which my driver executed an elegant U turn, avoiding the three feet deep monsoon drains which ran beside every road. I was mad to imagine this silly prank would not be traced back to me.

Boyldue again:

'Ambler, this time you have gone too far.'

'Not at all sir. It is all part of their necessary training. I had to show the Daimler driver what he should expect when he arrives at a guardhouse.'

Not very convincing you may think and nor did Boyldue.

The SEATO Conference concluded with a particularly fine party in our mess. However inebriated, it should not have been difficult to locate my cabin, a mere 20 yards from the bar. I therefore cannot explain why I was anywhere near the main road, still less lying at the bottom of a monsoon drain, gazing at the stars and wedged so tight I could not move. Oddly enough it was quite comfortable so I had a snooze and as dawn broke, scuttled back to my cabin.

SEATO aside, we also hosted units from up-country having a little R&R. We had an RAF group, known as 'Crabfats' to the navy, whose pilots got on poorly with our naval flyers. And we had the King's Dragoon Guards who proved excellent company not least because they were rather poor poker players. Chatting to Quill Greenwood, a friend and neighbour in Norfolk 50 years on, it emerged that he had been in that regiment in Malaya, albeit not R&Ring at HMS *Simbang*, and had had exactly the same monsoon drain experience, also with no ill effects.

As already explained, our company had been made up of soldiers no other unit wanted. Quite a few were from the Gorbals and many had criminal records. Always amiable with me they did not abandon their criminal ways with others. The trouble, often alcohol related, led to violence and some taxi drivers, sadly, were never the same again. Visits to see some of my chaps in Changi gaol were educational but they seemed quite relaxed about it. Their accommodation was little more that a rug, a water scoop and a bed made from leather straps. It would have been condemned in Britain.

Someone who should have been in gaol, in my view, was the Cook Sergeant, known to me as the Crook Sergeant. There were genuine complaints and although Aldershot food is not ideal for the tropics, it had to be down to the cooking as the raw materials were fine. I focussed first on the filets of beef. Beef arrived in whole quarters so there should have been a filet with every hindquarter. The cooks in the officers' and sergeants' messes assured me they never saw one and the Crook Sergeant himself was vague on the matter. Someone was selling them to local restaurants and perhaps much else besides. I set all manner of traps and had the guards search his car when he went ashore after a hindquarter had been delivered. Nothing untoward appeared. I will spare you the mashed potato affair but the bottom line was experienced Sergeant 2 – 19-year-old 2nd Lieutenant Nil. It was no contest really. I should have enlisted CSM James.

Nevertheless, with the aid of a middle-aged sergeant who had been up and down the ranks like a diver on speed thanks to his own misdemeanours, my unit got along very well. We were all in it together and determined to make the most of it. They were glad to be in Singapore, one of the nicest postings, and the town offered delights unknown in the jungles of Malaya or Glasgow.

The Military Police posted notices of out of bounds areas and lists of hotels which were out of bounds even though they were in in-bounds areas. The lads, especially those newly arrived, found this very helpful as otherwise they would not have known where to go. They were well equipped with condoms and were rarely caught by the MPs. The punishment was being confined to barracks which they needed anyway to recover and to await the next wage envelope.

The Captains knew of more sophisticated brothels to which they refused to take us. My fellow subaltern and I decided we'd play it safe, apart from the taxi dancing establishments which were brutal but not dangerous. The trouble with the more exotic places was not so much being caught by an infection or the MPs but the sheer embarrassment of finding our own men in the same establishment.

The lads' burglarious skills came in handy at one point. We discovered we were short of a motorcycle, possibly because one of them had sold it downtown. After conferring with my sergeant, he assembled them:

'We have a problem. It is a one motorcycle short kind of problem. Would whoever nicked it care to return it?' Nobody moved in the pause.

'Right, we are going to have to replace it.' The soldiers were in and out of the REME, army workshops, quite regularly having their vehicles repaired.

'I want no one to come out of a REME workshop without a motorcycle part we need.'

Within three weeks we had a fine new machine.

Thanks to Dennis's friends I had been able to join Tanglin. Sadly the Club is now a tower block with no hint of the colonial charm of the original. It had splendid open-to-the-breezes squash courts and was a great place to entertain. My fellow subaltern and I spent many happy hours there once we cracked the problem of how to get there.

Careful study of Queen's Regulations indicated that we could employ our military driver for leisure purposes at 6d (2.5p) per hour. The drivers were up for this too as it was a free trip downtown. Club members may have wondered why a military Landrover was so often waiting outside but nothing was said.

It had been noticed. I only ever met our Brigadier once when he turned up unannounced at my platoon's practice on the firing range. Having stomped about rather ominously, he took me to one side and told me off for wearing shoes and long socks on a firing range when any idiot should know the correct dress was boots and gaiters. Two days later he was on the phone:

'Ambler, I gather you are a member of the Tanglin Club.'

'Yessir'

'Any chance you could put me up as a member?'

I decided not to mention the matter of my shoes and socks.

The transport arrangement was soon blown. Accompanied by a couple of charmers, we were in a downtown movie house (the films at the mess were not the newest) when the film ground to a halt and a message appeared on screen for the owners of.... Followed by the number of our Landrover. Everyone watched as we scuttled out and the film resumed. Two MPs were standing beside the Landrover in the parking lot with no sign of our driver who would not have been expecting us so soon.

'Are you using this vehicle for leisure purposes, sir.'

'Yes but that is quite legitimate I am paying for it in line with Queen's Regs.'

'I think you'll find, sir, that army vehicles should not be left unattended in unguarded areas and ...' looking nastily at our rather nervous charmers '... they may not be used for the carriage of civilians.'

Next day, I was once again standing to attention in front of Major Boyldue.

We agreed that our next ploy was to drive the one ton van on the pretext of training. This was no good for civilians nor could it be left outside the Tanglin Club but it did get us downtown and could be parked in GHQ without being noticed.

Another snotty major, a friend of Boyldue's, asked him in passing why he allowed his subalterns to career wildly around the island in a one ton truck, not even in uniform. Apparently I had overtaken him doing about 60 in a 40mph area. Boyldue took a dim view yet again.

One way and another I was permanently in trouble. Much as I enjoyed our standard of living and the social life, the army and I did not seem to be well matched. I balanced the books with Boyldue to some extent, even though he would not have approved my methods. Some general told Boyldue that we managed our vehicle fleet better that any other unit in the Far East. He didn't know that our vehicle servicing was lamentable but I'd been up all night cooking the books in inks of different colours. The moustachioed Captain did smell a rat and asked how it happened.

And Boyldue was praised again when a General dropped in for a mess night and was impressed by the table gleaming with regimental silver. 'It is remarkable,' he said, 'that a newly formed regiment can have such historic silver.'

'Well we are No. 6 Company, sir, and that is well up the line.'

I doubt he believed him. The fact was that I had decided following a previous mess night that our table looked a little bare and took the matter up with our suppliers. Chinese vendors to HM Forces can take a hint.

This transport difficulty following the banning of the one ton van was solved by my deciding to teach myself to ride a motorcycle. Its L plates were easy to spot by the Tanglin Club front door but other transport had to be organised for friends.

Ordered down to the docks one dark morning to take a newly arrived infantry company up-country, the MPs at the gates demanded the identity card that I am supposed to carry at all times. Hand to pocket, no card. It had been a particularly good party the night before. Explaining what we were about, I point to the 30 trucks lined up behind my Landrover and ask if I looked like a Chinese communist terrorist. This may not have been the best question and things are looking ugly when an MP subaltern heaves in sight wanting to know what the problem was. He had been at the same party the previous night and we were through.

The battalion was all lined up on the quay and I give the Colonel my best salute. Apparently, due to the altercation at the gate, we were two minutes late and the Colonel was, to put it mildly, grumpy. I withheld my opinion that he was jolly lucky to be picked up in such style and offered him my seat in the Landrover. I could navigate from one of the back seats. 'Certainly not,' he replied. 'A Colonel rides with his men.' Clearly I should have known that. I was glad I served under Colonel de Stacpoole.

We more than made up the time because the drivers liked a good pace, never mind Queen's Regs, and we even found the delivery point without deviation. Some other transport platoon must have taken the outgoing battalion down to the ship as we returned empty. As usual I took the short cut through the Naval Base which, for some obscure reason, was also off limits.

The War Office then, and doubtless the MoD now, spent more time devising silly rules than training the military to win battles.

Mess dances were, by 1950s standards, posh affairs. Women in long dresses and men in mess kit. Mine was shrunk on – a sort of body stocking with stripes down the legs and the starched white top had brass buttons. The sanction for misbehaviour in the mess was being sent to Coventry which was slightly uncomfortable but one could catch up on one's reading and one's external social life was unaffected. It only happened twice during my time and I think it was an army thing with the RN officers looking on amused.

The first occasion was a sign of the times. The colour bar was still in operation in clubs like the Swimming Club and Tanglin and in officers' messes. It stopped two years later but in 1956 it operated although many disliked it and it was tricky when officers from Malay regiments visited – they were considered 'honorary Europeans'.

I don't know whether the moustachioed Captain knew the girl he brought to the dance was Eurasian. He certainly was not the kind to make a political point. She was a lovely girl, bright, fun to talk with and visibly upset by the cold shoulder she got from all the married officers and their wives. The other subaltern and I danced with her too.

Back on the carpet next day, Boyldue informed us that the moustachioed Captain had been sent to Coventry for a month and we were lucky not to have been given the same treatment. Apparently the wives decided we were too young to understand.

My own offence was more serious. The stuffy Captain's wife was a larky girl and a gym teacher. They were not well matched. Rock and Roll had just arrived and we younger ones rocked at every opportunity whilst the married ones waited for the next foxtrot – except for the gym mistress. Being slim and exceptionally fit, she seemed to float through the air. The world has seen the moves on *Strictly Come Dancing* 50 odd years on. Whatever they did, we did, or rather, she did. The next two or three mess dances were just great.

Dancing aside, she was fun to chat with. She was as uncomfortable with the other wives as they were with her, and therefore a little lonely. She invited me over for coffee in the morning and, with nothing better to do, I accepted. It was all entirely innocent. Needless to say, stuffy Captain returned just as the coffee was being poured. One of the neighbouring wives must have called him as he never normally did that.

A formal apology and a month in Coventry was my sentence and she, I believe, was similarly punished. Poor girl. I hope she found someone nicer.

My last summons by Boyldue was to give me my marching orders. He did not seem to have any regrets on that matter. Apparently the logistics unit down by the docks was short of officers as several had returned home on leave. For the remainder of my service, six weeks or so, I was to join that.

'What does it involve?'

'I have no idea. You will find out soon enough.'

Pleasurable as it may have been for Boyldue, it was sad for me as I had grown attached to the decadent life of HMS Simbang and doubted whether a bunch of grocers in uniform would be much fun. The other subaltern and I agreed that we would keep in touch once I had sorted out the personal transport problem; I was still on the motor cycle.

The logistics unit had very few officers. We were part of the GHQ mess around which table the shirts were more stuffed than Christmas turkeys. As the junior officer my sole duty was to propose the health of the Queen on mess nights. Unlike the mess on HMS Simbang, it was a place to be avoided.

Luckily Dennis had returned and was borrowing a large house from an executive relocated to Hong Kong. The army agreed I could move in with him. The very civilised accommodation was enlivened by Dennis's girlfriend. Not only was she beautiful but she was wise, witty and fun. She had to be because, being Eurasian and therefore something of an outcast, she had to make a living for herself and her child by being, I suppose, a courtesan. Dennis was not the only husband whose wife had refused to join him. She was mesmerising but not, of course, admissible to the Tanglin Club. Come to that, I do not recall any wives ever joining us for dinner but that suited Dennis's security wrap just fine and security was his middle name. It was hardly surprising that he was anxious nothing should get back to Patricia. Crockery would have been the least of her missiles.

Fortunately on my return, Patricia did not evince much interest in her husband's domestic arrangements. She just said 'Dennis must have been pleased to have someone else sharing the house.'

'Yes, he seemed to be.'

The other bonus from Dennis's arrival in Singapore was his introduction to the secretaries in the High Commission. They were several cuts above the otherwise delightful fillies we had been dating that far and we traded up immediately. And I had a borrowed car.

My military duties were a complete mystery. Under my command were the bakery, butchery and POL (petrol, oil and lubricants) depot. The Victorians had decided that fresh bread was bad for soldiers so the regulations stated bread had to be kept for 24 hours before being issued to the troops. In the tropics with no air conditioning, a dafter regulation is hard to imagine. Unable to overrule it across the board, I ensured fresh bread was delivered to our mess and acquired a few brownie points for so doing.

On the butchery front, quarters of beef or whole sheep or pigs tended to go missing – shades of my Crook Sergeant. My role was to count them in or out but unobtrusively so the coolies did not know if I was there or not. The sight of these tiny coolies, staggering along with beef quarters bigger than they were, was astounding. If any went missing, I did not hear of it.

The whole place seemed to run like a well-oiled machine. It was truly impressive. Everyone but me seemed to know what they were doing including my Major, and that was a step up from dear old Boyldue. It was a paper factory with chits for everything being processed, matched up, by 100 or so clerks. Their vast office was a sea of white shirts bent over desks.

The war machine requires massive amounts of fuel. Tankers drove in and out unceasingly. When supplies were short, or it was going home time, I did get to make the occasional decision on who could, or could not, have supplies. The units up-country not infrequently re-ordered too late so I made a few friends and enemies with my decisions. As the conversations were always with officers much senior to me, this provided some satisfaction.

Then the regular officers returned, I was redundant and put on the next available Comet – a bit too soon in my view. Comets had acquired a bad reputation in 1954 due to their habit of falling out of the sky. The public were reluctant to fly in them. So they were patched up and sold to RAF Transport Command as a job lot.

We flew to Aden where we stayed the night and next day we refuelled at El Adem in Libya and back to Wiltshire. Patricia was keen to hear all the news but discretion being the better part, she did not get much of it. With Jason at home, she had plenty else with which to distract herself.

# Chapter 4

# Salad Days

*Looking back, the Oxford summer vacations were more interesting than term-time, apart of course from punting which was marvellous. University life may have been painted sentimentally by the musical Salad Days but, so far as I was concerned, it was also accurate. We had so little to do with academic studies that they can be disposed of before more serious, social, matters. The chapter covers:*
- *Sums at Oxford*
- *The St John's College annexe*
- *Downside re-connections*
- *The North Quad and romance*
- *The Final Year*
- *Ideological marketing: Communism vs. Capitalism*
- *1960: Oxford University Expedition to Turkey*

Passmore, my headmaster at Downside, had said that maths at Oxford would be beyond me; I should read something simple like PPE. As he had never sent anyone to read sums at Oxbridge, I doubted that he knew; perhaps it was just a goad. In any case, sums involved less work than any other subject.

Getting back into the classroom, after two years of military mental slough, proved difficult. Lectures were so tedious that most of us ceased attendance after the first term. The worst was a mathematical genius who entered the lecture room with barely a glance at the class, turned to face the blackboard on which he wrote algebra for 55 minutes and then departed in similar fashion. Class numbers dwindled from about 80 at the first lecture to about 10 by the third after which I too departed. I have no idea if he ever noticed. Maybe the later lectures were given to an empty room.

The lecturer in question was Professor David Champernowne (1912–2000), a famous statistician who advised Churchill during the war and built, with Alan Turing, the first chess-playing computer. He must have had wonderful tales to tell but, sadly, our caravans passed in the desert.

My college, St John's, had no maths don. Roger Elliott, the physics don, did his best but his sums were little better than ours. And he lacked Page's skill in turning that to advantage. Elliott was a genial and delightful man and later helped me get to MIT. The college then subcontracted our teaching to maths dons in other colleges. They meant well enough but we were not their students and the weekly tutorials (all they were supposed to do) didn't work.

The tutor would set the term's textbook(s) and a few problems for the following week. One would rock up claiming rather pathetically to have done one of the problems (to show willing) but had failed to solve the others. After a quick scan of my one solution, with any comments, the rest of the hour was spent watching him (it was never a 'her') complete our week's work before one departed little the wiser.

Over the three years, I spent about four hours a week doing any academic work. No doubt things are different now and maybe they were different when the college did manage to hire a maths don, a topologist, for my final year, Ioan James. He reviewed our work, or the lack of it, and declared that, as we were beyond help, he would deal only with our successors. So we continued to be farmed out.

Ioan went on to become the top maths professor at Oxford and, in my opinion, deservedly so. Years later, John Ockenden, the maths scholar of the year after me, told me that Ioan was actually rather a controversial figure among the maths faculty. But then divisions between mathematicians are hardly new and topology is a tangled web.

A concentrated effort before Moderations at the end of year one harvested a modest second. The dons were not pleased: exhibitioners were supposed to get firsts. Rather similarly, a surge of actual work delivered the same result at Finals. There was an optional paper for those aiming at a first which I had been advised not to take. Diverting what little work I was doing, I was told, would compromise my expected second. When I took it nonetheless, the dons expected a first. All the compulsory papers would be done by the Thursday afternoon, so my view was 'why not?' and opened the optional paper textbook for the first time when the other exams were done. That evening, white tied and tailed, I took a pretty and long suffering girl to the Queen's College Commem Ball. When the Ball was over and the sun came up, we went punting, she doing the punting and me attempting to focus on the book.

After a good breakfast, the adrenalin was pumping. Throwing on a gown qualified my apparel as the 'subfusc' required for Finals. Luckily a couple of questions were straight out of the book and, or so they told me, I just missed the first. But then, everyone says that and the truth was that I was lucky to get a second. The eerie thing was that Dennis had done exactly the same 33 years earlier but I only discovered that in his papers when he died. I should have told him. I still have the red rose I wore on that last day.

Sloth can only partly be attributed to national service and there learning the art of the skive. I failed to see that university maths would be of any value later. That was wrong but no disaster.

Middleton Hall, an annexe just up the road from St John's, was my assigned abode for the first year. Walking further for everything was initially irritating but it turned out that the dons had selected the occupants with care. We had all done national service and mostly had gained a scholarship or an exhibition. David Bostock, the classics exhibitioner, had the room just below mine but our leader was John Crossley, the maths scholar. How the RAF failed to recognise his talent with a commission beats me but maybe it was class snobbery.

To back up a bit, about six of us sat for the maths scholarship in November 1954. Each paper had about 10 problems and the challenge was to solve as many as one could. There were some marks for good efforts, I think. Comparing notes afterwards, most did, on average, just one. Two or three of us solved two and Crossley solved eight. He was in a different league.

He did not much bother with our kind of sums and moved onto mathematical logic (philosophy), the stuff of Bertrand Russell, which was barely known at Oxford then. Even with Crossley's lucidity, mathematical logic made little sense to me. He was a great fan of Wittgenstein, then unknown to me and, having attempted his writings, unknown to me still. I also attempted Bertrand Russell and concluded that he was a randy old fraud. Being seen as intelligent is far more useful than being intelligent. As Crossley would have known then, and I discovered much later, Russell's life work, *Principia Mathematica*, was proved by Gödel, in 1931, to have been a load of rubbish. Very satisfying that.

Crossley and Bostock both became philosophy dons but by very different routes. Bostock (Charterhouse) was a national service subaltern in a good infantry regiment. He was slight, fair and good looking; Crossley was large, dark and only his mother thought he was good looking. They both were, and are, utterly charming and great company. Bostock arrived determined to become a philosophy don at Oxford. He got his head down on day one and could rarely be persuaded to lift it thereafter. But he achieved his goal and ended his career as the philosophy don at Merton, via Australia. Crossley got a double first without, apparently, working at all, immediately became a Fellow of St Catherine's after his doctorate and, a rare honour, a Fellow of All Souls three years later. Then he went to Australia. There's nowt so queer as folk.

Middleton Hall was a friendly place with late night coffee sessions putting the world to rights as undergraduates do. The pub immediately adjacent, the Lamb and Flag, served Phipps bitter, a nasty brew little improved when Watney Mann took the brewery over in 1960. The Eagle and Child ('Bird and Baby') across St Giles had better beer and better ambience and fuelled our creativity between dinner and nocturnes at Middleton Hall. At the time we neither knew nor would have cared that the pub was the venue for the closing years of the Inklings, a writers' club that included C S Lewis and J R R Tolkien. The pub was bought by St John's in 1962; the college already owned the Lamb and Flag.

The Eagle and Child was father to the Argonauts. None of the Middleton Hall set had ever rowed but some thought they should. The college VIIIs had turned up their noses at these come latelies so, as one evening at the pub wore on, we decided to launch our own VIII. It would remain bottom of the river but what was to be lost? I had no intention of sitting in the damn thing. Rowing requires great effort to go in the wrong direction watching an unattractive back, when one could have been watching an attractive front. I was therefore enrolled as official timekeeper and told to ride up and down the towpath shouting instructions as they had witnessed for other boats.

Aided by a few more beers, the boat was christened the Argo and we became the Argonauts. I didn't pay much attention thereafter apart from attending training meetings at the Eagle and Child.

I never gave the Argonauts another thought until, 50 years on, I received an invitation to celebrate the Argonauts' Golden Jubilee. An VIII would be made available for us to demonstrate our prowess. Apparently the club had faded and then been rediscovered. The Argonauts are now the top VIII and the smartest club in the college.

Middleton Hall was supervised, if that is the term, by my favourite scout,* Frank O'Donnell – 'garrulous, bibulous, jolly and kindly custodian, and his kindly wife.'†

It was always a joy to catch up with them both when returning in later years.

Not content with our VIII, we bought a punt. The college punts were fine but expensive to rent and had to be returned by nightfall which was precisely when a chap needs a punt. It cost us £2 each but was soon mortally wounded. Some idiot decided to jump into it from Magdalen Bridge. Strangely he was unhurt.

David Latimer and George Facer, chemists both, shared rooms on the college's handsomest quad, the Canterbury. As it was too old to have plumbing, the quad's lawn had some patches that were exceptionally green and expanded as term went by. Their sitting room was bridge capital for the college and boasted the world's longest continuous game of bridge. It continued for weeks, with players cutting in and falling out as meals, work and sleep demanded. Facer came from the same south-east public school background as Bostock, and possibly even the same regiment, but was tall with dark curly hair. He was, and is, more of an enjoyer of jokes than a joker. Latimer by contrast came from a grammar school in Goole, which I understand to be somewhere near Hull. Round faced, straight dark hair and a merry quip was never far away.

As well as sailing the Broads with Bostock, Facer, Latimer and Keith Gerrish (another northerner and a sums man), we sailed the Avon in April 1958. Keith too played bridge, an ideal occupation when the weather discouraged sailing. The point of inland sailing is to get from pub to pub with the minimum of exertion. The sun shines, the breeze blows and the peace is ethereal. One can hear bacon sizzling from far away. Well, sometimes.

Graham Barton was also a chemist and introduced me to fellow Catholic, Christopher Stevenson, a year ahead and with rooms con-

---

* A 'scout' at Oxford was nearly always a male domestic, unlike the equivalent 'bedder' at Cambridge who was a woman. Then anyway. Their conditions cannot have been that good, even supplemented with undergraduate tips, but they stayed for ever. The role was a sort of Jeeves-type valet, making beds, sometimes serving at table, but trying to keep the young master in check, combined with the eyes and ears of the college.

† Quotations from a memoir on the foundation of the St John's Argonauts. 'One aspect of Frank's consideration was his leaving the rear window open to facilitate access after climbing in over the wall, aided by the tree, for we were constrained by the College acting in loco parentis to be in by 9 p.m. or have a good excuse.'

veniently beside the porters' lodge. Barton was not unlike Latimer, a northerner (Lancastrian in his case), not tall but solidly built and strong in the merry badinage department. Stevenson's family lived near High Wycombe, his father was an accountant and he had been educated at Ealing. We now know that the teachers there were misbehaving but Stevenson may not have been good looking enough to merit their attention. He had a high pitched voice and was not one of the first to be chosen in the Paul Jones. But then, neither was I. He read, up to a point, history and he was often crumpled up with laughter. We cannot all have been laughing all of the time but that is how I remember them.

The Oxford chaplain was Valentine Elwes, tall, elegant, and a Monsignor from a grand family. Very 1930s. He was reputed to have a fine wine cellar. The thing to do, apparently, was to confide after some Sunday Mass that one had 'doubts'. An invitation to dinner would follow and the brilliance of the wine cellar revealed. This seemed like a good wheeze so I did as instructed and the invitation followed.

The two of us had a thunderingly good evening. He was good company and possibly a little lonely. We went through the card from sherry, 'oh perhaps one more', to white burgundy, 'I always think one bottle is exactly right for two people', claret, elegantly decanted. The port was about to arrive when Elwes said something like:

'Please tell me about these doubts of yours.'

This stumped me. By that stage of the evening I had no doubts about anything and could not remember ever having had any. I thought it rather a strange question. There was a long pause and Elwes probably twigged. I cannot have been the first. Be that as it may, he remained his convivial self and we enjoyed the rest of the evening.

Although that was our last *diner à deux*, he did include me in a small dinner party he gave at the Elizabeth, then easily Oxford's best restaurant, for André Simon, the creator of the International Wine & Food Society and probably the most famous wine critic of his day. Then 81 but not in the least pompous, he was good company and a good listener to the prattling youths around the table. André Simon believed that 'a man dies too young if he leaves any wine in his cellar' and there were indeed only two magnums of claret left in his personal cellar at his death aged 93. 'On what would have been his 100th birthday in 1977, 400 guests gathered at the Savoy to drink to his memory the Château Latour 1945 that he had left for the occasion.' (Wikipedia)

Elwes retired in 1959, much missed, and taking his cellar with him. He was replaced by the rather grey, earnest, but worthy, Fr. Michael Hollings. Or so we thought but we misjudged him. After Oxford and Sandhurst, he had fought through the war with the Coldstream Guards ending as a major and winning a Military Cross at Monte Cassino. In his 10 years as chaplain he cunningly purchased separate parcels of land at good prices which added up to a sizeable chunk allowing for major redevelopment.

One of the joys of that first year was reconnecting with the Downside contingent, notably Nick Sibley (Trinity), Denis Cross (Balliol), Nick Reynolds, John Clifford (Corpus Christi), Dudley Plunkett, Michael Maguire and, most of all, Paul Focke (Exeter). One of our sillier pranks was when we noted that St Frideswide's was both the name of one of St Anne's College annexes and a dairy farm on the Banbury Road. Suitably beered up, Barton, Focke and I shifted the large sign from the farm to the St Anne's entrance. It read: 'St Fridewide's Herd of Pedigree Guernseys.' The St Anne's ladies were not amused and nor was Peter Preston, then editor of the Oxford undergraduate newspaper and later of the *Guardian*. Reluctantly he ran the picture. Some of the ladies in the annexe suspected us but nothing was ever proved.

A rather more serious prank caused Focke's departure from Oxford. Our first year difficulty was the usual one: lack of transport. We signed up with the University Officer Training Corps, being lieutenants in the Territorials by then. We may have been supposed to help train the cadets but we did not get around to that. The attraction was their two armoured cars of which we had free use. The driver of an armoured car has restricted vision so whoever was not driving stuck out of the turret and, on a fine summer's day, it was most agreeable. We had several outings to pubs in the vicinity and were always ready to assist damsels in distress.

Young women were still hitchhiking in those days. Some blondes under 30 were disconcerted to find a military vehicle, sporting a large gun, reversing rapidly* down the road to offer lifts.

Well dined and ruminating upon the Exeter lawn, Focke and I

---

* Armoured cars travel as rapidly backwards as forwards.

decided that we were not putting our vehicle to proper use. It needed a challenge. The Americans had an atom bomber base nearby at Brize Norton. If an armoured car, we reasoned, rolled up at the gate, the guards would just wave us through. Drive up to a bomber, take the photo opportunity for future grandchildren and off we would go. Simple really.

The next morning was on the darker side of grey and I was not feeling too well. With the clarity sometimes brought by sobriety, this plan looked a little dodgy. At the very least, the Americans would not be any more amused than the inhabitants of St Frideswide's. Trouble would follow. Focke took my withdrawal with poor grace and set off on his own.

I agreed to meet him on his return to hear all about it. Astonishingly, it had all gone according to plan. When Focke appeared out of the top wearing his officer's uniform, he was duly waved through. He drove through until he found a bomber being loaded up with something that could have been an A-bomb, climbed out and took pictures. His return was just as simple. Having returned and changed back into civilian dress, he was in fine form. All would probably have been well, the Americans and the university none the wiser, if Focke hadn't insisted on phoning the *Daily Express* with the story and, later, the pictures. It was page one news (see opposite).*

Trouble there certainly was. The university authorities were mildly amused but it had taken them some time to pacify the irate US general and Focke's hide was his price. He was not impressed by Focke's claim that he had done the general a favour by testing the base's security. Trinity College, Dublin, seemed a suitable place to continue his undergraduate life, if not his studies.

The reasons for his departure from that august institution are a little shrouded. The culmination was reputed to involve a donkey arriving at a white tie ball being held on the rather grand hotel's first floor. The donkey apparently disgraced both itself and Focke. Some were impressed that Focke, a cavalryman after all, had persuaded the don-

---

* My recollection does not quite accord with that in the *Daily Express* of 23/24 June 1958 in which Focke was accompanied by the other armoured car, a Land-Rover, a 1-ton truck and a bevy of other undergraduates; albeit only Focke and Lt. Peter Jackson entered the camp in one armoured car. I do not recall anyone else being disciplined but I cannot be sure whose account is the more reliable, although if he was looking around from the turret he could not have been driving it at the same time.

# DAILY EXPRESS

## TUESDAY JUNE 24 1958

# VARSITY CADETS 'RAID' U.S. AIR BASE

### Express Staff Reporter

FOR an hour a party of Oxford undergraduates had the run of the best guarded American base in England—Brize Norton, from which the U.S. Air Force flies atom-bomb patrols.

It was all part of an initiative test by members of the Oxford University Officers' Training Corps.

With American slang and a Daimler armoured car the party—led by Lieutenant Paul Focke, a Cheshire Yeomanry officer attached to the O.T.C.—passed through two gates guarded by armed American airmen, passed observation towers surrounding the airfield, passed three thicknesses of 12ft.-high wire—and finally drove out unchallenged.

"This all started," Lieutenant Focke said yesterday, "because of an argument over lunch at Exeter College.

"Other undergraduates poohpoohed a raid we planned on Sandhurst as too commonplace and said a raid on a top-secret American base was impossible."

### Going in

Accompanied by another armoured car, a Land-Rover, and a 1-ton truck, Lieutenant Focke set out from O.T.C. headquarters in Manor-road, Oxford, and "on the spur of the moment" drove the 17 miles to Brize Norton.

"I left the other vehicles outside." he said. "Then Lieutenant Peter Jackson and I breezed up to a main gate patrolled by armed air force police.

"We were stopped, but I called out in as much of an American accent as I could manage. 'We want gas and water.'

"We were waved on, but a few minutes later another guard approached. I called out to him. 'Engine trouble, Mac,' and he let us go on. After that we were left alone."

**PAUL FOCKE**
*Gas and water, he said.*

### Looking round

And this, said Lieutenant Focke, was what he saw from the turret of the armoured car :—

Large planes, some with swept-back wings and jet engines ; Armed guards patrolling round camouflaged installations ;

A large black bomb on a trailer being towed to an aircraft on the apron. "My guess," said Lieutenant Focke. "was an atom bomb. It looked rather fearsome."

Then : "We fired imaginary shells from our two-pounder gun. Had we been armed for the real thing we could have shattered the place — and pinched that bomb.

"All the time we maintained radio contact with the other armoured car outside."

### Getting out

At one point the armoured car followed a convoy of troop-carrying trucks.

"Suddenly," said Lieutenant Focke, "they all halted and all the men jumped out and stood stiffly to attention all over the roadway.

"As we were both in British Army denims with pips clearly visible, Lieutenant Jackson and I sat tight.

"An American airman rapped sharply on our vehicle and shouted. 'They're lowering the flag.' But we stayed where we were."

Finally the raiders "wandered round a few offices," Lieutenant Focke said : "We were looking for a rubber stamp to make an entry in the log-book for our armoured car." They got it.

Exactly an hour after it went in the armoured car—painted green with Royal Armoured Corps signs on its side—drove out of the base for a rendezvous with the other vehicles.

**VERDICT** last night by Lieutenant Focke : "The exercise was a complete success."

### Checking up

A colonel of the Security branch of the U.S. Air Force said last night : "It is quite certain that these students did not enter the restricted areas of the base.

"Anyone in British Army uniform with military vehicles and passes is allowed in the general areas of the station.

"British civilians have business concessions within the general areas which include family housing, barracks, stores. shops, and clubs.

"American servicemen are in the same way allowed in the general areas of R.A.F. stations.

"These students could have seen no more than any motorist would see of our bases if he drove up or down the public roads adjacent."

key up the main stairs. Others were not.

Trinity Cambridge turned him down without so much as an interview. They were wrong. Focke went on to an impressive, and eminently respectable, career at the bar becoming a QC and then a Judge at the Old Bailey. What remained unchanged was his charm and good humour.

My second year provided palatial rooms in the North Quad: a large bedroom, sitting room and small kitchen, ideal for intimate dinners. With Moderations out of the way and with no further exams until Finals, I could get down to serious matters such as singing and acting, for which I have even less talent.

Graham Barton and I had joined the St John's choir in my first year but it was a bit short of altos and sopranos. The obvious solution was to meet the incoming talent by knocking on all the study doors at the women's colleges (we flagged after St Hilda's and Lady Margaret Hall). Second- and third-year undergraduettes were likely to be out so it was even money the opening doors would reveal the new girls. Most of them sent us packing, notably 'one of the leading debutantes of her day, society beauty Henrietta Tiarks'* who was already practising being a duchess. Alongside the setbacks, we had our successes and the choir improved in numbers, quality and pulling power. Our social group also improved albeit to a more limited extent. Christine Davenport (St Hilda's) had joined the choir in my first year and we added Elizabeth (Liz) McLaren and Patricia (Trish) Laugharne from that college. Trish played (rather well) more squash than I considered good for her which led to an exchange of rude verses. Hers were better than mine.

A few dates with the university choir followed of which the most memorable was a call from the Royal Opera whose touring company was bringing, inter alia, *Aida* to the New Theatre. They were seeking spear carriers to march across the stage several times in Act II scene ii and give the appearance of being an army. Being on stage with professional opera singers was good enough for me. Apart from the spear, my clothing was little more than sandals, a loin cloth and a great deal of brown paint. Not a pretty sight. As we were not required after the Triumphal scene for quite a while, Keith Gerrish, David Latimer and I repaired to the pub behind the theatre for a few

---

* Duchess of Bedford, MailOnline, 16th October 2010.

pints. The other patrons at the bar moved away from us.

Earlier on, stationary for a while, I asked the nearest chorus member if anyone would mind me joining in the singing. 'Go ahead, lad,' he said, 'no one is going to hear you.' And neither did they. The Canadian tenor, Jon Vickers, then in his thirties, sang Radames. It was only his second or third year with Covent Garden which was why, I suppose, he was on tour. He recorded the role with Sir George Solti two years later but I was not sent for.

Armoured cars being no longer available, I was delighted when Dennis and Patricia, returning to Singapore, asked if I would take care of the family car, a newish Ford Consul. The university proctors agreed and the then mandatory little green light, the 'flappers' warning', was added.

The car was most useful when Christine Davenport invited Graham Barton, Maggie Johnston and me up to her family's baronial mansion near Edinburgh for Hogmanay. It was huge but it was freezing and we were glad to escape into Edinburgh when we could. My one and only experience of Hogmanay was immense fun. The highlight was first-footing the author, Compton Mackenzie, who held court from his bed. He was then in his mid 70s and I didn't gather if he was permanently bedridden or just found it more comfortable (and warmer). As one might expect from the writer of *Whisky Galore*, he was highly entertaining but also welcoming even to the English.*

He also wrote *Monarch of the Glen* which became seven television series between 2000 and 2005.

Another name to conjure with from that year was Alan Bennett, then a post-graduate historian at Exeter. I had seen him perform in a smoke-filled room at some comedy evening and he was, of course, the star of the show. His two sketches were the 'life is like a tin of sardines' sermon and his attempts to communicate a telegram down the phone ending with NORWICH. 'Why Norwich?' says the telephonist and Alan's prissiest voice responds 'Knickers Off Ready When I Come Home' ..... 'Yes, I know Knickers starts with a K but KORWICH...'.

In the course of exploring various inappropriate careers, I had concluded that, since I was no actor, I would be an impresario. One has to start somewhere and mine was as organiser of the cabaret for the

* Although born in England, he was, in 1928, one of the co-founders of the Scottish National Party.

Newman Ball – the biggest Catholic social event. Paul Cheetham and another chap were quite decent singers and I recruited Caroline Seebohm, a stunning and much sought-after (the competition was too much for me) blonde. Anthony Wyatt, an elegant man-about-town, was her principal squire. The audience might not think much of the chaps but they would (and did) love Caroline.

Alan Bennett was persuaded, with some difficulty, to join this little group and to do two of his spots. They later appeared in *Beyond the Fringe* and made him famous. His reticence was not because he was too busy (he wasn't) but he was then massively shy. He did not want to appear before strangers. I was astonished, shortly before the off, to discover Bennett cowering in a corner suffering from dreadful stage fright. He had to be talked into going on and, although he came to terms with it, he continued to have stage fright for some time.

Of course I should have lined up John Wells but his talent had yet to emerge.

Our little group, minus Bennett, did a few gigs, including one at the Henley Regatta, with some success and a little income, until we had an absolutely disastrous evening at a dance on HMS *President* on the Thames. It would have been all right if the lights and the amplification system not both failed. When a bunch of City yobs and their molls cannot see or hear the cabaret they can become quite unpleasant. I was quite rightly blamed and our group was no more.

Caroline, the most talented of our group, became a successful and prolific journalist and then author and now lives on the banks of the Delaware.

When it was time for punting and picnics, the weather was perfect and, if it ever rained, I do not recall it.

That idyllic recollection may owe something to my being in love with Maggie Johnston for much of the year. I realise now that it was just a taster for the real thing six years later but, at the time, it was joyous. Birds sang as we passed, flowers blossomed and they were Salad Days, or perhaps one of Bertie Wooster's entanglements. My own Jeeves, in the shape of my scout, served supper in my rooms.

Maggie and I met at one of those dreary Oxford sherry parties one intends to miss. They were full of earnest suburban people making earnest suburban small talk. On this occasion there was one pretty woman, only one but one was enough. Maggie (St Hugh's) was wondering also why she had gone. Anyway, one thing led to another. As noted above, four of us went to Scotland together and it was all very sweet and innocent.

Maggie has an open face, a ready smile and a low, vibrant voice. We saw a lot of each other that autumn and spring. In the spring vacation, she stayed at Midgham with us. Dennis and Patricia were amazingly nice to, and about, her and asked no questions. Likewise, I stayed in Yorkshire with her parents and received an equally generous welcome.

Maggie married before Katie and I did. We stayed with them and Katie quickly spotted that this was one relationship that was not going to survive the two marriages. Sadly, she was right.

The third year is spent out of college and I was lucky to find a room at 10 Museum Road. The house, just along from Middleton Hall, has since been demolished and incorporated into the main college. If one climbed the garden wall, one was in college. Frau Hammerschmidt rented out her two top-floor rooms to undergraduates and we shared the bathroom there.

With hindsight we were all embarrassingly incurious about each other. Presumably her husband had been an academic at Oxford and had escaped Nazi Germany in the 1930s. To judge from Frau Hammerschmidt's accent she could have left the previous week. She was quite nostalgic about Germany, especially at Christmas-time, but I am sure there was a German circle in Oxford that she was happy with.

Richard Guy took the other room and, apart from a degree of idleness in the washing-up department, was an ideal partner. We were allowed to use the kitchen and dining room in the semi-basement provided we left it clean, so the devious thing was to leave before the other arrived. Faced by dirty dishes, the good Frau could be quite fierce. Guy had been in the Military Police for his national service. The unusual role may have been brought on by his wish to be a criminal barrister, as indeed he became.

He was at Wadham reading Greats and was therefore there for a year longer than me.

Dennis and Patricia were still away and I was asked to look after Willie, our Amazon Blue parrot. The Frau acquiesced and, as Willie and I were fond of each other, I was glad to do so. He disliked most women and especially Patricia whom he would bite given any opportunity. This sexist behaviour did not help any wooing I might have had in mind but he was otherwise an amiable pet. His daily exercise was to fly around for a while, but only indoors. Once before he had escaped. After days of worry, the postman reported a parrot on a phone line a mile or so away. He was delighted to be rescued.

Contrary to popular belief, birds like their cages and see them as protection, not restriction of freedom. When he had had enough flying around and destroying any paper he could find, Willie would return to his perch and wait to be entertained by music or conversation.

We were very fond of Frau Hammerschmidt, possibly the best landlady in town. At the end of the spring term, she announced she would be away for the summer. Although she did not wholly trust us to take care of the place, she was going to take the risk. We assured her of our reliability. We were to confine ourselves to our top floor, the kitchen and dining room. The cleaner would be in daily to ensure we did so and the washing up too. 'Absolutely,' we assured her, 'you can count on us.'

When the summer term arrived, things started to slip a bit. Guy had had himself elected chairman of the wine committee for the Wadham Commemoration Ball and he was in no hurry to appoint other members. To help him select the champagne, samples arrived from all the leading houses. Guy knew nothing about wine and saw little merit in a comparative tasting. He opened one bottle with a known name and a decent price and that was it.

It will not take you long, dear reader, to work out what we did with the rest. There were enough for a stonking good party in the Frau's garden. The trouble was that no one wanted to go home and fresh supplies were brought in when, amazingly, we ran dry. I was quite shocked at the behaviour and, naturally, left early. The panic in the morning was to get the last of the guests to leave before the cleaner arrived. Not to mention dealing with the empties, tidying the rooms which should not have been invaded and clearing all the cigarette butts before the gardener turned up. At least the dirty glasses could go back dirty.

That morning was a complete nightmare. Luckily, I did not have to face the music but, at the beginning of the next term, Guy did. The good Frau had had several weeks to develop her fury and she wasted none of it. She built up to her climax:

'Und,' she screamed, 'und you allowed that dreadful friend of yours, God knows who with, to sleep in my bed. MY BED.' This particular friend of Guy's was indeed rather repellent, large and smelly.

It was the only double bed in the house so there was always a good chance that someone would use it; it was just unfortunate that it had to be him. Whether his odour was still on the sheets when she returned or whether the cleaner had spotted him we did not know. Guy was still shaking when he told me.

She was a lovely lady and Guy was eventually forgiven.

The epilogue to our time together in Museum Road came years later when, shopping in John Lewis, I ran into Guy, now respectably married, and was introduced to his respectable married wife.

'Ah,' she said frostily, 'I've heard *all* about *you.*'

Guy was looking rather guilty and clearly I had been represented as a bad influence and the author of all his misdeeds. That was not the only time I have encountered hostility from new wives of old friends. No one expects life to be fair but when one has lavished support and protection on one's chums, a little more gratitude would have been in order.

Two of my summer vacations, and one during my articled clerkship, were spent as a pawn in the late 20th Century's Great Game. The usual term 'Cold War' is a misnomer. Neither side was about to invade the other, with the possible exception of the Cuban missile crisis. When Russian tanks rolled back into Budapest and then Prague, they were merely, in their view, repossessing their empire. The conflict lay in the marketing of opposing ideologies, communism *vs.* capitalism.

The 1958 instalment was at the Catholic Lublin University, the sole higher educational establishment in Poland outside communist control. It looked west, not east, and our invitation to teach English was part of that. The year before, Christopher Stevenson had visited via the Catholic mafia. This time Paul Cheetham (Stonyhurst), David Goodall and I went too.

The Berlin Wall had not yet been constructed and westerners had only to show passports at Checkpoint Charlie or other crossing points. The overhead railway, the S Bahn, ran freely between the sectors. I cannot recall how they managed to keep Germans in their respective sectors of Berlin but there must have been guards on the trains.

The contrast between the rich West, with its bright lights and shops of the Kurfürstendamm, and the grey, depressed East was staggering. We took a tour of the Russian Sector with a bus load of Americans.

The Russians, with a little help from the Allies, had mostly flattened East Berlin and although some rebuilding must have taken place in the 13 years since the war, it did not look like it. Some buildings remained flat; bullet marks and bomb craters were everywhere. Our guide, clearly a paid up communist, attributed none of this to the Russians, nor even the Americans. Each time we passed a bombed out building, the RAF were accorded the blame.

Our voices had given us away and, after a while, the Americans on the bus turned to glare at us, tut-tutting away as the guide nailed the RAF for another one. There was nothing to be said so we just cowered lower in our seats.

Lublin, by contrast, was lovely and so were our students. More than half were female and as keen to get to know us as we were to know them. One was Krystyna Zysiak, delightful, attractive, attentive and with long brunette curls. She later became Mrs Stevenson. Politics turned out to play little part in our visit; carousing did but I will spare you the detail.

Polish beer was agreeable enough but the revelation was vodka. The Poles dispute the origination of vodka* with the Russians and the truth may be obscured by boundary changes. Lwow, which some claim to be the birthplace, has been part of the USSR, as it was then, but also part of Poland in earlier times.

They start by distilling 96% pure alcohol[†], 'spiritus', and usually then reduce the strength with flavourings, fruit juice and/or water. Well of course we had to try spiritus straight as the Polish hard drinkers did, alternating with beers. This is its own art form. You have to tip it down missing the sides of the throat. If it touches the vocal chords, you sound like Micky Mouse, i.e. a complete idiot incapable of holding one's liquor. Weirdest of all, one can drink this stuff from 9pm to bedtime without getting in the least squiffy. The stomach cannot cope with pure alcohol. The next morning you toss down a couple of coffees, they dilute the alcohol and you are staggering all over the place.

Lessons over, we toured the country together, Warsaw, north to the Mazowsze region and thence to the south west of the country: Krakow, Częstochowa and Oświęcim (Auschwitz or Birkenau), both near by. We stayed at a youth hostel in Krakow for a tour of a city

---

* With typical Slav humour the word means 'little water'.
† UK gin and whisky were then 40% alcohol (70° proof).

undamaged by the war. The Russians had been persuaded to hold off and it is beautifully medieval, once capital of Poland, and with a wonderful castle. Moda showed us around which added to my interest.

Częstochowa and Auschwitz were, and are (not much has changed), both astonishing and astonishingly different. The first was and is a place of pilgrimage, full of people, life, love and hope. The second was empty, save only our guide, death, hatred and despair. It is a stark contrast between the worst of Nazism and the best of our traditional culture.

Today there are over a million visitors to Auschwitz annually. The Poles made it a museum in 1947 but in 1958 it was just as the Germans left it in 1945. Understandably, none of the locals wished to go there and few tourists then came to Poland.

Auschwitz was originally intended, not as an extermination centre, but as a work camp for the captured, and relatively few, Polish resistance fighters. The entry gate is marked 'Arbeit macht frei' ('work makes you free'). As the war progressed, the Nazis coped with the numbers by converting it to the largest of all death camps. The story is well enough known not to need recalling here.

We visited the huts each stacked in an orderly fashion with the cast offs of those who undressed, wigs in one hut, shoes in another, false teeth in another and so on. The Russians found 348,820 men's suits and 836,255 women's garments (why count them?) when they liberated Auschwitz in 1945 by which time the Nazis had emptied the camp and tried to obliterate it to cover up their war crimes.

It was a ghostly, grey day when we were there. No birds sang and we didn't say much either. Footsteps on the human ash paths were silent too. We stood inside a gas chamber and then on top of a demolished crematorium. I am not much moved by historic sites but this was an exception. It was horrifying, horrid and unforgettable.

For the last stage we were split up and stayed with separate families. We thought we were spoiled for choice but it turned out that we were raffle prizes. Janka Marylska was unlucky enough to draw me. Her family lived in Rabka, a small off-shoot of Zakopane, the Tatra mountains ski resort. If Zakopane was quiet in the summer, Rabka resembled a morgue. Janka did her best to keep us both amused but that involved a disagreeable amount of fresh air. Janka later married one of my bridge playing buddies, Andrzej Kaxuszinski, and, when I last heard, they were living happily ever after.

This venture into the Russian empire sharpened my appetite for involvement in the ideological marketing campaigns of the day. The Campaign for Nuclear Disarmament (CND) was set up in 1957 and there is little doubt that it was financed and influenced by the KGB. Few of the members of CND were aware of that but joining such a bunch of woolly-minded, pink liberal hand-wringers, even for subversion, filled me with horror.

Much more fun was to take up the suggestion of one of Dennis's MI6 cronies that we snoop around the World Festival of Youth which was sponsored by the Russians every two or three years as part of their global propaganda. The VIIth was to be held that year (1959) in Vienna. The government would pick up our tab. *The Third Man* film and a Vienna, still swarming with Russian military and KGB, seemed the ideal outlet for a little summer mischief. Graham Barton and Dudley Plunkett said they were up for it.

The biggest ever (before or since) of these Festivals was the VIth (1957) in Moscow with 34,000 delegates from 131 countries. Vienna managed 18,003, if you include us, from 112 countries. The Festivals still continue, on and off, with Quito (Ecuador) in 2013. Subverting enemy marketing campaigns is fun and contemporary history should be lived, not read about afterwards.

We were told to meet our minder in a particular café opposite the main cathedral, Stephansdom. 'You will recognise him as he will be carrying a copy of the *Daily Express*.'* He did not need to be: the sole Englishman in the café stood out from the central Europeans like a cardinal in a synagogue. Barton and I joined him for coffee as Plunkett had not yet showed up. Actually there wasn't much briefing. He handed over a good quantity of schillings to cover immediate expenses and a vague hope that we would report back on the proceedings generally. We were not there to check out the British delegation – that would have been an MI5 job.

At this point, Dudley Plunkett was still the infantry officer he had been in national service. His trousers were neatly pressed, his stride manly and his brown brogues polished to a high sheen. They had metal protectors on the heels. The next afternoon, a Sunday, was deathly quiet as the Viennese families digested their lunch and we lay on our beds reading our books. Suddenly, in the distance, we could hear brisk marching feet. As they grew nearer they grew louder and

---

* Or so Dudley recalls.

soon the old walls were echoing the left and rights. With one voice, Barton and I said 'Plunkett' and so it was.

We had acquired the programme for the Festival. Some of the events, like the opening and closing ceremonies, were open to all, usually on purchase of tickets, but most were restricted to official delegates which we were not. MI6 might have twigged that in advance, we thought. The idea was that we would socialise with delegates and capture intelligence vital to national security. We did try to chat up a few boys and girls but they were not forthcoming because we were not delegates, did not look like communist yoof, especially not Plunkett, and because they were under constant supervision. As far as the Russians were concerned, 'youth' is an elastic term. Anyone under 50 can be a youth, or yoof, with the right papers and badges. For the next Festival I acquired a pocketful of CND and other left wing badges.

Gate-crashing was the answer and these were the rules:

1 Always go in with a number of genuine delegates, the more the better.
2 Have something that looks vaguely like a ticket in your wallet which you open only briefly. If it looks like a ticket, it's a ticket.
3 Do not look at the guard and do not speak the local language even if you can.
4 Chat to one of the genuine delegates as you pass the guard. The delegate's surprise will not be obvious until you are through at which point one should move on rapidly.
5 Gesticulate to the guard to indicate that the leader in front has your ticket.
6 Keep moving.

We were never apprehended or refused entry although getting Plunkett through was sometimes difficult. Apart from the way he looked, he is a tremendously honest, God-fearing chap and rather disapproved of these nefarious tactics.

At a popular event delegates are likely to come out for more chairs. Grab a chair and there is no need to show a ticket. On one such occasion, we blended in perfectly – even with four foot high Indonesians.

Frankly, not much emerged in the meetings. It was the standard Russian (and a little Chinese) propaganda of the time. Most of the delegates were uninterested in the simultaneous-translation speeches (and they were very boring) and, indeed, uninterested in politics of any kind. 'Mir' (peace) was the most used noun. It is an odd phenomenon of propaganda that if you claim to be in favour of peace, you communicate that the other side must be in favour of war. In 1964, the UK Government renamed the War Office as the Ministry of Defence.

Be that as it may, these dozy delegates had been bribed to turn up with free holidays and were used to enduring boring speeches and the propaganda as the price. We, and a few others, did our best to liven things up by heckling but communist heavies don't do heckling. It was not so much the stewards as the ordinary delegates who thought it bad form. When they talked of Western Imperialism we shouted 'What about Hungary?' That was only three years earlier, still topical and quite effective. Even some of the torpid delegates perked up at that.

We also cited China's invasion of Tibet in 1950 which was compounded by the abolition of any Tibetan government three months after the Festival.

We reported back to our minder once midway and then at the end. He pronounced himself entirely happy with our (non-)findings and hoped we would be available for the next World Festival of Youth. That turned out to be Helsinki 1962*.

By that time I was doing my accountancy articles with Peat Marwick & Mitchell (next chapter) but Helsinki belongs here because the three vacation outings are all meddling in ideological marketing.

For the Communist Youth Festival in Helsinki, our MI6 sponsor was keen that Mike Strong, Graham Barton (now working with ICI) and I should be part of the official British delegation. That would save gate-crashing everything and take care of travel and accommodation. To get the inside story, we would have to be inside. Our briefing this time was six closely typed foolscap pages – far more thorough than Vienna. As contacting a minder would be tiresome for both parties, I would keep a detailed diary†. Not a good idea, in the event, as it loaded the bureaucrats with information they did not need.

The delegation leader (and full-time organiser for the previous six months) was Mike Costello, an impressive man who marshalled the 150 UK delegates in a methodical manner. By 1979 Costello was

---

* The title for Vienna was 'For Peace and Friendship and Peaceful Coexistence'. That for Helsinki was the same except they decided to dispense with peaceful coexistence.

† Used for these notes.

head of the Industrial Department in the UK Communist Party and credited with creating cells all across the country. No doubt MI5 took an interest in him. He certainly took an interest in us and interrogated us frequently.

Our brief was to be friendly with the British delegation and, when we did have to spend time with them, avoid politics. We were 'to explain the raison d'être and the objectives of the Festival to the following people: South Americans, Africans and Communist nationals', i.e. it was all propaganda to be taken with fistfuls of salt.

The train from the Hook of Holland took us straight to East Berlin and we were feted, in a low key kind of way, in three local towns by mayors, brass bands and lots of jugend – some delightful. The rest of the delegation tended to hang back a bit so the three of us disembarked to 'God Save the Queen'. After three days we were feeling positively regal. Presents were distributed according to the Stazi's matching version of our own briefing, namely Africans first, then Latin Americans, then any non-Europeans, then women.

At the Russian border, the change of track gauge* necessitated a shift to an even slower but more comfortable train. At every stop we were greeted by brass bands, flowers and girls† to dance with on the platforms. The most popular music was Kenny Ball's Moonlight in Moscow. Beautiful as it is to dance to, especially with a krasiva dyehvooshka, the tune began to grate after a while.

To merge, as I thought, with the proletariat that made up most of the delegation, I had brought my oldest clothes, some in a poor state of repair. This was a mistake. The Russians who were so wonderful to us at each station had dressed up in their Sunday best. Far more impoverished than we were, the girls tut-tutted over the worn patches and missing buttons and almost cried over their lack of time to make repairs. I felt bad about that.

The whole 18,000†† (same number as Vienna) party was accommodated in decent enough schools and hostels, apart from the Russians, Poles and East Germans who stayed on the ships that brought

---

* Russian is 1,520mm compared with 1,435mm in most of the rest of the world. Russian extends into Finland. They deliberately chose a different standard, or so we were told, to make life difficult for the invading imperialist armies of Western Europe.

† And, of course, boys for our girls..

†† According to the Russians; 13,000 according to the *Daily Telegraph*, 30th July 1962.

them, and, of course, the Finns who looked after themselves. The programme was massive: 38 close-typed pages covering the 10 days.

The most beautiful girl in our delegation was Barbara Amiel, later journalist and wife of [Lord] Conrad Black. Being a nice, we thought, middle-class girl, we were disappointed that, not only did she not support our trouble-making, she did not even give us the time of day. As she later married four times, our failure to get to first base was a little demoralising. Even Strong with his fine chiselled, Greek god-like features, got nowhere. It turned out that 'Amiel was an active communist'.* Her subsequent journalistic career could hardly have been further right of centre.

In the seminars we were mostly restricted to heckling as our requests to speak from the rostrum were ignored. Costello had probably marked our cards. The organisers broke their own procedural rules in order to exclude us. When I stood up in a gap between speakers to demand an explanation, answer came there none and several around us suggested we stage a walk out. My intervention had been rewarded with sighs and mutterings all around. 'Good idea,' we said and stood up to go whereupon our friends, and notably the wimpish Danes, said we were taking things too far.

Outside cameras and the press, including the BBC, were impressed by the great outflux of delegates apparently supporting our walkout. This was nothing to do with us: it was the lunch break.

For speakers from communist countries unused to heckling, our puny efforts had disproportionate effect. When a Chinese speaker claimed his country had never invaded anyone, our cry of 'rhubarb' disrupted proceedings very satisfactorily whilst people asked what rhubarb was. Overall, we probably did more good by being so conspicuously ostracised by the organisers than if we had been allowed to speak. We picked up a lot of sympathy and we made contact with other similarly-minded agitators.

The Russian, Polish and East German delegation ships had well stocked bars. Mike 'where is the bar?' Strong insisted we check this out. Security was, allegedly, tight but we had no trouble getting aboard the Russian ship using the flash the wallet trick. Unfortunately the passengers were all at lunch and the bar was shut.

We returned at drinks time to the Polish ship. This guard was at the top of the gangway, more difficult. We timed reaching him as he

---

* James Robinson (2004), 'For richer, for poorer?' *The Observer*, 25 January.

was distracted by a passing blonde, flapped our wallets and walked on fast. This guard was not so dumb and caught up with the straggler, me. Barton and Strong had disappeared. I was returned to the dockside and waited for them. A few minutes later they reappeared accompanied by a man with a lot of rings on his uniform. They had clearly been nabbed too but the outcome was different. The officer leant over the side and waved me aboard. Their bar was indeed well stocked and we had a very happy evening.

I doubt we did much to subvert the huge Soviet propaganda effort.

The final section of this chapter completes my Oxford story. The last summer term had gone with a bang and it was truly sad to say goodbye to friends one might never see again. I had secured an articled clerkship, thanks to an introduction by Nick Sibley's father, with Messrs Peat, Marwick & Mitchell. Partnerships were then limited to 20 with no more than four articled clerks per partner. So entry was tough. My paper credentials were deemed good enough but the interview was all important.

After the formalities with the staff partner, I was ushered into the leather-clad office of Henry Peat, a member of the founding family and potentially the man to whom I would be articled. He was tall, elegant and old-school.

'You are at Oxford, I see,' he said studying the papers that had come in with me.

'Yes, sir.'

'I was at Oxford. At Trinity.'

There then followed his story of being sent down after being found sleeping with a girl in his room. That could have been said, as I just have, in a sentence but I had the unedited version. Then, after a slight pause:

'Funnily enough I was sacked from Eton for exactly the same reason.'

He told these stories with wit and charm and I was enjoying myself. This was the sort of boss I could appreciate. When the Eton story concluded, he looked at his watch and said 'My goodness. Is that the time? I must go. Sorry to rush you but I'm sure you will be very happy here.'

And he was off. I had not had to volunteer one jot of information. The formal acceptance letter duly arrived. I asked the staff partner for leave to start a month later than they stipulated as I was driving a bus to Turkey. Amused, he agreed.

The bus thing had come about because a chap called Phillips had organised 'The Oxford University Eastern Europe Expedition' to Turkey. He had arranged the travelling party, borrowed an elderly charabanc free of charge, and sponsors to provide cash and kind. Kelloggs provided crates of cereals. Unfortunately he had not been able to find any drivers that the insurers would accept. It sounded fun and we explained to the insurers that with my heavy goods experience (3 tonners and armoured cars) I was well qualified to drive the bus. They accepted that with reluctance and even more reluctantly accepted Facer and Latimer as relief drivers. We had played up their national service even though, so far as I knew, it involved no driving at all. Having just left Oxford, we claimed to be mature adults, not irresponsible students.

The middle of Brussels had no signposts and we were lost. The driver waiting beside us at a traffic light, not only understood my French (rare that) but offered to lead us out saying 'Suivez moi!' He set off at a tremendous pace. Keeping up was terrifying. The colours of traffic lights were immaterial. Soon enough we were on the motorway to Germany and waving thanks and au revoir.

Germans can be quite pedantic at times. Our driving licences, they pointed out, did not cover buses. This must also have been true in England and France and although you might think that was obvious it had not occurred to Phillips or the rest of us. I have conducted many negotiations. Some have been disasters: the attempted acquisition of Martell cognac lay 30 years ahead and may have been the worst. This was one of the best. I had the advantage of not speaking German and the border guards' English was not too hot.

'This,' I said, 'may look like a bus but it is actually a car.' Puzzled looks.

'Are you Christian?' 'Yes, what does that have to do with anything?'

'Then you will know about transubstantiation.' More puzzled looks.

'In the Mass, what looks like bread actually turns out to be human flesh. We have the same situation here. This vehicle looks like a bus and at one time was a bus but, thanks to transubstantiation, it is now a car. If we thought it was a bus we would have bus diving licences but we actually have car driving licences because it is a car.'

This discussion continued for quite a while. Eventually the guards had had enough. It was no longer amusing and they had had a bad day so they waved us through. Bloody lucky that.

We thought we might have the same problem coming back or with other countries but the papers stamped by the German border guards saw us through the rest.

In Western Europe we had to fend for ourselves but once we got across the Iron Curtain, hospitality looked up. We were students and, as such, suitable targets for formal dinners and speeches. The Bulgarians could not have been more generous even though the Cambridge Middle East Expedition turned up in Sofia at the same time, rather wimpishly we thought, in a couple of mini-vans. We exchanged civilities.

The brakes failed in Yugoslavia and took a week to fix in Niš. A bullock near Rila also brought us to a halt and seemed to lie dead in the road. A crowd of peasants gathered soon enough and their murmurings were growing uglier and louder in contrast with those inside the bus that were fading nervously. At which point the bullock got up, shook itself and sauntered off. Everyone clapped. When we reached Istanbul we handed the bus over to a 20th century garage for proper repairs.

By this time, we and our passengers all knew each other well and the social side was going swimmingly. The talented Phillips had booked us into a delightful hotel in the centre of the old town, the Black Sea and sand were just what we needed after all that time in bus seats. The beer and shish kebabs were wonderful value.

Istanbul is a sightseer's paradise and, in small groups, we gawped at everything. There was no bridge across the Bosphorus then and the ferries were busy and fun.

Large green peppers in Istanbul come in two types: very mild and kill-you hot. They look the same. Russian Peppers is a game played by young men when they have had too much beer. The two kinds of peppers (five mild to one hot) are shuffled and put into a bowl so that no one can see which is which. Then, obviously enough, each player in turn takes a pepper and a large bite out of it. Quite why this game is hysterically funny played in a warm Istanbul street may have been the research question our Expedition set out to resolve.

Bus fully repaired, we took it on the ferry and then the 350 miles or so to our end point, Izmir.

I should mention a silly fad that had infected almost all the party. Two things, it seemed to us, characterised Turkish society. The first was the almost unceasing calls of the muezzin and the second was their wandering around in pyjamas. We adopted both customs. The noise was indescribable but the dress was comfortable in the heat. And the girls looked decorative in theirs.

Boarding the ferry to Athens proved a shock. Unlike the roll-on roll-off ship we expected, the ferry was a vintage cargo ship using derricks for loading from a barge alongside. When the cars were loaded, the derricks strained at the bus and gave up. Taking the luggage off made no difference. 'No problem' says the chief stevedore 'we'll lay a couple of strong planks from the dock up to the barge' which was about five feet higher. With no tides to speak of, the distance was not going to get less.

'Take a run at it,' says the stevedore, 'and be sure to brake when you hit the deck or you will go off the other side.' I had already worked that out. There were no protective rails on the far side. I suggested to Facer and Latimer that this was an opportunity to display their driving skills. No takers. This was a job for the self-appointed senior driver.

The bus was rear-wheel drive. The first time I did not take it fast enough and the back wheels were skidding on the dock before we made it. The crowd was enjoying this. The second effort was much better and I had the front wheels on the barge when the planks whizzed backwards onto the dock. There was an ugly crunch from the underside of the bus which was now swaying, exactly balanced on the edge of the barge with no wheels touching anything. After much discussion, the experts decided that the derricks with added manpower would be able to get the bus off the barge but not onto it. This was because there was more of the bus hanging over the dock than the barge. My mechanics teacher would have been proud of them.

We were now back to square one except the bus was seriously wounded underneath although not, as it turned out, mortally. There was a lot of talk of 'third time lucky' and this was definitely my last shot. Foot flat on the floor we surged up the planks and skidded as I stood on the brake. Fortunately someone took photos throughout the ordeal as the insurance company refused to believe our story and only the photographs convinced them. The bus was longer than the barge was wide. The last photo shows the bus projecting out from both sides.

# Salad Days

We were now tired and broke but we did have enough to tour the Peloponnese. We had overstayed the expected length of the expedition and we wanted to get home. The ferry to Brindisi was a roll-on job and most of the way back was motorway.

HM Customs welcomed us back with screwdrivers and spanners. We and the bus were all in such poor condition that they were convinced that we were smuggling drugs. Turkey was famous for hash. They took the bus apart, literally, and found nothing but a few bottles of Retsina and some legitimate cigarettes. Were they polite? No. Did they apologise or put the bus back together again? No. They just turned rather grumpily and walked away. With our one screwdriver it took us quite a while before we could cover the last leg to Oxford.

Welcome to Blighty!

# Chapter 5

# Accountancy was my life until I discovered Smirnoff

*My three years with Peats and then five years with International Distillers and Vintners were spent as an accountant and it was in that role that I went to MIT in 1968. That was a Damascene conversion to marketing but marketing is for later chapters. This covers:*

- *Articles with Messrs Peat, Marwick & Mitchell*
- *Fairey Engineering*
- *Squibb Pharmaceuticals*
- *Lotus cars*
- *Qualifying*
- *International Distillers & Vintners*
- *Career choices*
- *Joining the wine trade*
- *Early IDV*
- *Staff outings*
- *Establishing City Cellars*
- *Joining the 20th century*
- *Gilbeys take over*
- *The Showering bid*
- *Brackenbury creates Leisure Finance*
- *Launch pad for MIT*

The Peat, Marwick & Mitchell firm of accountants is now KPMG and the London office is a tower block beside London Bridge. Although it had local offices throughout the UK and internationally, the HQ was then a small family business in Ironmonger Lane, just off Cornhill. When I turned up with a tightly wrapped umbrella and Lock's bowler hat, I was directed to a rickety office above the barber's shop on the corner.

The department manager, John R. Wells (1925-2002), had been in the Indian Army and lost part of his left leg due to a motor-cycle accident. He was a dark, heavily-built man and seemed a bit fierce. He was certainly not pleased to see me. His opening words were something like, 'Who are you and what do you want?' He had forgotten I was coming.

'Oh God. I suppose you'd better get off to this small company,' he said, scribbling down the name and address. 'You can do the audit there.' He turned back to his papers, interview over.

'I'm sorry, sir, but this is my first day and I have no idea how to conduct an audit.'

I was now wasting his valuable time and I should, it seemed, have known the answer.

'Ask for the Chief Accountant. He'll show you what to do.' And indeed he did.

When I returned to the office Wells had caught up with my existence. He was crusty but kind, generous, accessible and helpful. Whoever led the audit would put together a file of the issues and a recommendation for the partner responsible to sign off the annual accounts. One would stand, hopping uncomfortably from one foot to another if the process wore on as long as it sometimes did, while the partner leafed through the file, asked questions and decided whether he was happy or not. One really did not wish to be sent back to the client to deal with whatever the partner was niggling about.

At one signing off ceremony my leader was long-qualified, thoroughly competent and about to become a manager. Most of the partners were amiable enough, none more so than Henry Peat, but a few were bullies who liked to throw their weight about. This partner was one of those and he had been particularly bloody minded that morning. The file had to be massively rewritten.

Our leader was particularly upset because he was due to go on holiday that Saturday and this was Tuesday. The rest of the team were going off too, not so strange as they'd timed it to fit in with the conclusion of the audit. On Friday our leader visits the partner again with me in tow and a rewritten file. He explains that he is leaving on holiday and if there are any details to iron out, I am the chap to do it.

The reaction was no better. The partner rants and raves and claims it's the worst piece of work he has ever seen. 'Cancel your holiday and do a proper job.'

'I regret, sir (this was 1960), that the bookings are firm and I have a family to take care of. I am sure Ambler here can deal with the amendments you require. He will return a week today.' After further acrimony, it seemed time to leave.

When we got back to our office, I asked, 'What am I supposed to do now?'

'I have no idea. The man is a bastard, and I don't think he knows what he wants either. I'm off. Good luck.' With which he took up his bowler and took an unscheduled afternoon off.

Next week I was none the wiser. I should have turned the problem over to Wells, but I did not think of that. Reading both files, I could not see much wrong with them. It was a routine audit and we had done it perfectly well. As the junior, I had nothing to lose so I put a fresh cover sheet on the first file and re-presented it to the partner.

All now smiles and charm, he congratulated me on doing such a fine job in so little time. Luckily he did not recognise it. Back from holiday, our leader asked what had transpired and was not best pleased to discover I had taken all the credit.

Auditing, aka 'ticking and blotting', is tedious work. We checked that the books had been properly kept with debits always matched by credits, that no one had made off with the cash or other assets and that the annual accounts represented a 'true and fair view' of the company's financial health. It was usually pretty straightforward.

My audits included a casings* company in Paddington, the London Metal Exchange which I did on my own, and the then premier Oxford Street furnishing store, Waring and Gillow, where the Chairman, Lord Mansfield, walked into his office, also the boardroom, to find us playing boardroom cricket. With shoes off to protect the table, a ruler serves as the bat and a rubber as the ball. After a good lunch, this takes considerable skill.

'Ah,' he said, 'I can see you are making better use of my office than I would.' He wished us good day and departed. A true gent.

Fairey Engineering was a popular audit because the three of us chaps lived in some style in an excellent Macclesfield hotel which had the further advantage of a beautiful and accommodating receptionist. The company had given up manufacturing airplanes and were building nuclear power stations. The operations were hugely inefficient

---

* Sheep's intestines which are washed through, then packed in barrels with salt and sent to sausage manufacturers.

and the management boring, if not brain dead, but the one thing they had got right, in their opinion, was building the power plants for the government on a cost plus 5% profit. So everything had to be smuggled into direct costs, no matter how extraneous. That included our expenses which added to Fairey's profits.

We were summoned to the Finance Director's office:

'You understand that we are lending you a car to save chauffeur costs. It is to be used strictly for travel from here to your hotel and back and for no other purposes. We will be checking the milometer to ensure you adhere to that.'

Needless to say, the milometer was never checked. All good things come to an end and, luckily, the audit was nearly complete before we were summoned again to the Finance Director's office:

'I don't care which one of you is responsible but please would someone explain how the inside of the front passenger door now bears the clear imprint of a lady's high heels. On second thoughts, the word "lady" is inappropriate.'

There wasn't much we could say. The grand and spacious Ford was replaced by a cheap and knackered Austin with barely enough room for the three of us.

Catching someone with his hand in the till is interesting but rare. I had a couple of near misses. The only substantiated thievery was at Squibb, the pharma company near Liverpool. My leader, John Finney, was an amusing Scot who had joined Peats three years after qualifying and was now senior. The rest of the team was me. The audit was quite straightforward. Peats paid for us to have a Mini, then only two years since launch and a revelation to drive. Richard Guy, my Oxford room-mate, had rooms by the Cathedral so I stayed with him. The building was a bit run down but it was still a surprise that, during a storm, the whole front of it fell off leaving the two residents staring into space.

The Fairey car experience not being far behind, we agreed that the Mini should be put to good use. The snag was that the only women we had spoken to were Squibb employees, nice enough in their homely way but not cut out for a spin in a Mini. Guy had been no use. There was one exception: the Research Director's secretary was a truly beautiful redhead. Auditors get to talk with almost everyone on the management floor but we could think of no reason at all to make an appointment with the Research Director, or rather, his lovely secretary.

Eventually some trumped up reason was found and, yes, she would be delighted to come out to dinner. It turned out she had no ties and maybe her beauty scared the locals off. Then she was delighted to come out to dinner again and the problem became how to unship Finney. He tried pulling rank and I told him the car was only insured for me. A few days later I picked him up in the worst of tempers:

'Where were you last night?' 'Out.' 'Who with?' 'That's none of your business.' 'It was the redhead wasn't it?' 'If that is what you want to believe ...'

It had been a little tactless to leave him solitary in his hotel room but there are some opportunities in life that have to be taken. And not necessarily shared.

By lunchtime, his spirits had soared: 'I've been on the phone to Wells and told him I can complete the audit by myself. You are to catch the train to London this evening. Wells has another job for you tomorrow.'

I had tea with my redhead and warned her about Scotsmen in general and Finney in particular: 'I believe he has been seeing a specialist recently but he won't tell me why. It must be something embarrassing.'

Time passes and I get a phone call from the new head of the Squibb audit, Finney having returned to Glasgow: 'Did you check the petty cash during your audit?'

'Dunno.'

'As the junior member of the team, it was your job to check it.'

'Read the audit book. If I signed I checked it, I did. If I didn't, I didn't.'

Whoever first does an audit, lists in an 'audit book' with columns for signatures over the years, all the jobs that have to be done. Each year thereafter, the team member who does each job signs for it. The book itself rarely changes.

'I have checked and you didn't. It looks as if the audit was incomplete. Why was that?'

'You'll have to ask Finney that. He wanted to finish the audit on his own.'

It turned out that the petty cash clerk had made off with £500, then quite a bit of money. I am glad to report that the redhead rejected Finney's advances.

Most of the work involved investigating companies wishing to go public. This was a lot more interesting than auditing. There was no routine, barring the tedious work of proof reading our final reports, and one was making a real difference to the wealth of the country – or so we imagined. Accordingly I rarely did the same audit two years running. The partners, Wells and the audit leaders provided continuity but fresh eyes were considered desirable for the juniors.

I was, though, part of the audit team for two consecutive years for Lotus Cars, a truly prestigious client for Peats. We were glad to be at the cutting edge of motor sport. We never saw the founder/owner and dealt with the Company Secretary, Fred Bushell. Although the partner felt that everything about Lotus was not just above board but truly splendid, we thought Fred was a crook. We had no evidence but he was too good at avoiding questions. He was downright shifty.

After the first year, we took our concerns to the partner:

'We need more time, sir. We are convinced Mr Bushell is up to no good.'

'That's a serious matter. Have you found any evidence?'

'Not yet, sir, but it smells wrong and we need more time.'

'Colin Chapman and Fred Bushell are two of my most esteemed clients. Malpractice is out of the question. You have already spent too much time on this audit so just wrap it up.'

The next year the smell was still there but we found nothing and there was nothing to say. Leaving Peats submerged all my memories of Lotus and Bushell until the enquiry into the demise of DeLorean in 1981. This was an ill-fated attempt to build the best ever sports car in Northern Ireland. Despite the millions thrown at the project, it failed utterly. Lotus had won the contract for technical advice and engineered all kinds of other back door payments which found their way to the bank accounts of Messrs Chapman and Bushell.

DeLorean himself escaped extradition and Colin Chapman died of a heart attack in 1982. Fred Bushell was given a three-year prison sentence although the trial judge considered him the monkey rather than the organ grinder. Chapman and DeLorean would have been given a lot more for this 'outrageous and massive fraud'.

Meanwhile there was the little matter of passing the Parts 1 and 2 exams. There could be no skiving now as my future livelihood depended on them. Foulks Lynch provided a professional correspondence course and lectures in Old Street. Peats provided time off and I had, for once, done my homework. Coming in the top 1% in Part 1 was due to good fortune which did not continue into Part 2.

The decision to quit auditing as soon as possible was easy. More difficult was finding a new employer. The obvious growth industry was computers. IBM was then a small firm and even such a junior candidate was interviewed at their HQ in Wigmore Street by Edwin Nixon who, I thought, was the MD although he only became that two years later. He was CEO of IBM UK for 20 years and knighted in 1984. I had been told to pitch for being a 'salesman' which is where the money was and avoid being one of the systems people who did all the work. Nixon was charming, the whole interview process could not have been more professional and the role of salesman was duly offered. No doubt I would have become a rich man had I accepted but there was an attractive alternative.

Dudley Plunkett's younger brother and also OG*, Derek, was rather grander than Dudley. Having dabbled in Lloyds (insurance) he joined Justerini and Brooks (J&B), the Queen's wine merchants. Derek was good fun, social and well-connected and mentioned that a job opportunity was coming up. J&B, four other 'fine wine' companies and an agency business, Twiss Browning and Hallowes (TBH) made up United Wine Traders (UWT) which had merged† with Gilbeys the previous year to form International Distillers and Vintners (IDV). TBH was agent for, inter alia, Hennessy cognac and Heidsieck Dry Monopole champagne. The back office functions of the fine wine companies were to be combined in a new company, City Cellars, and they would soon be looking for an accountant.

'Should I mention your name to John Brackenbury, the MD?'

'Yes, you certainly should.'

I consulted one of the partners at Peats, who, after perfunctory sorrow at my leaving, said this was a splendid opportunity. The J&B side of the IDV merger (United Wine Traders) were excellent managers but short of capital; the Gilbeys were none too bright but were financially robust. United Wine Traders would leaven the IDV mix and I would be getting in on the ground floor.

My interview was memorable, but only up to a point. The Chairman of City Cellars was Keith Stevens, CEO of Corney & Barrow, his family business. The interview was fixed with him and John Bracken-

---

* Old Gregorian, i.e. Downside old boy.

† This gave IDV a Stock Exchange listing via Gilbeys which already had one but it was a true 50/50 merger with four IDV directors from each side and Cecil Berens as independent chairman.

bury at 10am at Corney & Barrow's City office. Unfortunately the night before had verged on the excessive and I only rejoined the world around 9. Equipped with bowler and tightly rolled umbrella, but no breakfast, I made it on the dot.

'First things first,' says Keith. 'You'd like a glass of sherry? Which would you like?'

It was the last thing I wanted or needed but this was obviously some kind of test. We were in the tasting room and lined up in front of us were bottles of Corney & Barrow sherries numbered from 1 to 20. Sherry was a big seller in those days. #14 caught my eye. It was labelled 'Old Amontillado' but today would be called 'Palo Cortado'. Lucky it may have been but it was pronounced a good choice.

Back in Keith's office I was waved to the club fender beside an unseasonable roaring fire. We chatted about this and that. I had joined the Bath Club, largely for the squash and bridge facilities. Keith turned out to be a debenture member and also claimed to play squash there.

'Oh dear, my glass seems to be empty. May I top up yours too?'

I was feeling much better and another glass seemed just the ticket. I had failed to notice that the glasses were rather large.

No accounting matters were discussed as balance sheets, in those days, were *terra incognita* for Keith and John. Accepting a third glass was definitely a mistake. I have no recollection of finishing it but apparently I did. Much to their amusement, the interview then had to be terminated and a taxi called, or so John claims. Two sober interviews followed with John in J&B's Hatton Garden office and Colin Dare, the PE consultant advising on the building of City Cellars.

Somehow I passed muster. The promised company car did not turn up so I bought a Triumph Spitfire at the full asking price of £450. Wonderfully low slung and dark green, it couldn't do much over 90 but it felt like a lot more. In 1964, late at night, one could get from Brighton sea front to Kensington Gardens in an hour.

While the cellars were being built, space was found at the Hatton Garden office which also housed Derek and, newly joined from Fortnums, Christopher Pearman. Being at the sharp end of any business is illuminating and I took my turn to serve customers, but most of the work was on the phone. The best part was the lunchroom which operated one or two days a week with an outside caterer. Favoured customers, prospects and celebrities, e.g. wine writers, were mingled to make enjoyable occasions. Beyond pressure to identify the (decanted) wine, business was not discussed.

We would obviously need a similar facility at City Cellars. Nat Leslie in the Silver Vaults, then dark and dingy, supplied the silverware: 12 of everything plus obscure serving spoons cost, after extensive negotiation, around £200.

One of our early festive lunches was for the Old Codgers, a self-elected club of, what seemed to me, very elderly importers. I boggled at how much fun these ancient buffers were having and thought I'd long be in my grave before I got to that stage. In fact they were only in their late fifties or early sixties and I did indeed become one in due course. They were discussing a libel case then in court when Bep Salvi (Seagrams) piped up with a typical contribution:

'I know a libel when I see one. It's what you put on a bottle.'

My other early despatch was to the wine and spirit auction house, then the old family firm of Restalls* in the City.

'Go down to Restalls and buy the hogshead of 1962 Hennessy cognac.'

'How much can I bid up to?'

'Don't worry about that. Just bid.'

This seemed a bit strange. When the cask of cognac came up at the auctioneer's suggested price, I raised my hand. No sooner had I done so when the gavel banged on the counter.

'Sold to Justerini and Brooks.'

How did he know who I was?[†] Twenty years later, now MD of the UK side of IDV, I had the (almost forgotten) cognac bottled and bloody marvellous it was. The UK is the only country in the world that can import, mature and then bottle vintage cognac, provided it is imported before it is three years old. Only a few English merchants are given the privilege of labelling the cognac with its vintage, two then being J&B and Corney & Barrow. All other cognacs are blended and bottled in France with fancy names.

Cognac starts life at original distilled strength of 60-70% alcohol

---

* Michael Broadbent MW was taken on by Christie's in 1966 to create a new retail auction house. In the boom years for trading vintage wines, it proved far more successful and took over Restalls, which had been for the trade.

† Reflecting on this 50 years on, I think I know. Hogsheads of vintage cognac were valuable but rare. The French might have suspected Twiss, Browning and Hallowes of the Old Pals Act in the price to its sister company, J&B. Selling it in a public auction, or appearing to do so, and this is only a guess, was a ruse to reassure the French.

(120°–140° proof) as does malt whisky but that is reduced to 70° proof by adding water, a criminal act for cognac. The trick is to keep the barrels in wet cellars so that it gradually reduces to 70° by absorbing water. In the relatively hot and dry conditions in cognac warehouses, the cognac loses 3% a year by volume but the strength stays high.

The West End wine trade, like J&B, was very different from that in the City, like Corney & Barrow. Most of the trade clustered in the City has now gone. The main reasons are the entry and now domi-nance of the supermarkets and disintermediation as the textbooks call it, i.e. there are fewer layers of business between grower and con-sumer. The importers were small family businesses, with the mer-chants gathering for lunch at the Wine Trade Club. Little business was done in the afternoon as they would still be at their lunch tables. Given the amount they (we) all drank, it is astonishing how long most lived.

The Gilbeys were regarded as grocers and, as such, virtually excluded from the wine trade. Even so, most of the directors (Gilbey family) would typically arrive at a gentlemanly time, soon after 10, deal with their correspondence and go home to Henley, without trou-bling any of the staff, immediately after lunch. Different attitude but same results. The entire Gilbey board in 1962 was family members but after the two takeovers by Watney Mann and then Grand Metro-politan in 1972, not one family member remained.

The Peats partner had been right that IDV was a merger of unlike businesses. Gilbeys was stodgy but they had done some bright things for the mass market, notably taking on Smirnoff vodka for all their countries around the world (the major Commonwealth countries). The stodginess was due to layers of management. Profits were stag-nant. United Wine Traders *per contra* had very few managers and a brand, J&B Rare whisky, soaring in the USA. The tills were ringing but they were having difficulty finding the whisky or the organisation to support the cash flow.

The two unequals had been brought together by Cecil Berens, a Hambro banker who became non-executive and very part-time IDV Chairman, and the Hon Freddie Hennessy, Chairman of UWT who became IDV's Vice Chairman. The other UWT directors joining the IDV board were Geoffrey Hallowes, Keith Stevens and Ralph Cob-bold, of J&B. Everyone loved Freddie and when he died soon after the merger, the cement crumbled. The UWT side looked down on the grocers and the grocers boggled at the amateurs. They were barely on speaking terms and Cobbold, whose disdain was manifold, rarely attended a board meeting. This was not UWT yeast leavening the Gilbey dough, as the Peats partner had envisaged, it was oil and water.

When one of the IDV directors crossed the Atlantic on the *Queen Mary*, he was glad to see a rich American drink nothing but J&B Rare.

'What is it,' he asked, 'that so attracts you to J&B?'

'It is the variety. No two bottles ever taste the same and I can't wait to try the next one.'

The Gilbeys did get the whisky supply side sorted out but in terms of early integration that was about it. They really hankered after taking over the J&B exports. They had international spirits experience with Gilbeys gin, some whiskies of their own and now Smirnoff, whereas the other side were UK wine people. It made sense but not to J&B it didn't. A previous generation had made a fortune for J&B selling VSOP cognac to India. Recognising that Indian independence was likely to mean prohibition there, they set about trying to establish a VSOP* whisky in the USA which looked likely to shed prohibition quite soon.

Justerini & Brooks had been founded by an Italian immigrant in 1749 but until the 1950s had operated at the top end of the market. J&B has had Royal Warrants from every monarch since its founding.[†] Eddie Tatham, MD until he retired at the formation of IDV, was a leading member of the glitterati. His charm, contacts and powers of consumption attracted much, perhaps most, of J&B's wine business.

Ralph Cobbold, initially Joint (with Tatham) and then Sole MD, an old Etonian and one of the 12 best shots in the country, was equally successful with the aristocracy and his networks of the moneyed classes. J&B was based at 2 Pall Mall until, in 1954, they sold out at a hefty price to make way for New Zealand House and moved to the Piccadilly end of Bond Street. Two of their best customers, also glitterati, were having difficulty paying their bills. Tatham agreed to let them off provided one designed the new premises and the other redesigned the labels. So it was that Oliver Messell designed the shop, which became known as the 'tart's boudoir', and Cecil Beaton

---

* Very Special Old Pale.

† See *1749-1965 The Eight Ages of Justerini's*, Dennis Wheatley, The Dolphin Publishing Co, Aylesbury, 1965.

designed the elegant but unusual wine labels.

Smuggling booze into the US was not a skill learned on the cricket field and it was not until prohibition was over that they made any progress. Unfortunately the smart English men-about-town they hired, David Niven, the film actor being one, as agents did not cut the mustard. Then came a letter from Charlie Guttman who had a distributorship ('Paddington'*) in New York and had recently been fired as the agent for Cutty Sark, owned by Berry Bros – J&B's main rival. It was similarly pale and accessible for non-whisky drinkers, unlike Johnnie Walker.

Guttman was almost illiterate but the letter, written by a friend who had an ad agency, was elegant enough to gain him an interview. The Pall Mall wine merchants were appalled by the thug who showed up and if he had done so sooner, the interview would not have lasted long – but Tatham was clever enough to recognise the failure of their US agents thus far and decide to hire the opposite. Guttman got the job.†

In the 1960s, the US 'beverage alcohol' industry was run by people who got their stripes during prohibition. Some Cosa Nostra but mostly Kosher Nostra. Guttman's successor, the brilliant Abe Rosenberg, recounted how they started. Bottle stores were mostly small outlets with dodgy insurance. When the Paddington rep called he would express disappointment that J&B was not in prime position in the window.

'When I return next week, you will either have J&B in your window or a brick through it.'

The skill of the Pall Mall team was to make Rosenberg a friend and provide unceasing admiration – as indeed he deserved – and the banned Cuban cigars he loved. I walked in on a rather grumpy J&B secretary one day messing about with two boxes of cigars.

'What are you doing?'

'Mr Rosenberg is returning to New York today. I'm taking the bands off the Jamaicans, putting them on the Cubans and putting them into the Jamaican box.'

This was the least of the kindnesses J&B undertook. The Gilbeys would undoubtedly have screwed up this business but fortunately

---

* He got the name from the front of a London bus, believing that European brand owners would think it respectable.

† The ad agency kept the business for the next 40 years, despite being hopeless at advertising.

J&B hired Dorrien Belson from Harveys who was enough of a wine merchant to get along with the fine wine side and commercial enough to pacify the Gilbeys.

J&B maintained, nevertheless, that the Export and UK businesses were integral and indivisible. The Royal Warrant, essential for the export trade, was for the Palace's wine, not spirit, business. About a year after City Cellars opened, I was at a J&B board meeting vainly attempting to explain the accounts. The phone rang and the MD, Ralph Cobbold, irritation was his middle name, held out the receiver to me. In his opinion, new boys should not attend board meetings and certainly not interrupt them with phone calls. The rest of the board were merely interested.

'Mr Ambler? I have Mr Burns for you.'

Sid Burns was our stock clerk at City Cellars: 'Sid, what the hell are you doing interrupting a board meeting?'

'Yes, I knew you were in the J&B board meeting and I thought that was a particularly apposite time to call.' It was not Sid Burns but C. Berens, the IDV Chairman. 'I'd like you to visit me tomorrow morning.'

Putting the phone down, I explained, 'Mr Berens wants me to visit him tomorrow morning but he did not say why.' This was greeted with ominous silence.

The next morning's meeting did not take long. 'I'd like you to divide the accounts between J&B Export and the UK business. Can you do that?'

'Easy enough. When would you like it, sir?'

When I returned and explained, I was in trouble. J&B had been hiding the loss-making UK business in the profitable export accounts since the IDV merger. There was nothing to be done and the two parts of J&B were soon separated much, probably, to Belson's satisfaction.

The annual stock-take and the dining room aside, the J&B cellar staff were abstemious but this was not the case at Corney & Barrow, where, probably sometime in the previous century (the business was founded in 1780), the management discovered that the best way to stop the cellar staff drinking the claret was to have a barrel of beer on open access at all times. It had the additional advantage of not having to worry much about pensions. Cellar staff did not live long after retirement.

Similar paternal airs were adopted by the two sets of directors for their annual staff outings but they were expressed in different ways.

# Accountancy was my life until I discovered Smirnoff

Both J&B and Corney & Barrow would hire well-victualled chara-bancs for the day. The Corney & Barrow directors would send a telegram of good wishes whereas the J&B outing included a cricket match. Some of the staff were useful players and Cobbold especially*.

Frank was Cobbold's other middle name. On one occasion, he congratulated our cellar staff on 'working like blacks' as indeed they were. They were, luckily, much amused. He was a member of White's, whose white burgundy business was with J&B for as long as he could remember. The Chairman of their wine committee was also equerry to the Duke of Edinburgh. Cobbold was incensed when J&B's tender was not accepted and wrote something like:

'We are immensely disappointed by the rejection of our white wine tender and cannot understand how this could have come about. Our white burgundy is far the best value in London. I can only assume that the Chairman of your wine committee has had his nose so far up the Royal arse for so long that he can no longer distinguish white burgundy from Blue Nun.' It took a while to restore relations.

His conversation was liberally decorated with the word 'fuck' or some variation thereof. His secretary, so grand that she had her own lady's companion†, was well used to editing his dictation but she had not initially taken kindly to it:

'Fuck, Mr Cobbold?' she said sweetly. 'I am unfamiliar with the word. How do you spell it?'

Two other J&B characters were Colonel Ronnie Lambert and Dick Bridgeman, an Old Harrovian and enthusiastic practical joker. Today the Colonel would be in gaol: so far as young women were concerned, he was generous with his hands. Dick had two bowler hats made, identical to the Colonel's including his initials inside, but one much smaller and one much larger. The Colonel would return from a good lunch purely to collect his bowler. He was routinely nonplussed by finding it shrunken or expanded and was never the wiser.

The poor man was usually the butt of Bridgeman's ingenuity but on one occasion it went too far. This was the age of the telegram, the

---

* He captained Eton and obtained a Cambridge blue.

† By the 1960s, paid companions were uncommon. A rich widow or spinster from a good family would retain another single woman from an equally good, but impoverished, family to provide company in their later years. Although the practice goes back to the 18th century, the loss of menfolk in WWI brought it to its peak. They were not supposed to be treated as employees, as governesses, for example, were but as near enough equals. Some rich women treated their companions well and some as glorified skivvies.

least secure form of communication ever invented. The Colonel was bidden to some immensely grand Scottish baronial house and his hostess was a Lady-in-Waiting to the Queen Mother. As they sat around the drawing room, the butler entered with a telegram on a silver salver.

'It is for you, Colonel Lambert,' and then as his purpling face read it, 'Will there be any reply, sir?'

Bridgeman had arranged the telegram, ostensibly from a Harley Street consultant and it said something like, 'Regret tests confirm gonorrhea.' The poor man took the next train back to London.

Less cruelly, Bridgeman was later found, after a particularly good lunch, with a golfing iron in hand standing, or rather swaying gently, on the parapet of the veranda outside his second-floor office. He explained that he was trying to hit a ball through a window of Boodles, the gentlemen's club just across St James's. He failed: he may have been using the wrong club, a common fault.

Mischief-making aside, Bridgeman was a lovely man and a great rackets player. The Tennis and Rackets Association charity is named after him.

We were integrating three distribution systems (Corney & Barrow, J&B and Chalié Richards) which had been under an office block in Old Broad Street, Charing Cross station and next to a strip joint in Soho (Ronnie Lambert, it was said, had a Life Peerage). The first was methodical but Victorian. The open beer barrel doubtless contributed to the air of calm. The clerks worked on pen and ink ledgers on high stools. J&B's was simply chaotic, especially at Christmas time when they had to work 24-hour shifts. Chalié Richards, a subsidiary of J&B, was too small to be inefficient but, per case, it was costly and the premises valuable.

J&B had sought to deal with the chaos by prioritising the most urgent orders with red stickers. By the time I arrived, all the orders had red stickers. I was told that an order without a red sticker would not be delivered at all. The cellars were in a constant state of panic. Bringing the stock into City Cellars, in Shoreditch, enabled J&B to find out, probably for the first time in many years, what their inventory was. They did have an annual stock-take in which the front office took part but lunch was too liquid for the results to be more than a guess.

J&B had another means of simplifying their distribution. Their wholesale side had struck a number of unwise deals with the likes of Angus Steak Houses. They were major users of clarets and burgundies but the margins had been set too low. J&B could only make a profit through, and there is no polite word for it, malpractice. The cellars had two large bins of unlabelled bottles, claret-shaped in one bin ('Bin 66') and burgundy-shaped in the other ('Bin 65'). A wide variety of labels were kept above. If the customer ordered Aloxe Corton, then the pristinely labelled Aloxe Corton would arrive on the next van. If Beaune was ordered, Beaune would arrive, except, of course that they both came from Bin 65.

Transfer to City Cellars was the end of that game at the expense of some customers. The patrons of Angus Steak House liked their burgundies full and affordable. Whether they came from North Africa was not an issue. No doubt plenty of other reputable wine merchants were playing the same game. J&B did, of course, also have the real wines to sell to the gentry but at higher prices.

A similar situation applied to customer reserves throughout the industry. When a customer bought wine and left it with the merchant for safe keeping, one might have thought it commonsense to separate the customers' wines from the merchant's. With perfect book- and stock-keeping that might not have been necessary. Corney & Barrow's records were reasonably accurate but J&B's were not. We separated the stocks, made good the deficiencies as best we could and were left with quite a large quantity of unaccounted old and valuable wine.

What to do? We consulted our lawyers who said that we should write to all customers whose reserves we had found and advise them of the stocks we held for them, asking them to confirm the accuracy thereof. Then we should run ads in *The Times* and *Telegraph* for several days saying something like: 'If you believe you have wines being kept for you by J&B and have not heard from us recently on that score, let us know'. Some did and they were straightened out but we were still left with quite a bit of old claret and port. We didn't want the auditors asking awkward questions so there was only one thing for it: we had to drink or secrete the wines before the audit came around. Our lunch room was well supplied for a few years.

When City Cellars was up and running, our immediate Chairman, Keith Stevens, decided we should have an official opening, pulling out all the stops. A stone was carved and laid at the front door, concealed behind the customary velvet. Two hundred guests arrived to enjoy a splendid lunch washed down with Château Cheval Blanc 1947*, but we had a problem with protocol. We were half a mile outside the City walls and the Lord Mayor could officiate only at the invitation of the Mayor of Shoreditch. As I was the only IDV person who had met the Mayor of Shoreditch, the introductions to Stevens and the other bigwigs lined up on the pavement fell to me.

My stammer was a lot worse in those days especially on occasions like these. It came on badly and I was later told I said: 'Oh bugger it, you'll have to introduce yourselves.' The Mayor smiled happily and did so.

City Cellars was trying to reconcile modern methods with traditional values. Whereas Gilbeys pumped the wines from the hogsheads to the bottling lines through filters, we eschewed both pumps and filters. The former pressured the wine and allowed oxygen in and the latter took the guts out of the wine. Maturation of the best wines required the sediment to drop out naturally and then remain in contact, hence the need for keeping the wine still and decanting before drinking. The traditional hand method just involved holding the bottle under a tap in the hogshead as J&B and Corney & Barrow had still been doing.

With fine ingenuity, a mobile bottling line was especially constructed. The whole thing was wheeled up to the barrel so that the bottles were just gravity fed with no filtration. The 18th century Samson brewery in Bohemia is also entirely gravity fed but I have never seen another. The barley receiving barn was at the top of a hill. It was malted there and every further stage, down to the lagers in the cellars, was gravity fed. Electricity and steam power had not been invented when the brewery was built.

We bottled all our requirements of classed, except first, growth 1962 clarets there and the 1963 ports apart from Croft which Gilbeys owned and wanted to bottle in Harlow. They were both excellent, high volume years. The traditionalists told us that vintage port should only be bottled on a fine dry day when the moon was full. The pipes† should be taken down and rolled to ensure the sediment is fully

---

* As it happens, this particular wine was bottled separately in England by J&B and Corney & Barrow and at the Château. According to John Brackenbury who compared them, there was no discernable difference.

† A pipe of port, or a butt of sherry, amounts to about 56 dozen bottles, and a hogshead of claret or burgundy has about 24 dozen.

mixed with the wine. We thought that was going too far and, *per contra*, used egg whites to fine (clear) the wines. By the end of the 1960s, almost all classed growth clarets and all vintage ports were bottled at origin using methods sympathetic to what we were doing – if not so extreme.

Operating the cellars was simplified by being granted the first ever 'Open Bond' facility. The traditional 'Closed Bond' warehouse required officers from HM Customs and Excise to check every import into bond and then out, ensuring that the right duty was paid when the goods left. In an Open Bond, there would be no physical checking, HMCE would rely on our records. Given IDV bookkeeping skills to-date, it is truly amazing that the Revenue were prepared to rely on them and maybe they had not done their homework. Their enthusiasm for the new system was, of course, based on reducing their manpower. In the event the system worked very well, not least because there could be no discrepancies between reality and the paperwork: there was no reality.

The other technical development was the IBM360 computer. The previous generation of computers kept the files on magnetic tape which meant the endless and messy running and re-running of tapes. A seminar soon after the launch showed how the hard disk provided near enough simultaneous updating of all files. IBM quoted £4500 for installing the system and we were sold. We sent punched paper tapes to Welwyn Garden City once a week and everything was up-to-date the next day. Probably the biggest single advantage was providing the sales staff with a real time stock list so they knew, for the first time, how much of what was available for sale.

This was great for us but not so great for IBM. It was still very early days for the 360 and it cost them a fortune to deliver the system. Good learning experience for them and their salesman, Bob Nordlinger, who played a large part in getting me to MIT in 1968.

Whilst we were setting up City Cellars, Gilbeys had been moving their far larger operation from Camden Town to Harlow. The Roundhouse was built in 1846 in order to turn railway engines around but by 1871 the engines became too big and Gilbeys took it over as production and distribution centre. By the time they moved out in 1964 it had become a spooky horror movie setting.

Gilbeys was a family business made up of the heirs to the original founders. Jasper Grinling had succeeded Freddie Hennessy as IDV

MD, Walter Gilbey was IDV Finance Director and Bobby Gold was, in effect, IDV Marketing Director, with George Bull, ex TBH (United Wine Traders), and a relation of the Hennessy cognac people.* George, like my flatmate Peter Molony, is one of those right first time people and utterly charming with it. Sporting precision brushed hair, shiny shiny shoes and (then) a military moustache, it was no surprise he was deputy head boy at Ampleforth and commanded the display platoon of the Coldstream Guards.

Walter was the youngest and most diffident director. The casual observer considered him too immature to be FD of a major public company, but that missed two factors. He shared an office and all corporate meetings and responsibilities with Stanley Lee who was a sound FD in his own right. Secondly, Walter was and is very astute in financial matters. He has never been, or pretended to be, a technical accountant – he had Lee and the auditors for that – but he has always been very canny about where to place, and when to withdraw, his money. He is now one of the big financial players in the Isle of Man.

J&B's loss making UK business was put into the care of the 'Gentle Giant' Geoffrey Jameson. He fought with the Rifle Brigade in the war and had been badly injured. It gave him a lot of pain but he was a brave man. The J&B and Corney & Barrow wholesale businesses were transferred to Morgan Furze, which had been owned by the Peppercorn family until they sold out to the Gilbeys shortly before their IDV merger. Morgan Furze moved their distribution to City Cellars which offset the loss of the Corney & Barrow retail business which returned to the Stevens family.

Keith Stevens had wisely decided that a Gilbey dominated IDV was not going to do his traditional City wine business any good. Corney & Barrow weren't making any money either so he persuaded the Gilbeys to give him his business back more or less for nothing. Keith was a great friend, my first Chairman, generous supporter and father-in-law of one of my closest school friends, Nick Sibley, but this was a remarkably one-sided deal. IDV had funded Corney & Barrow's pension liabilities and returned the stock at no cost.

In 1967, Showerings made a surprise and unwelcome bid for IDV. What put it beyond the pale was not the price offered but the delivery of the envelope during Ascot week. To the Directors of IDV, only

---

* Nephew of the Hon Freddie.

one* of whom was available that week, that timing meant that Showerings were cads and bounders.

Walter Gilbey summoned all senior accountants to an all-Sunday meeting in Harlow to review the profit forecasts and see how they could credibly be improved. No one wanted to mention Walter's pet and not inconsiderable expenditure: the Gilbeys' coach and four was supposedly part of the company's promotional campaign but in reality it was a family tradition†. I raised the matter diffidently. The others looked shocked but without a moment's hesitation Walter said:

'Of course you are right. In future I will pay for them personally.' And he did.

IDV directors found a White Knight in the shape of Watney Mann who received 30% of IDV's equity in new shares, enough to ward off Showerings, in exchange for their wholesale wine and spirit business, Brown & Pank, which largely engaged in wholesaling to pubs and their chain of second-rate off-licences called Westminster Wine. Their agency business, main brand Bols liqueurs, Brown, Gore & Welch came with the deal. Watneys promised not to convert their equity into a majority holding, a promise they subsequently broke, albeit in mitigating circumstances.

Showerings had already, the year before, acquired Harveys of Bristol which provided much of the rationale for the IDV bid and then later, in a reverse takeover, Allied Breweries, #2 in the UK. In later life I got to know Uncle Francis (Showering) and liked him a lot. Mild in manner and clear minded, he was not unlike Anton Rupert, the tobacco king, and Jack Keenan, Diageo's marketing supremo in the 1990s. I admired them all for their style and marketing skills.

By this time I was General Manager of City Cellars and John Brackenbury had become Chairman of Morgan Furze and was starting Leisure Finance which was financed 50/50 by IDV and Watneys. The deal was that IDV would provide venture capital in return for equity, interest on loans and sole supply of wines and spirits.

The first major clients were the Roux Brothers. Their success

---

* Jasper Grinling did not care for Ascot.

† Before they entered the wine business in 1857, the Gilbeys had been in the coaching business but steam trains undermined them and they turned to wines, keeping a coach and four out of nostalgia. Some of the UWT snobbery can perhaps be traced back to the fact that the Gilbey brothers had been, in the interim, civilian clerks in the Army Pay Department in the Crimea War, see Four in Hand, Alec Gold, published by W & A Gilbey, 1957.

story, with their flagship restaurants, Le Gavroche and the Waterside Inn, needs no telling here. Albert remains a close friend of John Brackenbury.

The second was at the other end of the restaurant scale: Billy's Baked Potato, a chain of cheap and cheerful fast food outlets. Billy Walker had achieved fame as amateur boxing champion and then in the top league of professionals. His older brother George was accredited with the most brains and the third brother, John, with the least. They were a classic Essex family. George put John in charge of stock-keeping because 'he's the only person I can trust'.

George had been a successful boxer himself and boxing manager for Billy and then ran their joint businesses. After making a fortune from the Brent Cross shopping development, Brent Walker opened casinos and catering outlets and became one of our most valuable clients. Then betting shops proved a disaster. George wasn't everyone's cup of tea but he was mine. In his youth, he had been caught up in the Kray Twins' gangland and served nine months in prison. He very nearly went back again after the Brent Walker collapse when he was charged with stealing £20m. He certainly had a colourful career.*

The customer that got away was the Penthouse Club founded in Shepherd Market by Bob Guccione as a follow up to launching the magazine in 1965 – both a bit raunchier than the *Playboy* equivalents. Bob was as stereotypically New Jersey as George was Essex. He was a Catholic of Sicilian extraction but not linked to the Mafia.

Guccione took all the photographs himself – not, be assured, for the pleasure of staring at naked beauty queens but so that he could apply his artistic talents and the soft focus which (nearly) made the photos inoffensive. And he had no money to pay professional photographers anyway.

Guccione needed £1m to launch the business and the initial discussions, according to Brackenbury, were with Guccione and his glamorous partner, Kathy Keeton, both in bed. Brackenbury had difficulty concentrating on the return on investment. Guccione met the Watney investors, dressed all in white but open to his navel revealing excessive hair, gold chains and medallions. Amazingly, the Savile Row suit-

---

* See *Daily Mail* obituary:
http://www.dailymail.co.uk/news/article-1369741/George-Walker-From-gang-land-high-society-champion-boxer-East-End-gangster—married-daughter-Prince-Philips-cousin.html

14

ed brewers agreed the deal. The Pooterish IDV board, however, did not which was a pity as the £1m would have turned into £17m over the next three years.

When the Gilbeys took over City Cellars to merge UK distribution, I was out of a job – but Bobby Gold had been making encouraging noises and everyone told me just to hang on. So I did. Then I tried to reach Bobby for a chat but he was always in meetings and did not respond to memos. Eventually I sent him one that read: 'I'm not sure why I am sending you this by office mail when it would have a better chance of response if I put it in a bottle and chucked it in the Thames.' Bobby did respond with an invitation to become the FD of his Marketing Division.

On paper this was promotion but the job had little substance. In particular I had no responsibility for computer systems. We ended up friends but the man then in charge, John Westerman, and I came from different planets. Once the City Cellars integrated 360 finally worked, it worked very well and cheaply. Westerman's approach was to create a mosaic with hundreds of small pieces fitting together. Each piece was therefore easy for the programmer to write and amend, but they did not fit together and the overall complexity was a nightmare.

To compound matters, when Gilbeys moved physical operations to Harlow, the computers and their acolytes went to Uxbridge – about as inconvenient (with no M25 or M11) as they could be. Westerman had persuaded the Gilbeys that no programmers* were available in Essex, as they all lived in Middlesex. How anyone could believe such a balmy tale tells you a lot about the top management of the day. The truth was that Westerman's wife had a good job in West London. The computer operations remained a shambles for six or seven years.

As recounted in the next chapter, Katie and I were married by then and it seemed a good idea to further my education in the US. The Fulbright people turned me down but that led to the Department of Trade who were, until the UK built its own business schools, offering scholarships. John Brackenbury and my St John's tutor Roger Elliott wrote generous supporting letters. The interview panel could not have been nicer and I was in – subject of course to gaining business school acceptance.

The then fashionable belief was that advanced mathematics could

---

* Today we buy packaged systems and adapt those and/or the business to fit. In the 1960s, systems design and programming were mostly bespoke.

solve all the problems of business. Cybernetics* and operations research had had some successes such as understanding why three number 11 buses start at intervals and then arrive together. Stafford Beer made extravagant claims for cybernetics but these subjects never realised their ambitions although they are still making contributions.

As MIT was the world HQ of management science, and arguably still is, that was the offer I accepted. When I told IDV's MD, Jasper Grinling, he was furious. Apparently I was the very last on his list for business school. I was sacked on the spot. Bobby Gold and Geoffrey Butler, our Personnel Director and ex Rifle Brigade it need hardly be said, patched things up and I was duly awarded one year's unpaid leave of absence but with pension contributions continuing. This proved valuable.

---

* Wikipedia: 'Cybernetics is a transdisciplinary approach for exploring regulatory systems, their structures, constraints, and possibilities.' This includes business systems. Stafford Beer was the lead guru of the day.

# Chapter 6

# Domesticity and MIT

*This chapter covers:*
- *Mount Carmel Chambers*
- *The Molonys*
- *Wiltshire shows up again*
- *Julian Cotton*
- *Katie gets her man*
- *The Wedding*
- *33 Temple Sheen Road*
- *Katie's brother Roger*
- *And Marah gets hers*
- *MIT*
- *Outward bound*
- *I get my head down*
- *Jay Forrester*
- *Harvard Business School*
- *21½ Inman Street*
- *Other MIT Faculty*
- *The Moon Shot*

After spells in British West Hampstead, commuting from my parents' house in Kew and the top floor of Nottingham Place (opposite York Gate), I agreed with school friend Peter Molony that we needed a place of our own. A leasehold on 17 Mount Carmel Chambers, just off Kensington Church Street, was available at £525 a year. That was cheap even for those days as it was on the third floor with no lift, central heating or porterage. On the other hand it overlooked the Carmelite church, handy for Sundays, the rooms were all decent-sized and it did not need any heating as, in winter, the flats above and below were kept at tropical temperatures. Peter and I took the nicest two bedrooms and we let the third to

Martin Wells, a Beaumont friend of Peter's from Cambridge. Martin's father, William, was a QC and an upmarket (Lancing and Balliol) Labour MP. They had a fine country house, garden and tennis court with a private, but well used, chapel. Martin had been in Cyprus for his national service but had the good sense to be in the Intelligence Corps and thus not in the line of fire. He married Peter's sister Mary. His cheerfulness has never diminished and I am godfather to his third son, Jonathan. Mary takes after her mother, equally lovely but fiery.

The 1994 film, *Four Weddings and a Funeral*, perfectly captured a typical summer Saturday morning at Mount Carmel Chambers. At 10 o'clock one would roll out of bed, groggy and bleary-eyed asking:

'Oh God. Whose wedding is it today?'

'XXX'

'It can't be. That was last week.'

'XXXX'

'Where is it?'

'XXX'

'That's bloody miles.'

After struggling into a morning suit and adding a fast fading carnation, one raced off struggling to make it on time. Two of these occasions, both in East Anglia, proved disastrous. I blame them for being on the wrong side of London. By the time I got to the first, the service was so far gone that entry would be both obvious and embarrassing. I went to the house where the reception was being held and hid among the rhododendrons until the entry queue was moving well. Saying hello to an old friend, I slipped in alongside him. On reaching the bride's mother, I said as smoothly as I could muster:

'Lovely service. The music was beautiful.'

'How would you know? You weren't there.'

The second was worse. The groom was my grandest wine trade colleague, John Armit, who I did not know very well. The bride was the daughter of Lord and Lady Caldecott whom I'd never met. I was surprised to have been asked but I did accept. That Saturday morning was even worse than usual and the wedding was in some God-forsaken part of Essex, a village called Debden. I knew I'd never make the reception, still less the service, rolled over and went back to sleep.

That afternoon I faced the conundrum: did I write a grovelling apology with some implausible excuse? If they asked me, there must have been hundreds there. Lady Caldecott cannot have noticed my absence and I decided it would be undiplomatic to draw it to her attention. I did apologise to Armit when I next saw him and he took it with his usual gracious sangfroid.

You can guess what happened next. Eight years later, when I had forgotten all about it, Katie and I bought a house in this same Debden. Caldecott was still lord of the manor. At a party soon thereafter, I was introduced to Lady Caldecott:

'How'd you do?'

'I know who you are. You are the man who didn't show up at my daughter's wedding.'

In 1963, Mount Carmel Chambers, with its 22 flats, came up for sale. Peter and I thought we, and the dwellers in the other flats, could capture the freeholds. It was a good time to buy. We had an apathetic response from the other inhabitants but we could set up a housing trust to cover the unsold purchases so tenants could buy or not as they liked.

Peter and I moseyed out in Mary's car to see the manager of my bank, still in Harrow-on-the-Hill. The agent said we would need £80,000 comfortably to cover the expected price. The gross income was £6692 but with early reversions, that was likely to rise steeply. We explained the situation and our own lack of any money or any security. 'Would the bank cover the full purchase price up to £80,000?' 'No problem,' was the immediate response. 'Just keep me informed.' We were out of there within 15 minutes and wondering what to do with the rest of the day.

We bid up to our limit. There had been just two bidders after £60,000 and the other man got it. With hindsight we should have taken the risk and continued or asked for £100,000 in the first place. Even in 1963, £100,000 was not a lot for 22 flats in Kensington.

Peter had escaped national service by a year but he did four years at Cambridge so we were doing accountancy articles simultaneously. His father, Joe, was a very successful QC* with an Irish fondness for debate. He didn't mind which side he took so long as it wasn't yours. Mealtimes at their spacious Edwardian Wimbledon home could be quite challenging.

Peter's marriage to Lizzie in Cambridge was memorable in many ways but not least for her being blessed with her many equally pretty

---

* In 1963 he was elected Chairman of the General Council of the Bar.

sisters. Her father and uncle were identical twins, a mild embarrassment as whenever, as chief usher, I approached one for the promised
purse to cover the ushers' night out. I was told the other one had it.
They thought it was funny. One, very well liquored by this time, drew
me aside and made me promise not to relate the story to Lizzie or her
mother. 'What story?' '25 years or so ago, on our wedding night, I
changed places in bed with my brother to see if my bride would
notice. She didn't.'

Peter went on to an illustrious career including being Finance
Director successively at the Post Office, Scottish and Newcastle Breweries and Rolls Royce Aero.

Peter's younger sister, Angela, takes after her scientist uncle. All the
family are tennis players and Angela reached Junior Wimbledon. She
qualified as a doctor but never practiced preferring research into
muscular and, more recently, brain matters (or maybe one cannot distinguish the two). At one point she was using nuclear material but
never seemed in the least perturbed that she, and her children, caused
any Geiger counter they passed to get so excited it fell off the table.

She became a hugely successful professor (neuro immunology) at
Oxford and a Fellow of the Royal Society. Female professors at
Oxford are rare enough but what is truly amazing is that her daugh-
ter, Tonia, is now also a professor (musculoskeletal biology) at
Oxford.

Husband Pip (New College) was a contemporary of mine and we
have been involved together in jaunts, pubs and From-Scratch singing
at the Albert Hall. He introduced me to the Surprise in Chelsea, my
then favourite pub in all London. It must have been the last to have
a proper public bar patronised by local tradesmen, with cheaper beer
and a dartboard. From there we sallied forth to the Star of India for
curries.

The fourth Molony sibling, John, is not unlike James Wiltshire, see
below, but very unlike brother Peter. They are well named: like the
apostles, on Peter you could build a church whereas John is more
loveable than rock-like. Since coming down from Cambridge, he has
been immersed in the art world in various capacities. Like James
Wiltshire, John used not to be a model of sobriety. At a Cambridge
party I introduced him to an elderly don who turned out to have been
his supervisor 30 years earlier. The don looked very puzzled and then
light dawned:

'I've been trying to work out why I did not recognise you. Normally I have no trouble. The answer is that this is the first time I have ever seen you sober.'

My final flatmates were James (JFTO) Wiltshire and Julian Cotton, both extraordinary in their different ways. James I had not seen since the SS *Empire Orwell* en route to the Far East but he had not changed, still falling about with merriment.

Unwisely, in my parents' view, I chose James to be my best man when Katie and I married. On account of being even more inebriated than the rest of us, he was, apart from providing the right ring at the right time, completely useless. In the canon of worst and longest best man speeches he was supreme on both counts.

James did not initially adapt well to commercial life. Indeed, he did not adapt at all. Luckily he fell on his feet. A friend from national service founded a business called 'Breakmate' which supplied a machine and the comestibles to brew tea and coffee for small and medium sized offices. The business needed a trustworthy Company Secretary. James was a quick learner and sobered up just as fast.

The business prospered mightily and when it was sold out, James received a ton of cash. He departed beyond the reach of the Inland Revenue in some haste and toured the Continent in a camper van. The Inland Revenue ultimately treated him as their Prodigal Son and happiness was restored.

My last, but equally eccentric, flatmate, Julian Cotton. A friend of Peter, Martin and James from Cambridge, he took his Ampleforth background very lightly. The rest of his family were pious Roman Catholics, and one is a Benedictine monk, but Julian has never allowed his faith, any faith, to prevent him charming birds off any perch.

When he joined us, he was a salesman for Rank films in general and the 'Carry On' films in particular. For an avid follower of the poems of Rainer Maria Rilke and all that is beautiful, Carry On films were beyond the pale. The end came when he was asked to sell *Carry On Up The Nile* to Egypt, a country not long on humour or the recently invading British. Even Julian's gifts could not pull that off and he decided to quit.

Julian's charm has brought him important friendships with high-level people and his native cunning has made him a fine bridge player. On my sole foray to the roll-up bridge night at the Arts Club, Julian came as my guest. We were regarded with some suspicion by the regulars but did well mostly thanks to Julian and the mini-bombshell he dropped. Zia Mahmoud was, at the time, the most famous bridge player in the world. In a lull in the conversation, Julian said:

'Did I tell you I was playing with Zia Mahmoud last week?'

Jaws dropped round the table, especially mine, and we won the next rubber comfortably. Out of earshot by the bar at the next break I said:

'What's this with playing bridge with Mahmoud?'

'Oh no. I don't play bridge with him. Golf. He's a member of my golf club.'

I have never been sure how much to believe of Julian's accounts of his amatory successes. All his life, it seems, has been fighting off the women dying to sleep with him. Just when one thinks a particular story cannot be true, one meets the other party and it turns out that it is. Julian used to claim that taking a girl out for an evening never cost him more than the half pint of bitter he bought at the beginning. He was pretty stingy in those days, albeit not now, but even so that is not credible.

Eventually he found a girl who was beautiful, charming and making lots of money, Penny. Not only that but she ran a model agency, with a string of lovelies all of whom, according to Julian, adored him too. Penny was in love with Julian who reckoned he had got to heaven. With a fine house in Holland Park and two lovely children, we thought he had too.

Some men (this is predominantly a male disease) believe that nothing is so good that it cannot be improved with a little tinkering. If it is a sports car, no problem. If it is the wife's successful business, we are into dangerous territory. Both Julian and my brother Jason would insist, if quizzed today, that their salesmanship and improvements to the business were entirely beneficial. Their wives told other versions and all, no doubt, were true. Be that as it may, to an outsider mixing business with marriage seemed to contribute to the break up of both. And then Penny died of breast cancer.

After marrying another beautiful and commercially savvy blonde, Carole, with a similar outcome and another delightful daughter, Julian decides the bachelor life suits him better. The old charm is still as productive as ever.

Move the clock on, we are now both 70 and Julian still has his successful photographers' agency business. I get an agonised phone call. He needs my advice:

'I'm in a terrible pickle and I don't know what to do.'

'What's the problem?'

'I have this American girlfriend and she wants me to move to Wichita with her.'

'So?'

'The thing is that she's only just 20, her father is a lot younger than me and they are making difficulties.'

'I'm with the father.'

Julian goes off to meet the family most of whom are very agreeable but the father is not, at least initially. Julian's poker skills and charm do the trick. The parents want him to make an honest woman of their daughter and run the family business in Wichita. As a confirmed Londoner with a bus pass, this was a step too far.

What they did not know, and nor did I initially, was that he concurrently had a live-in lodger in the shape of a Swiss professional dancer. Her dance partner and all her other men-friends were, according to Julian, gay and she needed hetero company. Each time the American came to London, Julian went to church (she was Roman Catholic) and the Swiss dancer moved out. When the American departed, the previous arrangements resumed.

The dancer's mother took as dim a view of these arrangements as the American father had. She flew into London to read the riot act but such words bounce off like racquet balls from the end wall. Julian sees himself as merely dispensing human kindness.

He may not have liked the Carry On movies but, in his mature years, he was living them.

My own *coup de foudre* was love at first sight but it took a while for Katie, then Cathy, to get around to the idea. She was very young (21) and I was very old (27). Our first meeting came about like this.

Cousin Marah had completed a secretarial course in Cambridge in high style although not so substance high, she claims, as her father believed. She was now a secretary at Mather & Crowther, one of the leading London ad agencies of the day.* Her parties were always excellent – not least because she commissioned me to fix the drinks. The Mount Carmel cocktail was half gin, one-third Martini Dry and one-sixth cognac, with the occasional lump of ice to water it down a bit.

Sooner or later a drink like that was going to cause trouble. The

---

* Now Ogilvy & Mather, part of the WPP Group.

first was when my father fell down the stairs when leaving our Mount Carmel flat – no harm done. The second was a party given by Marah and her then boyfriend at his parents very grand flat in Gray's Inn (father was a QC). Marah and I both left early but the next day I heard that the flat had been trashed and I was getting the blame. Moral: if you mix the drinks, do not leave early.

At this 1965 party in Marah's flat overlooking South Ken station there was a lovely blonde, tall enough to be seen across a crowded room. I demanded introduction. Marah said Cathy was a colleague. At a party where one cannot hear a word, one smiles a lot and pretends to listen. It was one of those. As it drew to a close, I offered to drive her home and was pleasantly surprised by her acceptance.

'Where do you live?'

'Reigate.'

Being in no fit condition to drive even a few hundred yards, this was dismaying. I compensated by taking the Spitfire's roof off. On arrival, the house was dark, barred and shuttered. After a great deal of battering on the door and lights coming on in the neighbouring houses – it was about midnight – an irate father appeared at the door in his dressing gown. Expecting due thanks and appreciation, I said:

'I've brought your daughter home, sir.'

'Home? HOME? She's got a perfectly good home of her own in Ebury Street.' With which he stomped off back to bed. Ebury Street is a few hundred yards from Marah's flat.

Katie shortly moved to the lower ground floor flat at 19 Queen's Gate (handier for Mount Carmel). She shared a bedroom with Maggie Beaumont, the beautiful but mad daughter of a Russian father and sensible English mother. The other bedroom was shared by a dreamy girl from North Carolina, Norcott Pemberton, and a rather homely, hysterical, privately educated English girl, Sue Smith. They could hardly have been more different.

My eyes were only for Katie but this was difficult when Norcott drifted around wearing nothing but a hairdryer. Norcott was shapely. The noise of her machine somehow prevented her noticing my presence.

I still feel guilty about poor Sue. She was aggravating but we should not have been beastly to her. On one occasion she and Maggie had a spectacular cat fight – nails and hair flying as they rolled around the floor.

My courtship of Katie followed conventional lines. Katie accepted flowers, dinners and dancing. Early on I had acquired a kid fur coat. It was a lot more glamorous than expensive but I could hardly admit to that. Katie was reluctant to accept it – I suspect she thought her father would get the wrong idea. Having acquired it in circumstances that would not bear the light of day, I could not return it. Thankfully she acquiesced and gifting was more cautious thereafter.

Introducing Katie to Dennis and Patricia went as well as could be expected. We were not then engaged; it was just the usual preliminary skirmish. Patricia was nice to me about Katie but, I found out much later, not to Katie. As recounted earlier Katie was subjected to the trial by ferrets, not something one would expect to meet at a Sunday lunch in Richmond. Anyone not selected by Patricia would have come in for the same treatment. Dennis thought she was wonderful and was his usual courteous self. Katie and I agreed to keep our parents away from each other as long as possible.

The claret was always decanted for dinner parties at Mount Carmel Chambers. The wine for the chaps had a black sewing thread around the neck; the otherwise identical decanter held the wine for the women. These were straitened times and one had to make savings where one could. Katie has always had a beady eye when it comes to wine. Inevitably we were rumbled and the conversation became quite disagreeable. The practice stopped.

On a happier note, when Katie and Maggie grumbled about the cleanliness of the flat, we engaged them as cleaners. They needed the money and the place had indeed become a little grubby. Before that, Angela Molony had been our cleaner. We only employed the highest class of cleaner.

By early 1966, I was even more certain that Katie was the girl for me and I detected some signs of domesticity – but I wasn't much of a catch. Short, fat, short-sighted, an accountant with anarchic tendencies who stammered and had a none too profitable job. I thought my beautiful dark green Spitfire must be a plus but no; Katie has never liked open cars.

Hatton Garden had its advantages as a workplace and I had been introduced to a delightful old-school jeweller. He made everything he sold and one dealt with him in his tiny workshop. I explained the position. I would like to do things in the traditional way, down on one knee, whipping ring-box out of pocket and all that.

'What happens,' said I, 'if she turns me down?'

'She won't.'

'How do you know? You have never met her.'

'I'll take the chance. If she turns you down, I'll take the ring back and you will have a full refund.'

With that we sat down and designed a three-banded platinum ring with a good square-cut sapphire and diamonds each side. I never saw another one like it until we had to make a replacement 40 years later and it was our very own ring.

Of the various places we dined and danced, the 55 Club in Jermyn Street was our favourite. On 4th March 1966, we went to *Arsenic and Old Lace*, laughed in the usual places, dined at the 55 and then I went down on one knee and plighted my troth. The diners nearby were taking a keen interest. In films, the girls say yes and all the other diners applaud but it was not quite like that. They were simply embarrassed that a chap should be doing it in public. Luckily the ring was a great success and I got a cautious 'yes'.

The next day we had people to tell and particularly the jeweller. He could keep the money. 'Never doubted it,' he said. We stayed with the Hatton Garden connection and chose St Ethelreda's in Ely Place which, thanks to a cut-through, was only 20 yards from J&B's premises. The church is small, lovely with a great ambiance and the only Catholic pre-reformation church in the country thanks to various Bishops of Ely being a bit slow in turning to the prevailing wind.

First the Preston and Ambler parents had to meet. Over tea, Patricia had been banging on, as some middle-class women do, about the people she knew and did the Prestons know them? That is about as irritating a habit as putting invitation cards on the mantelpiece. After a while, Katie's mother sweetly asked if Patricia knew the Derbyshire dales. After a pause for thought:

'I don't think so. To whom are they related?'

Her mother sat back with a happy smile.

We settled on the 4th of June for the wedding, not least because it was a date that I was likely to remember. Katie's father, Lawrie, insisted on picking up the tab – fortunately modest – and I bought the champagne. That proved to be a challenge. I love old champagne and scoured London for the 1943s, Katie's birth year and also a good champagne vintage. I think I bought every bottle, luckily enough for the reception.

Passmore, now Abbot of Downside, agreed to take the service and we met him for lunch at the Bath Club. He was in his customary black habit liberally splattered with past meals. Like most of his pupils, she found him terrifying but actually he was at his gentlest.

My preparation for the wedding proved unfortunate. In those days the stag night was the evening before the wedding and not a week in some distant capital. After being thrown out of the Surprise pub at closing time, and then the curry house, the details are unclear. Even less clear is why we were walking towards Mount Carmel Chambers from the wrong direction but we did find, as one does, a steamroller parked in a square just off Church Street. The ignition key was in the lock.

There are various versions of what happened next but mine is that I climbed aboard and got it going. We were slowly building up speed when a police car pulled in alongside us. It didn't take them long to size up the situation.

'Excuse me, sir, but do you have a licence to drive a steamroller?'

'Er, no officer.'

'I think we should put it back, don't you sir?'

The next morning took a while to get going but things perked up with a splendid bachelor lunch at Brown's with much talk of hair of dogs. By the time Wiltshire and I got to the church and stood before Passmore, I may have been swaying slightly. He hissed:

'You're drunk.'

The service otherwise continued in the customary fashion with wonderful music. The organist hammered out Widor's Toccata in F and a Handel March as we variously arrived. One of the hymns, presciently as our son Gus was to marry a German girl, was the English version of the German national anthem. We hired a trumpeter from a London Orchestra to perform part of Telemann's Heldenmusik (Honour, Love and Vigour – one can but hope) and Purcell's 'Trumpet Tune', aka Voluntary.

The lunch caused one other casualty. At its conclusion, Katie's brother Roger was persuaded to have his first and, as it turned out last, cigar. His car had the back-up case of champagne and the flowers for the cake. He never made the church and there was still no sign of him at the reception. Katie and her mother fussed about the flowers and I was much more worried about the champagne. The butler, who came with the house, picked some flowers from the tubs on the terrace and Roger arrived, pale and anxious, before the champagne ran out. The speeches, Wiltshire's apart, passed off smoothly.

IDV had by now come up with the promised company car. They refused to take over my beloved dark green Spitfire and replaced it with a Triumph Vitesse. As a reluctant concession, it was both sporty and soft-topped. The limo took us from the reception a mile or so to the parked Triumph and we set off down the M4 at speed. The motorway was fairly empty in those days and, with the roof down, it was joyous, at least for me. Katie grumbled a bit and suggested that the 70 mph speed limit would be more acceptable.

Booking what I thought was a love-nest in the New Forest was, I thought, inspired. In reality it was insane. We should have gone to the Savoy to sober up. Our hotel was about as romantic as Dracula's castle. It was very dark and a single light swung from the ceiling of reception. We were starving but it was half an hour after last orders and the harridan in charge was implacable. Leaden sandwiches eventually appeared but it was a horrible hotel, a horrible room and a horrible wire-sprung bed. Marital bliss did not arrive.

The next day went from bad to worse. With nostalgia for the sea and Scandinavia, nothing could be more delightful than a summer channel crossing on a ferry serving smorgasbord. Except that, being June, it was blowing a gale. All the better for me but Katie, it turned out (how was I to know?), gets seasick crossing the Thames.

She sat moaning gently at a quiet table whilst I went to the buffet for provisions. Eschewing the more exotic offerings, I returned with a variety of easy foods on two plates. As the ship rolled and pitched, so did the food on our plates. Eggs are particularly volatile. Her first (and last) large cognac did not help.

Life looked up when we got to France and made our way, now more responsibly, down to Château Loudenne, near Bordeaux, where IDV, which owned the property, had generously made the honeymoon suite available. Loudenne was totally blissful. We picnicked for lunch and had glorious dinners with even more glorious wines.

The hotels there and back proved to be all one could want on honeymoon with no disasters apart from a close encounter with a marvellous cheese. I have never had it since but a blend of Roquefort and cognac is delicious. It is also unwise at the end of a liberal dinner.

Patricia, in a determined effort to be helpful, had found us a sunny, corner house in East Sheen. An easy stroll to Richmond Park, it cost £7200* and the mortgage company obligingly coughed up £7000 of it. Roly Pennefather, the City Cellars lawyer and friend of Keith

---

* By 2013 the market price had increased a hundredfold. If only... rice had increased a hundredfold. If only...

Stevens, gave us the conveyance as a wedding present. My other favourite present, though not Katie's, was a Lalique ashtray from Dennis's friends in the CIA. His last job with MI6 was liaising with the CIA and we had had an outing together to the big annual Burgundy feast at the Château du Clos de Vougeot.

Driving to Shoreditch every morning was easy then and especially quick when the City Cellars' alarms went off at 2am. The neighbourhood was criminal. The Council provided money-boxes on sticks. Every time a parking meter filled up, they sawed it off and took it home to be emptied. The Shoreditch police came from Scotland, or other distant parts, as not a single member of the local community would join them. As a result, their detection rate was well-nigh zero. Our security was good and after a while they gave up. Later still, thanks to the locals we employed, we were accepted into the community.

SW14 was a bit embarrassing as I had spent too much time at Oxford being rude to Liz McLaren about her SW14 home being the pits of suburbia. I should not have knocked it. Her family had a comfortable house near Richmond Park and my visit there had been fun although my disdain may have slipped through. Her bright, but then diffident, brother ended up as our Ambassador in Beijing. Liz still lived there but, quite rightly, did not welcome us.

The one undeniable downside of the property was the neighbour, a Scottish shrew much given to screaming at Katie. A gentle conversation only made matters worse. She had a screw loose and there was nothing to be done about it.

Katie's brother Roger provided transport, in his little red Sprite, to Queen Charlotte's for Gus's arrival as I was unforgivably detained. When I did get there, Katie was comfortably ensconced in a six-person ward and one of the others, astonishingly, was the wife of my one-time flatmate, Richard Hopking, and their daughter-to-be, Scarlett. Nothing much was happening on that front either and the Sister suggested Richard and I made ourselves scarce.

Fortunately there is a pub just outside and we filled in the time as best we could, checking in by phone from time to time. At chucking out time there was no progress and Richard and I applied our beer-fuelled brains to whether we would wait in the hospital corridor or go home to our beds. Sister supported the latter option. In those days, fathers were not expected to witness births.

The phone went at about 8am. Gus had arrived in the early hours. 'Why didn't you call me then?'

'The last time I spoke with you, you sounded like you needed a very long sleep. How was the pub?'

Roger decided not to go to university but to join the Royal Navy and to get the equivalent of an electronics degree at Her Majesty's expense. He had a year at Dartmouth followed by two years at RNC Greenwich. I enjoyed at least one Trafalgar night there and Katie and I attended some magnificent balls. The painted hall is one of the world's best places to dance.

One such evening there was a shriek of 'Tim' echoing round the walls. The voice belonged to cousin Valerie who was with a jovial submariner. It turned out they had just got engaged that evening and Miss Swabey was about to become Mrs Jeremy Davies Webb. The sparkling wine served on these occasions is rarely more than adequate and it was certainly below the standard required to toast the forthcoming nuptials. The CPO in charge of wine agreed completely and led me down to the cellars.

As luck would have it, odd bottles of champagne were gathering dust because each variety was too few to meet the numbers for any catered event. I chose a couple of bottles of Krug and we agreed it would be good to get them off his hands. He was a pleasure to deal with. It was always going to be a splendid evening but this family coincidence made it unforgettable.

Mather & Crowther also provided the link to cousin Marah's matrimony. John Armitage was one of their top account handlers, otherwise known as 'suits'. Middle height, dark and handsome enough, John was an attractive prospect who, thus far, had resisted permanent attachments.

The wedding was in the Henry VII chapel and the reception in the Jerusalem Chamber, both in Westminster Abbey, following a splendid ushers' lunch at a Wiltons-type restaurant beside Victoria station. Only Wodehouse would have been able to do justice to the ushers' conversation. The central flaw, as we saw it, the worm in the apple, of the impending marriage was golf. John was not just addicted to golf, it was an obsession. Office hours between Mondays and Fridays were a waste of the daylight that should have been devoted to waving golf sticks around.

John did not devote two weeks of honeymoon to teaching Marah golf only because John had only scheduled two days for it. Golf lessons did indeed await her return and she became an elegant golfer with a handicap large enough to offset his minuscule one. They moved to a beautiful Georgian home in Charing, Kent and all was in Himmelreich. By day they developed their own interests and by night presumably did whatever young lovers do. After a few mishaps, son Edward duly arrived.

John's father had been Rector at St Bride's, the journalists' church off Fleet Street, and music ran in the Armitage genes. His uncle Noel had always played the trumpet. Even John, when he retired, recognised that golf should not be played ten times a week and went to read music at Kent University, focusing on the trumpet. When he died too young, Edward created the John Armitage Memorial Trust which has run top level concerts (principally brass, choir and organ) for over ten years. It has continued John's interest in helping new composers, of any age, achieve performances for their music.

Fate plays funny tricks in our lives. I was rude about SW14 so I was sent to live there. I failed to show up at a Debden wedding so I was sent to live there. So it was with MIT. Just when I thought I was the only person in London to be going there, it turned out that two of my friends were doing the same, at the same time (1968).

Bob Nordlinger had been the IBM salesman handling the computerisation at City Cellars. An ex-US naval officer he was tall, lean and dark just as one would expect from Hollywood. His wife Angela was Australian, ruddy, round faced with short dark curly hair. We had a week's sailing on the Broads, great fun as ever, but the naval skills were not in much evidence. Broads sailing is not to be taken seriously and is, as I've observed before, merely a way of getting from one pub to another without risking the breathalyser.

Max Boisot was married to the younger of Peter Stevens's two blonde and svelte daughters, Virginia. He was a master of conversation in the sense that you did not actually have to join in. Max solo flowed in a highly entertaining fashion. Max was half French and never drank alcohol but he sounded as if he did. His parents had separated and his mother had long owned the Saddle Room, an upmarket night club at the southern end of Park Lane. She was rumoured to have had an affair with the Duke of Edinburgh and there is little doubt about that. Max's friends all reckoned he was the progeny but he vigorously denied it and had evidence to prove it. He did, though, look like the Duke.

Bob had missed out on university by joining the navy and was going to MIT to do an undergraduate degree. Max had been at Cambridge and now wanted a doctorate in town planning. I was down for the master's degree in business at MIT's Sloan School. The doors back into IDV would close after a year and I wanted to keep that option open.

We agreed to split the jobs. Max would go early and secure three apartments, reserving the best, it went without saying, for himself. Katie and I were going by the *Queen Elizabeth** and could therefore take everyone's heavy luggage. With Bob's help and an IDV van the luggage went to Southampton, and Bob would meet us at the New York dockside with van and trailer. Between us we had 31 items, trunks, tea chests, suitcases and packages of all sizes, in addition to our cabin baggage.

The ocean was rough and Katie was seasick. As she lay moaning on our bed, the steward kindly brought Spam sandwiches. Not a good choice. Luckily that was only two of the five days and overall it was great. The architect of the QEI knew his wines and the cellar was at the fulcrum, i.e. the exact middle of the ship – so the wines were not disturbed no matter how much the ship pitched and rolled. Most passengers were not fine wine drinkers so with the help of the steward I discovered some clarets that had been crossing the Atlantic for many years and were in peak condition for us. That did not work on the QEII ten years later.

On our arrival, the Customs Officers showed a remarkable lack of enthusiasm for inspecting our 30 plus trunks and chests on the dock. Two hours later, we found ourselves alone apart from the two officers who had not gone to lunch. Their new-found enthusiasm was not so much pity as revenge for a late lunch.

Responding to hostile questioning was complicated by having no idea what was in two-thirds of the cases. We should have numbered them and got lists of contents from Bob and Max.

'Did you pack these yourselves?'

'Yes' – wrong I know but any other answer seemed to be worse.

'OK what is in this one?' Inevitably they had not picked one of ours.

'It was so long ago and there are so many cases that I honestly cannot remember, Officer.'

---

* The QEI was the biggest passenger ship in the world.

After a few rounds of that he had one opened up. He poked around and said:

'Are there any weapons in here.'

'Of course not, Officer.'

'What's this then?' he said brandishing a very large black revolver. I nearly died. Only a US naval officer could have done something that stupid. Funnily enough the Customs man was not at all bothered. It would have been different in Southampton. Having made us look foolish, he brightened up and waved us through.

The welcoming area was solely occupied by very worried Nordlingers.

'We saw everyone else come through except you. We thought you must have been taken into custody.'

'We very nearly were. I take it that the revolver is yours?'

'Yes. Everyone has guns here. You should get one yourselves.'

The Nordlingers had by then established themselves in their apartment but did not know where Max's or ours were, and Max, true to form, was nowhere to be found. We stacked up the cases with Bob and returned the van and trailer. It was not a good night on the floor.

Max turned up the next day all bright and breezy and unremorseful. He took us to our apartment, the first floor of 21½ Inman Street, ideally located midway between MIT and Harvard Square, an easy walk to both. The sun shone on burnished wood flooring without a stick of furniture. We had not anticipated that. Cambridge had though and the down-and-out shops had a good supply of down-and-out furniture. Slats had to be bought to put under the mattress and a door to go on two tea chests to form the desk.

Max had a much grander solution for his apartment. He designed a whole suite of furniture to be made by the MIT support technicians from new wood as, he claimed, a design project for his PhD. Free of charge he had new furniture IKEA could not have bettered.

Much to the annoyance of other universities, an MA comes automatically at Oxford and Cambridge four years after a BA. MIT, however, required serious work. Miriam Sherbourne ran the admin at the Sloan School more or less single-handed and had done so for a generation. The professors were in awe of her. As is so often the case, once past the brusqueness, she was kindness itself. Having listened to my plan for completing the master's in 12 months and not the customary two years, she was brisk:

'It has never been done and it cannot be done.'

'Is there any harm in trying?'

'I suppose not.'

Lectures were far more interactive and fun than at Oxford and were pretty much compulsory. Operations research (maths) quickly seemed to be marginal for business whereas marketing was central. Company boards do three things: make money, count it and spend it. Any idiot can count it and spend it; the difficult bit is making it in the first place and that is marketing. Too many accountants not only join boards but become CEOs. They promote the belief that the more often one counts a pile of money, the bigger it gets. At best accountants keep score: they do not make runs. My Pauline conversion from accountant to marketeer had taken place.

One disappointment in moving away from operations research was not being taught by Jay Forrester, a senior faculty member and the inventor of 'Industrial Dynamics'* which is what operations research had become. It is a really useful field of work. For example, he showed that, in a multi-tier distribution system, the first tier should base its production forecasts not on its own sales but on final demand. Stock levels at the intermediate levels go in and out like a concertina distorting and amplifying the peaks and troughs. I had arrived at the world centre for my chosen subject and walked away.

The Forresters came from Nebraska, a highly self-disciplined community. If you live with no electricity and in the middle of a field stretching so far in all directions that you can see the curvature of the earth, you have to be. Jay, in 2013 still going at 95, was only 50 when we were there but seemed a lot more. He was tall, slim, austere and serious, very serious. He kindly invited us to his home for a weekend.

On arrival we were warmly greeted and offered a cup of hot Bovril (or its US equivalent). This seemed a little odd but we'd come through heavy snow and the outside temperature was minus something nasty. Luckily I'd packed half a bottle of Smirnoff as a precaution so we could take our cups to our room and make them more interesting.

The room was an icebox: 'We know the Brits like to sleep with the windows open so we thought we'd make you feel at home.' It took until mid the next day for 'room temperature' to be achieved.

By this time it was clear that the Forresters were not just teetotal but deeply hostile to alcohol for religious reasons. I did my best to circumvent questions like 'What did you do before MIT?' 'I was an

---

* Roughly the same as what is now called 'System Dynamics' both are part of what is now known as Decision Science..

accountant' was met with 'but in what kind of business?' We had to fess up and there was a bit of a frisson. But they were lovely generous people and normal service was resumed soon enough.

Katie's employers were at the other end of the alcohol scale. She had obtained a job in the Doctoral Office of Harvard Business School and we thought that would provide a neat counterpoint with the Sloan School. She had two charming workmates, Carolyn Stanfield, the glamorous one, had a delicious slow Southern drawl and a dachshund called Otto. Kitty Galaitsis was a larky Midwesterner. Carolyn was married rather unconvincingly to a tall physicist doing a PhD and Kitty to an entertaining Greek.

Fridays would be the problem. At both business schools, serious drinking began at 4pm sharp. The MIT lot divided into non-drinking but otherwise civilised people and those so dedicated to the stuff that ambiance was for cissies. Barrels of beer were rolled into some dark cellar where plastic cups were held under the frothing taps and then upended over one's face. Some civilised brews have since been developed but then it was just the dreadful Budweiser, Miller's, Coor's etc.

The professors for whom Katie worked had a totally different approach. 'Party-time' involved a large number of two-foot diameter pizzas in cardboard boxes and free flowing Dry Martinis. Conversation would peak early and slowly decline to slurred mumblings. Have you ever noticed that what one has to say feels more important the more inebriated one is, and is at the same time less memorable? By 6pm it was all over, both the party and the whole evening.

Katie's professors tried to persuade me to do a doctorate with them. Whether or not they were inebriated at the time does not matter, we were going to achieve the Master's in one year and go home. And that was final.

I did one course at Harvard just for comparison but I did not like the case study method then – or, much later, at London Business School. 90% of MBA students do like it and, though I had to use it at LBS, I did not warm to it. MIT did not then use cases at all and had a far more intellectual, rather Oxbridge, ambiance. When I returned to academia 20 years later, I found that almost all the US academics I got along with best were either at MIT or had been. Lucky again.

The 1960s were probably the peak of US affection for alcohol. Prohibition had ended only 35 years earlier and the Manhattan business lunch involved at least two Martinis. In general wine hardly featured apart from dominating the larder at 21½ Inman Street.

Road-building has swept it all away now but there was a thriving Italian market area just where the Callaghan Tunnel emerges from Logan Airport. Zinfandel* in gallon jars, at a price barely above that for water, was delicious and met our needs and those of all our guests save the Masters of Wine (we didn't have many of those).

Unlike the Forresters' home, our apartment was over-heated and the only means of cooling it down was to leave the back window open. Soon enough, this was discovered by Mr Simpkin, a long haired, scruffy but very affectionate cat. He joined us every night for supper, his being a saucer of milk and a few titbits. A bunch of friends were knocking back the Zinfandel with us one evening when a very annoyed female voice shrieked, 'What are you doing with our cat?' Mr Simpkin turned out to have quite a few owners, or rather, quite a large staff. We did not need to worry about him when we left. What really annoyed the woman in question was that Mr Simpkin was quite happy with cold milk with us but insisted on having it warmed up by her.

We did not see much of the Nordlingers but we kept in close touch with the Boisots. I got frostbite walking down to them for Christmas lunch and we drove out to see the 'Fall Foliage'. The latter was a bit of a disaster as the rain never let up. New England is a pretty part of the world and it has always been my favourite part of the US, Manhattan aside. In some ways it is more English than we are with better manners and just as much Ye Olde.

Now students again, Max Boisot and I decided to take part in political protest. 1969 was a high water mark for the feminist movement in the USA. Marches were being held and bras were being burnt. We knocked up a couple of placards and joined a Women's Liberation Front meeting – but not for long. Two large and aggressive women asked us to leave. Due to some mix-up our placards read 'Liberate Women's Fronts'. When we got back, well pleased with our contribution, Virginia and Katie told us we were childish. Don't mess with the sisterhood.

In Plymouth we ate shrimps and watched the rock on lovely warm evenings. By that time Katie was pregnant. Apart from complaining about the level of shrimp consumption, her doctors were marvellous

---

* Californian dry red wine from the zinfandel grape.

and Harvard paid for everything. We discussed whether our son (we knew that by then) should be born in the US which would give him the option of citizenship.

Consulting was profitable for business school students but I lacked the necessary diplomatic skills. One job came out of a course we had had with an engineering firm. Curiously the sales function of this family business had been contracted out to a delightful pair of old buffers, friends of the CEO's father. There was no friction but sales were not as good as they should have been. I was summoned not to adjudicate so much as suggest how sales could be increased. A budget was set for two or three weeks' work and both sides told me how tough the assignment was.

It turned out that the answer was elementary. The salesmen called on their friends. The customers or potential customers complained about lack of calls, and that was attributed to 'customers are always grumbling'.

On day two of the assignment, I compared call records with the customers according to the sales ledger and there the answer was. A seasoned consultant would have spent the next two weeks softening the clients up and helping them take credit for the solution, whilst at the same time determining future work that needed the consultant's services. Idiot that I was, and delighted to be saving them so much money on consulting fees, I rushed in with the solution. It was obvious, too obvious, and I was instantly *persona non grata*.

The deal on my scholarship was that earnings should be split with the UK government which seemed fair enough. When I got back I sent them a cheque for their share and got an astonished phone call. No one else had ever bothered. Idiot again.

The Sloan School faculty were all remarkable in their different ways and included a couple of Nobel laureates. My thesis supervisor, Arnie Amstutz (PhD 1965), had written an amazing book showing how to model the entire business process*. I had read it, or rather struggled with it, coming over on the boat.

He was believed to be the richest faculty member as a result of automating buy/sell decisions on the New York Stock Exchange, the earliest venture of this kind. He was not a nerd, nor did he look academic. Middle height, with light brown hair he could not have looked

---

* *Computer Simulation of Competitive Market Response.*

more ordinary. You would not have spotted him in a crowd. His model worked well, albeit not initially. The printer permanently linked to his, or maybe MIT's, computer was located on the floor of the New York stock exchange. All his brokers had to do was to take the printouts and do what they said.

Amstutz was puzzled why orders were being executed late and sometimes not at all. That was costing him, sitting in Cambridge, serious money. He went down to investigate. Stock markets, and indeed any other markets, are primarily places for social networking and only secondarily for doing business. Brokers hated the computer and the robotic actions required of them. Anyway, they were too busy chatting to friends.

Amstutz reckoned that chastising the brokers would only make matters worse. Instead he hired two female models, working in alternate shifts, to chat up the young brokers and hand out each instruction with a smile. On his next visit he found the brokers clustered round the, er, printer and instructions being promptly executed.

Amstutz only had three or four students of his own and we were delighted when he invited us to lunch. Surely such a rich man would book the finest eatery in town. We cleared our diaries for the afternoon. On arrival we were greeted with Cokes and brown bags of Burger King Whoppers.

His approach to computer modelling in marketing, unlike his share modelling, would never work in most businesses: it demanded huge amounts of data to be fed in, much of it unavailable and therefore requiring guesswork.

At the other end of the attention scale was Michael Scott Morton. Neither as bright nor as rich as Amstutz, he was generous with his time. He was from Argyll, small and dark. Maybe because we shared the UK heritage we had quite extensive discussions. His field was also decision control systems but not from a marketing perspective as Amstutz's was.

I mention two more, Dave Montgomery and Al Silk, as I had many happy times with them at conferences when I returned to academia after 1990. Today many business academics are teetotal, or near enough, but this has never applied to [most of] the MIT faculty. Dave (MIT 1965-70) taught statistical methods for marketing, not one of my favourite subjects and, from the back of the classroom, I was subversive. He had only completed his PhD two years earlier but rode the punches in his jovial way, before hitting back. He was a Stanford man and returned there for most of his career. Many business schools, including London Business School, have a rule that PhDs have to go out into the wider world before they can return. Monasteries with schools attached do the same. Dave's final flourish was two years in Singapore where he spent 2003-5, after he officially retired in 1999, creating the School of Business at Singapore Management University. His budget was so large that, much to his own sorrow, he was unable fully to spend it.

Al Silk arrived at the Sloan School the same year as me and the three of us are about the same age. Al had quite a flattering beard but Dave's was not. In 1989, Al moved to Harvard Business School and his prodigious output still continues. Both in 1968 and more recently, he is always very encouraging of one's point of view and one's work.

One can summarise my main interest at MIT, and at London Business School 20 odd years later, as being how managers and consumers brains work in making decisions. My thesis* tried to connect what market research firms bought with the value they thought they received. In simplistic terms, if the value exceeded the price, it was a good decision. But value comes in different dimensions: one car may be faster and another more comfortable. The rationalists try to trade these off against each other and reduce value to a single dimension. In 1969, that was the conventional wisdom but my findings cast doubt on it. A whole science has since been built around that.† Re-reading the thesis 44 years later, it was not a great piece of work but it was certainly both pioneering and on target.

As I had nothing left to do in the summer term apart from my thesis and Katie had gone home to have Gus, I took on the role of teaching assistant to John Rockart in the accounting course for the Sloan Fellows. That is a one-year Master's for experienced executives in their 40s. As I had obtained an exemption for myself, it was interesting to see how accounting was taught.

The students were great. Quite a few had been sent by NASA as a thank you for their development of the lunar module for that first

---

* Entitled The Value of Market Research Information: A Multi-dimensional Study.

† Professor Paul E Green, Wharton, was a leader in this area and my research was built in part on his work. In my view he went too far, e.g. with conjoint analysis, toward seeing the human brain as a computer. His multi-dimensional scaling assumed metricity (i.e. $2 + 2 = 4$) whereas my methodology was non-metric (i.e. $2 + 2 > 2$ but not necessarily equal to 4). My research used a, perhaps the first, non-metric scaling program: MIT's TORSCA.

landing on 20th July 1969. So it was a thrill for me to be included in the party on Cape Cod being held to watch and celebrate the landing. My memory of the party was starting on the beach, digging for clams and drinking beer until it got dark and then drinking more beer and eating the clams whilst we watched on a very small black-and-white television set. The NASA people were outwardly confident but it was obvious that they were really very nervous.

My memory does not accord with the official timings: Apollo 11 landed Neil Armstrong and Buzz Aldrin on the moon at 20:18 GMT (15:18 US Eastern Time). 'Armstrong became the first to step onto the lunar surface 6 hours later.' [Wikipedia]

Perhaps the serious watching only began with Armstrong's stepping onto the moon and we watched on from there. I remember it being a late night and a wild night with joshing and insider jokes at each other's expense. These people were truly professional. Their confidence came from expecting things to go wrong and building in enough back-up systems to ensure that those problems could be by-passed.

# Chapter 7

# Booze brands

*Rather generously, the two key IDV decision-makers, Bobby Gold and George Bull, accepted me back from MIT as a trained marketeer. The CEO, Jasper Grinling, maintained his distance. Apart from the MIT incident, he probably recalled my presentation to the IDV board on pricing vintage wine using Gus's wooden bricks to show the added interest costs and therefore the need for annual price increments. More sophisticated explanations had failed to register. Some directors found it amusing, a few even found it helpful, but Jasper and others were offended by the childish bricks. Luckily I had moved from accountancy to marketing and my time with IDV thereafter was devoted to launching and building brands.*

*Take vodka for example. It is just ethanol ($C_2H_5OH$) and $H_2O$. Smirnoff, in particular, prides itself on being nothing more. Yet Smirnoff, in the US, is twice the price of store brand vodkas and the super premium vodkas are twice as much again. The consumer is not stupid: she knows that but still mostly buys Smirnoff, the largest spirits brand in the world.\* The job of the marketeer is to ensure the consumer gets enough pleasure from experiencing the brand to return again and again even though cheaper options are available.*

*This chapter covers:*
- *Gilbey Vintners' Marketing Director.*
  - *Brown & Pank*
  - *12 York Gate, Regent's Park*
  - *The key to Smirnoff*
  - *Lift off for Croft Original*
  - *Dealing with the Dutch*
- *Debden.*
  - *Gus starts school*

---

\* 25 million 12-bottle cases in 2011. Economists have never caught on to the fact that most buying is driven by emotion (anticipated pleasure), more than by logical analysis of the facts. They think volume is driven by lowering price whereas almost all the biggest brands are premium-priced.

Watneys' rescue of IDV from the Showerings in 1967 had brought in Brown & Pank and the Westminster Wine off-licences. By the time I returned, the rather obvious decisions had been made to amalgamate the rag-bag of off-licences starting with the original Gilbey's off-licences called 'Fosters'. The premier chain, Peter Dominic, bought from its founder Paul Dauthieu, was a different kettle of fish. Peter Dominic was a wine merchant in that it focussed on wine rather than beer and also sold to restaurants. 'Off-licences' by contrast focussed on beer and tobacco: such wine as they sold was the bottom of the range. Few supermarkets then had alcohol licences.

By 1969, IDV's retail management had managed to drag most of the better off-licences up to the Dominic level but then they were swamped by 200+ Westminster Wine off-licences. With hindsight IDV should have kept the better stores and gradually sold off the rest. Be that as it may, Alistair Eadie, a tall and charming man from the Northampton Phipps brewing family, was put in charge.

My concern was with the brand marketing and wholesaling side of the business where the merger of Brown & Pank and the Gilbey interests* made more sense. After a well catered conference at the Bell in Aston Clinton, Gilbey Vintners was formed with George Bull as CEO, John McWhirter, an old school Brown & Pank man, as Sales Director and me as Marketing Director.

---

* These included the old Twiss Brownings agencies, such as Hennessy and Heidsieck Dry Monopole champagne and the Watney-owned, but independent, Brown Gore and Welch, including Bols liqueurs. The latter was a very traditional City agency business held together only by the alcohol they consumed.

The UK operation was housed in 12 York Gate across the road from HQ at #1. David Peppercorn and I discovered a cellar under the road which we used for the fine wines we did not wish the auditors to see, nor the Gilbeys come to that. There was a car park for seniors and that, together with the new A40 Flyover, halved my commute.

We were a strange bunch. One brand manager had an aristocratic English name but was actually Polish and had very little idea of how business in the UK proceeded. Dennis Ing had been brought in as brand manager for J&B. He came from Lyons Ice Cream and somehow we all got the idea he was an Eskimo. Like so many new brand managers, his first move was to try to change the packaging. Dorrien Belson, the J&B Export supremo, jumped on him from a great height. Every other change he proposed was similarly nixed. Why did we have a J&B brand manager at all? Ing had other brands too and, for an Eskimo, was exuberant and extroverted. When this was remarked upon his response was:

'I'm not a fucking Eskimo, man, I'm a fucking Chink.'

In 1973 Oddbins, a small chain of quite high level wine shops founded ten years earlier by Ahmed Pochée, got into financial trouble. Pochée started by rounding up parcels of wine and selling them cheap to restaurants and consumers. He was a rogue but a likeable one. 1973 was the start of the 70s slump and many companies were in difficulty, including us. We stopping supplying them, which pulled the rug and NatWest were going to be the big losers. They persuaded Walter Gilbey that it would be a favour if we could suggest a couple of bright young wine men to keep the show afloat.

Ing volunteered and so did Nicholas Baile, who had recently left being the head of wine marketing for our own chain, Peter Dominic. A more unlikely duo is hard to imagine. Baile was immensely grand and a lot brighter than he pretended to be. NatWest cut them a friendly deal, Baile put in some family money and the business was theirs.

Much to our surprise it prospered. Their HQ and cellars were in a sort of Beau Geste fortress in, of all unlikely places, Wapping. Ing had an office at the top of one of the corner towers and Baile had his in the one diagonally opposite. It transpired that they had indeed fallen out but decided how decision-making should be split. On the rare occasions a decision needed both of them, runners were sent with messages. So far as I know, they never spoke, still less met.

The chain built up to 278 stores and then had a succession of downs and ups, being sold to Seagrams and then resold, including latterly to Nick Baile's son Simon. It still exists with, at the time of writing, 37 stores.

Ian Lockwood looked after the main IDV brand, Smirnoff, and was the only real pro. Young & Rubicam had taken over from Mather & Crowther as IDV's main UK agency and therefore had Smirnoff, Croft sherry and, not that they did them any good, the lesser brands such as Gilbey's gin, J&B Rare and Old Grand Dad. Brown and Pank had brought in MCR of which Winston Fletcher was CEO. They had Justina Portuguese wines and Bols Advocaat.

Winston became a true friend and, despite many vicissitudes, our account man as he moved through many London agencies, usually as CEO. He had the great gift of enjoying life in a way that ensured all around did too. Hired from Cambridge as a copy-writer, management was his forte and he became the *éminence grise* of advertising, becoming chairman of all the advertising organisations in turn and finally of the Royal Institution. Copy-writer to the last, he churned out a dozen management and advertising books and became a visiting professor at business schools.

The Gilbey Vintners' open-plan marketing department was a buzzy place except when Kathy Keeton came to sell space in *Penthouse* magazine. With a perfect figure, micro skirt, boots up to her thighs and blonde hair down to the waist, all chatter abruptly ceased and the lads queued up to buy.

Smirnoff's key selling point was purity and the 10 tons of charcoal Smirnoff went through to ensure it was the cleanest spirit on the market. The brand had taken off well enough but by the late 1960s it was flat-lining at 300,000 cases a year. Word of mouth was good and the most popular usage was as a screwdriver (Smirnoff and orange). The upper classes used it in Bloody Marys and Bullshots (consommé and Worcester sauce). The Young & Rubicam advertising was risqué, although quite what the couples were doing in the hay stacks was left to the reader. It had little impact on sales.

Y&R kept changing creative teams and presented one campaign after another. Each was deemed utterly fantastic until the client rejected it. Finally, one team made the breakthrough. Purity was known but not wanted. Every other vodka could, and did, claim purity to some extent but the consumer was not interested. Never mind 'good, clean fun', consumers saw vodka in general, and Smirnoff in particular, as *potent* – virile Russian noblemen downing their vodkas in a gulp and chucking the glasses into the fireplace, and all that. Vodka was seen, in the elegant language of the day, to be a knicker-dropper.

Smirnoff's key attribute being potency was ironic as it was actually weaker than the other spirit categories, 65.5° compared with 70°.

From this insight came the 'shattering' campaign, e.g. 'I was the mainstay of the Public Library until I discovered Smirnoff ... The effect is shattering.' Ian Lockwood, George Bull and I thought the campaign was terrific, apart from one which I took personally: 'Accountancy was my life until ...' It turned out that Y&R were not taking the piss. The Accountant became the most successful ad and we developed a lucrative sideline selling the various ads as posters.

First to land us in hot water depicted a naked – but with naughty bits air-brushed – woman running through a cornfield leading a stallion. The line was 'I was a suburban housewife until ...'. We ran it on the underground and I'm not sure whether London Transport or our own main board was the more irate. The ad was rapidly withdrawn.

The one that amused us most was, with a picture of the book: 'I thought the Kama Sutra was an Indian Restaurant until...'. We had to take that down when we discovered that the majority of our target market thought the Kama Sutra really was the name of an Indian Restaurant.

The mid-70s saw a furore about advertising causing young people to drink and to create drink-related problems in general. It was all nonsense of course but we had to bow to the wind. I was on the committee that drew up the first ever code of advertising practice for alcoholic drinks. It must have been reasonably sensible as it has been little changed since and copied around the world.

Dealing with the anti-alcohol lobbyists occupied a large chunk of my career. After the anti-tobacco fight was won and lost we were bound to be next. In fact the anti-alcohol bandwagon rolls out every 20 years or so, always with a new twist. It has little merit because most sensible people and doctors know that moderate consumption does no harm and may well do good. Forty years of academic research shows that alcohol advertising does not materially increase alcohol consumption in aggregate. By encouraging the consumption of premium brands at the expense of larger quantities of cheap commodities, advertising may even decrease total volume consumption – as happened in France.

The right trade strategy is to make friends with the opposition and find common cause. We did that then but the drinks trade top management today does not.

'The effect is shattering' had to come off the advertising but otherwise we could, and did, continue the campaign, leaving the consumer to fill in the missing bits. The best one had us in further trouble. It depicted an elegant girl dressed for a party and holding a cocktail glass, except she was in the ocean with a SS *Titanic* lifebelt around her. The, not very witty, line was, 'Well, they said anything could happen.' We considered whether it was in good taste but *Titanic* jokes had been around for ages and the tragedy had been 70 years earlier. The ad provoked a number of complaints to the Advertising Standards Authority. It turned out that the then IDV group CEO, Geoffrey Palau, lost an aunt in the tragedy. He was not amused.

Be all that as it may, it was one of the most successful ad campaigns of the decade and sales rose from their 300,000 case plateau to 1M. Ten years later they were about 2M.

Croft Original had been launched in1966 to compete with Harvey's Bristol Cream. Sherry was then a major market and Harvey's was by far the brand leader. Unconsciously, IDV's marketing team (Bobby Gold, George Bull and Colin Hession*) working with the Mather & Crowther people (including Anthony Tennant and Tom Jago of whom more anon) followed the model established by J&B Rare. Both are pale in colour as that is seen as smart (fino in the case of sherry and VSOP – Very Special Old Pale – in the case of brandy). Both Croft Original and J&B Rare are blander than their competitors.

The team launched the brand with the crude tactic of adding a case of Croft to every order for Smirnoff, whether the customer wanted it or not. On the positive side that gained instant distribution which provided a base for advertising – something Mather & Crowther were keen to do. And it encouraged sampling, a key feature of any successful booze brand launch. On the other hand, it did little for its reputation in the trade.

In the following years, the price was pushed up from the rock bottom it started at (well, if it goes out free, what do you expect?) and, because the product itself was so good, the word of mouth was very positive. The advertising for its first eight years or so was poor and Y&R were no better.

---

* Colin soon after succumbed to a crisis of conscience when he concluded that peddling booze was immoral and left the business.

Harvey's like most cream sherries is dark in colour. That originally came from both its aged components: Oloroso and Pedro Ximenez – a different, very sweet, grape that loses much of its moisture as do the Sauternes grapes and those used in the Reciotto wines of Italy and German spätlese. Pressures on costs have reduced the ageing, and thus the quality, of cream sherries and one does not ask how the colour has been maintained. Croft Original, by contrast, is a blend of Fino and Sweet Moscatel. In the early days, IDV was accused of using Tate & Lyle's excellent products to achieve the sweetness without adding colour. I doubt that was ever true but if it was, it was not for long.

The breakthrough, as for Smirnoff, came from advertising. In the first eight years or so the emphasis was on difference (from Harvey's). Guests at smart drinks parties, for example, were shown tipping dark brown sherry into pot plants, causing them instantly to wilt, in order to empty their glasses for the arrival of our hero, Croft Original.

Y&R, after much flagellation, put a new, American creative team on the brand. Sometimes it takes foreigners to see the British as we really are and sherry was, at the time, the most British of drinks. Y&R's London boss, Joe DeDeo, also an American, should take some of the credit.* Their first insight, like the one for Smirnoff above, was that telling the consumer what she already knows is pointless. Any consumer or potential consumer of Croft Original was already well aware that it was pale and the label said so. More importantly, Croft should not dwell on *difference* but appear to be *better*. They did so by showing an immaculate dressage rider and horse going through their paces in front of a stately home, Wilton House.†

The creative team had noticed that posh English people say 'one' in place of 'I' so the copy line became 'One instinctively knows when something is right'. It was the definitive campaign for Croft and the first ad was never bettered. The brand took off, overtaking Harvey's Bristol Cream in due course until the whole sherry market went into decline. I have always blamed this on the Church of England. When vicars called on the parishioners, a bottle of sherry was always on hand for the vicar and the cook would have a little taster from time

---

* He ran Y&R's London Office and then the part of the Y&R group headquartered there for 15 years. Sadly he died of lung cancer in December 2000.

† My London Business School colleagues, Professors Patrick Barwise and Sean Meehan, would have been delighted with this case history. They wrote a best selling book *Simply Better* on this better rather than different theme.

to time. When vicars stopped calling, the cooks no longer got their tasters.

A small success from this period was the introduction of women into the salesforce. Apart from the obvious equal opportunity issue, we wanted to bring graduates into marketing via sales. And it was a way to break up the locker room atmosphere of sales – although in the UK, but not in Ireland, they had stopped boozing with the customers as they went around. The official objection to women was that moving cases around was part of the job and they were too heavy for women to lift. There was some truth in that up to the 1960s when cases weighed 20 kilos. By the 70s, wood had been replaced by cardboard and lightweight glass introduced. The weight of a case dropped 15%. Furthermore, the women in pubs had no problem shifting them.

Sucking of teeth notwithstanding, women were recruited and the chaps were delighted, for good reasons and not so good. The biggest objections came from the publicans' wives. They were mostly 'stately as galleons', to use Joyce Grenfell's phrase, and were displeased with having our attractive young things chatting up their husbands.

Our two main import agencies were Hennessy cognac and Bols liqueurs. The Hennessy family, led by Count Alain de Pracomtal, were old school gentlemen and a delight to deal with. If they wanted a meeting but did not wish to travel to Harlow, not their favourite town, they sent their corporate jet. We never cracked the advertising despite being given a free hand to do so. The St Bernard dog advertising from 30 years earlier still hung around and cognac consumers were set in their ways.

The Dutch were also charming but, in other respects, could not have been more different. In particular, they were stereotypically mean. When salesmen's expenses became troublesome, we started publishing the cost per call and gave the 'Plastic Dutchman Award' to the person with the most calls with the lowest average cost.

The most spectacular example of the Dutch care with money concerned their quatercentenary in 1975. A couple of years earlier, I asked how they planned to celebrate the event. Bols was one of the oldest, maybe the oldest, booze business in the world. 'Nothing special. 500 years will be the big one. I expect the board will give a cocktail party for the managers.'

Sales conferences are expensive things and being parsimonious myself, I liked to offload the costs where I could. So: 'Nonsense. This is a great event which must be properly marked. We'll pay the costs of bringing our salesforce over to Amsterdam and I'm sure you would like to provide the hospitality.'

With ill grace initially, but great generosity once they got into the swing of it, they did. Terry Wogan provided the cabaret by compèring the final of the Spoejf* competition. Surprisingly he had never played the game and had to be taught during one of the canal trips. He was last seen happily bowling a large round cheese through the market square on his way back to bed.

At the big dinner, we were all given masks each showing the original 16th C Lucas Bols. We were told to put them on for the group photograph The point of a photograph of 200 Lucas Bolses escaped us but we did as we were bid. As the dinner was being held on the edge of the red light district, we should please leave our masks on the tables as we left. They would be very upset, they said, if any images of their dear founder were seen where they should not be seen.

Needless to say, not a single mask was left on a table. The usual denizens of the red light district must have been perplexed by being transported to a different era. The best account was of a live sex show. As I am sure you, dear reader, know, these take place in small, rather intimate rooms, with sexy red lighting, subdued to make it difficult to recognize the participants. I was not there myself, as you will appreciate, but apparently the girl performer at one point turned from her partner to look at her audience and then screamed. The room was full of apparitions from 400 years earlier.

We did a decent, if not spectacular, job on the brand but the negotiations of the annual plans and the discussions of the results were protracted and tough. In this we had a secret weapon: my secretary, Bineke McLaughlin, had lived in Harlow since it was built 15 years earlier but was Dutch. She was a keen swimmer and a good sense of humour once she detected what the joke was. The two doors between our offices were left open and we shouted at each other through them.

One morning Bineke's phone rang. I should explain that the most

---

* Spoof, to which we added Dutch heritage, is a pub game played usually to determine who buys the next round. Each player round the table puts between 0 and 3 coins in his hand and then they take turns to guess the total number of coins. The winner on that round drops out and the last one in buys the drinks. Good players rarely have to do so.

famous girl in the land at that time was Fiona Richmond, who was devastatingly beautiful and removed her clothing whenever possible. I heard Bineke call out:

'It's Miss Richmond for you.'

'If it's Fiona Richmond, I'm in. Otherwise I'm out.'

'Mr Ambler says that if you are Fiona Richmond ...'

By the time I ran into her office, wrested the phone from her and talked to Dick Bridgeman, he was nonplussed.

As the Dutch had a habit of breaking off our meetings to confer with each other in their own language, I introduced Bineke, as my secretary, to take notes. When they returned to English we took our own break and caught up on their discussion. As we never learned much of interest and my colleagues thought the ruse unsporting, we desisted before we were rumbled.

We bought the Debden house on a gloomy, wet February day. In 1971 the property market overheated. By the time we drove up to north west Essex on a Saturday, the property we had discussed with the owners that morning was likely to have been sold. Some people then accepted higher offers (gazumping) and some didn't. We bought from the Parkers, an extremely decent Scottish couple, and the only wrong note in the discussion was when I asked if it had a cellar. They looked horrified. At the time, the Parkers were teetotal, although they reformed later.

We paid the asking price: £24,000 was high* by the standards of there and then because the wood at the end of the garden had planning permission for another house. Built for the village doctor in the 1950s, with Crittall windows, the house was not attractive, but the position was spectacular. Debden may be the highest point in Essex – which is not saying much – but the house looked south onto rolling Constable-style meadows. We think the hillside beside the house was a vineyard in medieval times. When the sun came out and the larks sang, it was heaven, especially for Katie who is really a country girl.

Gus was now between two and three and attending Miss Grey's playschool. He seemed to spend much of the time on the blue stool in the corner and was threatened with expulsion. We were faintly pleased he could be as big a pain there as he was at home.

His next school, Dame Johanna's in Saffron Walden, had seen bet-

---

* But then we sold our £7200 house in East Sheen for £17,500 so we weren't complaining.

ter times. After a year, a parents' committee took over. They were talented professional City folk and although the school turned the corner, it did not get back to where it should have been by the time Gus left.

Dame Johanna's chief excellence was the pulchritude of the mothers. On a scale of 1 to 10, they were 10. Skimpily clad, they lounged on the grass waiting for the children to come out and I regularly volunteered to pick Gus up. *Desparate Housewives\**, still less the swinging sixties, but the dances verged on the amorous. Maybe they did everywhere but they sure don't in North Norfolk in 2013. Around Saffron Walden in the 1970s, men were reliably absent and marriages collapsed like dominos, each one knocking over the next. Two friends of ours were incensed when their son, aged about 20, was taken over by a newly divorced, but very attractive, 40-something, a 'cougar' in today's idiom. It had its ups and downs but, 40 years on, the marriage has proved successful partly because the young man turned out to be a whiz in the City. No couple, as Ogden Nash observed, is incompatible if he has income and she is pattable.

Minimal research told us that Moor Park should be Gus's prep school. It was a main feeder school for Downside for which his name had been down since birth. Shropshire was far from convenient but a boarding school was essential. He was not good at being an only child. Moor Park had joint headmasters, one academic and one genial, and was moving up into the top league. Mercifully, no exam was needed, just an interview with the parents.

The joint headmasters were Hugh Watts and Denis Henderson. Watts had been games master at Downside in my time. He and Henderson had met at a drinks party and woken up the next morning to discover that they had agreed to buy and run Moor Park together.

I was fairly sure Watts would not remember me as we had only had two brief encounters. The first was at the beginning of my time at Downside when I explained that, even though boxing was compulsory, my excessive weight and shortness of arm made that inappropriate. To everyone's surprise, Watts immediately agreed and returned his attention to proper sporting matters. Three years later he spotted me in the boxing ring, flapping a towel as chief second in the house competition. Absence of experience is no bar to consultancy expertise, as any McKinsey employee can attest. That was not Watts's view:

---

\* An American TV series (2004-2012) where secrets and truths unfold through the lives of female friends in one suburban neighbourhood.

'Ambler. What the hell are you doing in there. You know nothing about it. Get out at once.'

Twenty years on we were sitting in his study enjoying gins and tonics – we had been warned to avoid his (home-made) sherry – and a light dawned.

'I know you. I let you off boxing.' Schoolmasters never forget. The rest of the interview was jolly and all was well. According to Katie, I was very impressed by the computer lab. The gin must have been speaking: they did not have one.

Moor Park was a huge success in all ways. After the inevitable initial tears, Gus was happy there and did well academically, socially and on the fields of play. Watts did warn us that Downside was not what it had been but the hint was too subtle for us at the time.

Most of our friends commuted into the City. But commuters then were few. When I took the train from Newport, if the duty porter saw my car coming down the hill, he'd hold the train until I could get parked and on board.

Keen to participate in village life, I was suckered into taking on the chairmanship of the village hall. Despite many efforts to pass the job on, I only stepped down when we left the village. In fact it was a useful way to keep in touch. The first AGM did not go well. All the records and minutes had been lost. We had a large turnout and a decent agenda of items of general interest. I opened the meeting:

'Thank you all for giving up your time to be here. We have a full agenda so let's get straight into it and take the minutes as read.' At all the other meetings I had attended, the members were only too keen to get onto the new stuff and not mess with the old.

Voice from the back of the hall: 'No, we want to hear the minutes.' General assent to that.

'Well, I'm sorry but you can't. We can find no trace of them or any other records come to that.'

'Well why didn't you say so?'

'I was trying to avoid the embarrassing exchange we have just had.' It rumbled on a bit but peace was restored.

We had another contretemps a few weeks later. Villagers were getting steamed up about how the chairs were set up in the hall. We tried them this way and that and someone always objected. At the next committee meeting, somewhat irritated, I said, according to John Mawer:

'Each hall user will have to set out the chairs any way they want.

We've tried more positions than the Kama Sutra and none of them satisfy everyone.'

The current Smirnoff advertising must have been on my mind but, Mawer aside, my remark passed them by.

My next mistake was to get through the committee's agendas as rapidly as possible so that I could get home for supper. All my business meetings aimed for rapid conclusion. Mutterings developed and I was told that they had all had their suppers and regarded the committee meetings as their nights out. Gossip could be exchanged and matters considered in a leisurely fashion. My suggestion of holding meetings in the pub was turned down as a surprising number were teetotal. In the event, they were right, our ruminations made the village a better place. Especially when we added one of the country's first volunteer village shops.

The original village shop may have been a safety hazard with the unkempt cat sitting on the bacon slicer but it had been the blessing that village shops are. When the shopkeepers died, no-one would take it on so we extended the village hall and villagers took shifts to man it. A great success, it is still running 30 years later.

Our commuting friends restricted socialising to the weekends. As they were fed up with City suits and 'smart casual' had not been invented, Saturday night dinner parties were usually black tie. Most people gave an annual thrash, ours were fancy dress. As, in the mid-70s, the country and the economy were in terrible shape, we gave a Wake with everyone told to come in 'mourning suits'. A couple of bankers regarded that as a buy signal and did very well out of it. Almost the next day, the stockmarket started surging up but I don't think we should take all the credit.

One of the better events, after a bad start, was a surprise birthday party for Katie. I said I'd take her out for dinner and the Gus-sitter duly arrived. In the restaurant bar, I slapped my pockets and announced I'd left my credit cards at home so we would have to go back. After absorbing the incoming flak, we return to find a very over-excited Gus leaping up and down by the front door. He was in the know and his security had been exemplary, but he should have been in bed. By now thoroughly riled, Katie's tirade would have been rated child abuse by Social Services. The lights went on and the planned triumphal 'hurrah' was replaced by silent horror on the faces of the other parents.

Perhaps the most inebriated dinner party followed the discovery that Baileys made excellent ice cream just by pouring it into a freezer tray.* It had been bibulous well before we got to the pudding. That was the *coup de grâce*. When frozen, the alcohol is hidden and only takes effect when the stomach warms it up. One guest had a second helping and slid gracefully under the table where she was only noticed by her husband when he wanted to go home.

In August, Debden decamped to North Norfolk. After some resistance ('I see them the rest of the year, why August too?'), I capitulated and we discovered Cley, partly thanks to the cookery writer Mary Norwak who had the Old Hall and had moved her family up there permanently. It is a wonderful house and garden with masses of space but after a few years the pressure went on for a place of our own. Gus† purchased a cottage for us by the windmill. But North Norfolk is for the end of my book.

In 1971, the Watney Mann group battled with GrandMet to take over Truman's, the high profile brewery in London's East End. Watneys lost and a year later, Max Joseph, founder and Chairman of GrandMet, announced their bid for Watneys. City opinion was divided: some thought it was too much too soon. Joseph was not interested in beer or brewers, he was a property man and his calculations were based on the huge estates then owned by the brewers.

The Watney board, with the agreement of some but not all IDV directors, decided that absorbing the whole of IDV would make them too much of a mouthful for GrandMet. It was a close run thing but they were proved wrong.

The months under Watney control were unsettling. The top brass, and notably Julian Crawshay their Marketing Director, tried very hard to be nice to us and they no longer had a wine and spirit business to merge us into. Julian generously took George Bull and me to the opera. There was no doubt that it was the opera. Watneys had boxes and debenture seats everywhere (Albert Hall, Wimbledon, Lord's and Ascot to name but four) so it was no surprise to find ourselves in their box at Covent Garden. Boxes there are not that comfortable but they do allow a continuous flow of lubricant.

We hadn't checked the programme and were taken aback when the

---

* This no longer works with the modern formulation of Baileys so don't try it at home.

† As he was at boarding school and then university, it was his main residence and therefore the gain tax free, as that from a second home is not, when sold.

curtain went up to reveal dancers performing Anastasia. Katie loves ballet and goes when she can. I don't and don't. I know opera can be ridiculous but I love it whereas whenever ballet is as ridiculous as it often is, I get the giggles. The lubricant may have been partly to blame but when the Russian guardsmen ponced on, I took one look at George's face and collapsed. Coldstream Guardsmen take their manliness very seriously and George is no exception. Crawshay pretended not to notice and we went on to a very jolly dinner.

Despite these blandishments, the marketing network was alive with rumours that I was for the chop. Some of my informants seemed quite pleased; I was not a good customer. Crawshay owed his position to immense charm and also to being a member of the beerage; Watneys had taken over his Norwich family brewery. The professional marketeer was his deputy, an ex-Unilever man. I tried to be nice to him then and for the next 20 years of our acquaintanceship but it was to no avail. He was oil and I was vinegar.

Personal chemistry aside, his marketing skills were open to question. Watneys' reputation for beer had been damaged by Watneys' Red Barrel, one of the first keg beers, i.e. it was fizzy and not in a proper wooden barrel. Not only was the product poor* but it was marketed like a Unilever margarine. In 1971, as an associated company, we were invited to the Talk of the Town to see the launch of its replacement to see, *inter alia*, how real marketing was done.

It was true that we had never seen such a spectacular launch. 'Watneys' Red' was a better beer but everything about the launch was flash and silly. The Chairman, Micky Webster, came on stage revealing his red socks. How exciting was that? There were gimmicks galore including red footprints on pavements leading to Watney pubs. Marketeers have a little more licence with lager but bitter drinkers care deeply about their beer and Watneys clearly did not. As we walked out of the presentation we were sure it would fail. It did.

When Watneys were in charge I was sufficiently unsettled to demand to meet their Personnel Director, one of the Mann family. He was as charming as could be but I wasn't sure if his reassurances were real or if his marketing director had not briefed him. GrandMet's success took the matter out of their hands.

The GrandMet acquisition of Watney Mann was a near run thing, maybe just 0.5% of the shares swung the issue and it was Watneys

---

* The joke at the time was, 'Why is Red Barrel like making love in a punt?' 'Because it is fucking near water.'

that messed it up. About half the IDV directors had opposed the Watney bid and having been sacked when Watneys succeeded, they supported GrandMet. Hennessy, with about 5% of the shares, had favoured the Watney bid but they switched to GrandMet as offering more opportunity for their brand. Watneys had failed to court them.

The Watney supporting IDV directors were sacked when Grand-Met succeeded which meant a complete clear out. Three IDV seniors were promoted: Robin Kernick, originally with Corney & Barrow but latterly with IDV Europe to CEO, Stanley Lee to Finance and Simon Bradley, Ampleforth and Rifle Brigade, to MD of the UK (Home Trade). Geoffrey Palau, Guards and more recently CEO of Seagram UK, was imported to look after the main profit-making section IDV Export (mostly J&B of course).

We were glad to see back of the Watney top brass, nice as they tried to be. GrandMet, in contrast, had a reputation for financial astuteness and toughness. Joseph in particular was held in awe and his two lieutenants, Stanley Grinstead and Ernest Sharpe, a.k.a. Pinky and Perky, were accountants. The whole outfit was Kosher Nostra. Sharpe was extrovert but Joseph and Grinstead were not. Indeed he refused a knighthood until his wife Eileen made it very clear that she should be a Lady. Joseph never liked the title.

Apparently, in the early days of GrandMet, Joseph decided he needed an accountant and asked his auditor for suggestions.

'I have just the man for you,' and Grinstead appeared for his appointment a few days later. Ushered in by a secretary and given cups of coffee, the two sat in silence. Neither then nor later did either ever start a conversation. Eventually Joseph cracked:

'I think you are just the man I am looking for.'

They worked happily together ever after.

Soon after the takeover, the IDV team was summoned to hear a brief, always very brief, talk by Joseph. As with all the quotes in these memoirs, they are not the exact words but they give the flavour of the occasion as best I can:

'As you know, I am a property man and we purchased WMTB for its extensive property portfolio. We had not intended to acquire IDV but you are a fine business and we regard you as the Green Shield stamps on the deal. Thank you for your attention.'

We weren't sure whether to be pleased or insulted by being the Green Shield stamps nor whether we should be pleased when he decided to set up his office in IDV's HQ rather than GrandMet's. In the event, both worked out very well and IDV could not have had a better friend than Joseph. A few years later, Heublein (or maybe their parent company Reynolds Tobacco) approached Joseph with a view to buying IDV. With us merely Green Shield stamps and Joseph being a trader by nature, they might have been successful but they did not understand their man.

Anyone would dismiss the opening offer as standard negotiating tactics but Joseph did so in his diffident manner that they mistook for weakness. Confident in their own strength the Heublein team threatened him with what they would do to Smirnoff, which Heublein owned, if Joseph did not agree. Joseph was not a man to threaten and they never darkened his door again.

Soon after the acquisition, Brackenbury and I lunched with a brewery high flyer, Miles Broadbent. Miles had a Harvard MBA and was probably the only other GrandMet person with a business degree. It was on the first floor of a Wigmore Street pub and a stonking good lunch it was. The conversation got around to the furthering of our careers. Brackenbury has always insisted that Joseph and his team were more positive about Leisure Finance than I recall. By then it was a big business and a partner with the US Marriott Hotel chain in Europe. Whoever is right, Leisure Finance ceased to be and Brackenbury decided, rightly as it turned out, that the grass was greener elsewhere.

Broadbent claimed to have a much better plan. Joseph's secretary Judith was exceptionally charming and good-looking. Broadbent asserted that no woman had ever resisted him:

'It's quite simple. I will woo her and she will put in a good word with Joseph.'

'Miles, I don't think this is a very good idea. Anyone with Judith's natural assets will be more than capable of repelling boarders.'

'Nonsense. It's a brilliant idea. Can't fail.'

What Broadbent had failed to calculate was that Max Joseph fancied her himself and was only restrained by his wife Eileen who had previously been his secretary and knew the score. Joseph spotted the move at once and Broadbent was looking for a job.

The story had two happy endings. When Joseph died, Judith and Eileen became great buddies and worked together on Eileen's business (hotels) and charitable projects. Meanwhile Broadbent teamed up with David Norman to create one of the UK's most successful headhunting agencies, Norman Broadbent.

A final story shows Joseph's liking for certainty. I have no idea why but he decided I was a wine expert. He lunched with us in the Harlow directors' dining room from time to time and I lunched with him in the York Gate canteen because he thought the main directors' dining room too snooty. I knew he liked Burgundy in general and, in particular, the Bouchard Père & Fils, Beaune Grèves Vigne de l'Enfant Jésus, for which we had the agency. When he appeared in Harlow, so did that.

Messages from Joseph appeared on little bits of pink paper typed by Judith and known as 'pink perils'. They could be ominous but in my case never were; they were only wine questions.

When Joseph bought a large house and larger garden between South Ken station and Sloane Avenue, he installed one of those vertical, cylindrical cellars where you walk down a spiral staircase with wines sticking out like porcupine quills all around. Needing to stock it up, he took expert advice and then sent me the list he received for comment. I phoned Geoffrey Jameson, MD of J&B, Master of Wine and the Queen's cellarer:

'Geoffrey, can you do me a favour?'

'That depends.'

'A chap has had proposals for stocking his cellar and wants my comments. You know I haven't much of a clue so would you mind looking it over. Just very briefly, I only need a couple of comments.'

Grudgingly: 'Very well. Send it over.'

A couple of days later my phone goes with an irate Jameson on the end of it. It was only the second time* I ever heard him even mildly irritated:

'That was the stocking list I gave Max Joseph. What the hell is he doing sending it to you of all people?'

'He has this fancy I'm a wine expert and it would not be wise for either of us to prove him wrong.'

'Well there's nothing wrong with my list so you are on your own.'

He eventually relented, provided some improvements to his own stocking list and Joseph gave me a tour of his new cellar of which he was very proud. I was in Jameson's debt. And not only on that occasion. A true gentleman. He published the story of his war but it did not, according to his colleagues, do justice to his bravery on the battlefield or in hospital. He was badly wounded and in pain for the rest

---

* The other time was when he discovered I'd borrowed some of his Buckingham Palace headed writing paper for a spoof I was running at the time.

of his life.

Two other Joseph stories help describe his style. As he did not like board meetings, still less chairing them, he left that to Stanley Grinstead and tended to sit at the end of the table saying little if anything. He did speak up on one occasion:

'You know I was in Copenhagen the day before yesterday?'

Silence.

'I stayed at the Angleterre and was shocked by the bill. To cut a long story short, I made a few phone calls and I am pleased to tell you that we now own the hotel.'

The other directors' jaws dropped. The rules about acquisitions were immediately changed but the Angleterre proved a good investment. He knew what he was doing.

At another meeting, the directors were agonising about the poor returns from their newly bought flagship hotel, the Carlton at Cannes. There was a muffled grunt from the end of the table:

'It's the girls.'

'What about the girls?'

'All my friends are complaining. You've thrown out the girls.'

It emerged that the GrandMet management, in an effort towards respectability, had removed the local *belles de nuit* from the bar. They were restored and so were the profits.

IDV's relationships were never too strong with the pubs and brewing side of GrandMet but there were pleasures associated with other parts of the Group. Express Dairies provided the cream for Baileys and Mecca Bookmakers provided racing in style with glamour girls to place one's bets. Intercontinental Hotels provided suites when travelling, sometimes even Presidential Suites. To be honest, and it is ungracious to say so, that became less of a thrill. Travelling on business one typically checks in late, leaves early and all one wants is a shower and a comfortable bed. A Presidential Suite has three bedrooms, the attached palatial bathrooms, sitting room, dining room and kitchen. In one's besozzled state, one cannot remember which bed is supposed to be yours and where the porter put your luggage.

Top of my pleasure list was Mecca's Miss World competition. At the Albert Hall, fighting one's way through crowds of baying lesbians in dungarees to one's box was probably the best bit. It has always seemed to me that if a dungareed feminist was pretty enough to stand a chance of winning, she would have no objection. The competitors, by contrast, were easy enough on the eye to make the proceedings endurable. Afterwards the Coronation Ball was at the Grosvenor House. The wine was good, the food and services were fine and we chaps were expected to dance with the contestants. These girls were bright as well as beautiful and had been equally bored by the proceedings. Now they wanted to let their collective hair down. There was just one problem: our wives were sitting at our tables drumming their nails on the table cloth and suggesting it was time to go home.

The admirable Eric and Julia Morley (Mecca CEO and manager of the event respectively) had a solution to this problem too. Those GrandMet executives who had been prepared to put themselves out for the sake of the contestants, were invited to the annual riverboat shuffle. Boarding mid-morning at Westminster and motoring slowly to Greenwich for lunch, a guide tried to explain the places we were passing. No one was interested. The bar below deck had music and a dance floor. These outings were probably the most I have ever done for international relations.

On getting home, the routine question 'Did you have a nice day at the office?' was easily answered: 'Yes, thank you.'

But those pleasures came after 1973 which, for GrandMet, was a Force 12 Storm. The country was in a mess with three-day weeks, industrial unrest, low and declining productivity and an oil price hike. The stock market had plunged. It was worse for GrandMet who had overleveraged in the Watneys acquisition (or paid too much), interest rates and inflation were soaring, and the property values on which their debts were secured had also crashed. The shares had gone from over £3 a share to about 17p. The general opinion was that GrandMet was about to go under and Joseph wasn't saying much. But then, he never did. Our company secretary had the wit to see 17p as an opportunity, not a threat, and bought accordingly. I wish I had. The price climbed steadily back to £4.

That year was equally dark, for IDV's UK business albeit for more parochial reasons. It had been making a loss since heaven knows when and some members of the board thought it should simply be closed down. The problem was compounded by the high costs of the Harlow HQ and warehouses. They had won design awards but were poorly built. The lack of ties in the walls caused some to fall down. This was British architecture at its worst. A rectilinear warehouse on an industrial estate has no lasting aesthetic appeal no matter how much mutual admiration it may attract from the Architects' Union.

To compound that with excessive costs, poor specification and worse supervision was a disgrace. We progressively replaced them with warehouses at half the cost and found that even they were twice as expensive as our competitors'.

The problems were further compounded by the business being a mash up of Gilbeys, Brown and Pank, two brand agency businesses and a bundle of ill-fitting retail chains.

The creation of Gilbey Vintners tidied up the agency and wholesale businesses so far as sales and marketing were concerned but the tail was heavy, expensive and incompetent. Invoicing was wrong, deliveries were not what was ordered. Customers and the salesforce were up in arms. George Bull got out his steel helmet from his army days and wore it to a conference where he took questions on distribution and accounting. The humour was appreciated but the business was a mess.

If all that were not enough, the York Gate HQ thoughtfully provided a series of consultants to investigate our problems and suggest solutions. We were sent one of the major firms every nine months or so. PA and Boston Consulting Group were two of them. If you are struggling for survival in the Atlantic Ocean, the last thing you want is some busybody taking the life raft away for closer examination. The time given in explanations to the consultants was time not given to the real problems.

The consultants had to be creative so they could not accept our solutions and theirs, thankfully, made no sense. Eventually we persuaded York Gate to let us do what was necessary with independent help from Andersen Consulting (now Accenture). Stanley Lee, the Group Finance Director, was marvellous all through this long process. He was sensible and down to earth, as indeed he always was. Bobby Gold was supportive, as ever, but I cannot really blame the others for being sceptical.

The Home Trade Review Group, as it was called, worked by using the best and brightest managers to challenge the working practices of the other departments. The conventional wisdom of the day was to go for staffing cuts but we were working the other way around: modernise processes first and people savings would follow. The trouble of course was that the Gilbey business, around whom the rest was built, was very set in its ways.

'We need five days for a delivery.'

'How about next day delivery?'

'That's impossible.' But of course it wasn't. For several weeks, we spent 16 hours a day debating similar problems and solutions.

It was exceedingly hard work but it had the supreme advantage that the resultant managerial team owned the new arrangements. We did have to lose quite a few people and the process exposed those who needed to leave. They were often glad to do so as it was no longer 'their' company. We also cross posted managers across functions where the process had shown them to have wider skills.

Andersen Consulting nudged and brought light where there was friction, which was often, but they did not actively design any solutions as the other consultants had tried to do. Graham Reddish provided the steadying hand through all this trauma and became a lifetime friend.

The Home Trade Review Group turned the business around. It became reasonably efficient, integrated and profitable. Success with the key existing brands, mentioned above, and three new brands, mentioned below, drove the business up but, before that, I should mention IDV Europe which was, frankly, a pain in the butt.

In the 1960s, IDV came up with the superficially reasonable idea that the group, being international, should expand from the UK to the EEC. The three flaws in the plan were the unsatisfactory base in the UK as described above, lack of resources and building the business around Gilbey's inadequate production sites in Oporto for Croft port, and Château Loudenne, just outside the Medoc.

The success of Croft Original sherry allowed the construction of a grandiose bodega in Jerez, since demolished. Piat (Beaujolais) was bought in Macon and a nondescript winery in Germany. There was little or no concept of marketing, i.e. selling to the consumers in these countries. On the contrary, the idea was that the UK wholesale and retail businesses would buy all their needs from these Europe outfits who would thus become fat and happy from this tied trade.

From the UK perspective these suppliers were expensive, unresponsive and could not supply the wines we wanted. To them we were tenants whereas we thought we were customers. It is best not to name names in the mini-warfare that resulted. The bottom line was that they failed to have me sacked as they hoped, thanks to support from Stanley Lee and the Home Trade team.

In the 1980s, proper marketing companies were formed in Europe initially with George Bull as MD IDV Europe and then Christopher

Pearman. They had both been through the Home Trade 1973 experience and learned the practical skills on top of the marketing and selling skills they already had. Since his Fortnum days, Christopher was not only a top class salesman in his own right but he was able to impart those skills to others. He really understands customers. Christopher played a key role in bringing the UK company back to profit.

When it was back on the rails but not yet doing well enough, three new brands made the difference, the first of which was the biggest.

David Dand, CEO of Gilbeys Ireland, may have been a small man in a small country but he was a well connected dynamo. In one of his last important contributions, Bobby Gold returned from a visit to Dublin to report that, the Irish Finance Minister, would give us a ten year moratorium on taxing the export profits if we invented a new brand for that purpose.

IDV's innovation team at the time was led by Tom Jago, who had joined from Mather & Crowther, Mac MacPherson, our #2 technologist (chemist that is) and David Gluckman, a South African innovation consultant. Tom is Cornish with a first class degree from Oxford and a truly daunting wife, Penelope. When chairperson of a bench in South London, a role she was born for, she handed down a severe sentence which was met with

'Fuck you.'

Imperturbably: 'Thank you for the offer but I find my husband quite satisfactory in that department.'

It didn't take them long to identify two Irish ingredients: whiskey and cream. But it needed flavour and chocolate was added. The not-dissimilar Brandy Alexander had been a popular cocktail in the 1930s but in both cases the cream separated from the whiskey. Tom went round with their mock-up in a Schweppes soft drink bottle and had to shake it up before every sampling. No one on the IDV or Home Trade boards liked it except, luckily, Christopher Pearman. He said that Mac had cracked 'the technology to bring an unbelievable taste sensation to a host of new consumers'.

Mac cracked the separation problem roughly in the way milk and butter can be coalesced into cream by squirting the mixture through a very small hole, i.e. homogenising it. The GrandMet merger provided a bonus in the shape of the Express Dairies subsidiary which also had a big business in Ireland. They could assemble all the cream when and where we needed it. Initially only the summer cream (cows eating fresh grass) was suitable. Cream from the winter feeds was not – but the technologists solved that soon enough. Express Dairies also had the homogenising equipment needed and, as a sister company, they refused assistance to anyone else.

We could now market research the newly christened Bailey's Irish Cream. Hardly anyone liked it. Our new brand operation in the Home Trade had by now become quite sophisticated: we knew that favourable market research implied familiarity, i.e. the product was not that different. If you asked the sales force what innovation they wanted, the answer would look like whatever the competition had just introduced. In the case of a radically different product or ad campaign, dislike meant it either was potentially great or truly lousy. The only way to decide was to try it on consumers to see if they would re-purchase.*

The main board hating it was a positive signal and even better was that the group MD, Robin Kernick, had originally turned it down. When he recovered from his irritation, Jago went back in and said he had heard a competitor was about to launch a similar brand. Untrue, of course, and it was not the only time we pulled that stunt.

The consequence of this marketing strategy was that launches had to be small, low key and involve much sampling. Any idiot could sell something once but if customers came back for more, you were onto something. To keep the costs down, no parsimony was spared – Dublin used old bottles ordered for Redbreast Whiskey which had failed to sell. The crest on the glass was covered over with sealing wax and a Baileys crest. It looked well enough and the original package was progressively enhanced until recent Baileys' management got clever – maybe too clever.

In order to launch the brand, we obtained approval from Bols, who were very lordly about it. The UK's north-west region was chosen as inexpensive, out-of-the-way and full of the Coronation Street ladies we envisioned as the target market. Pearman made me nervous when he broke out of strategy and sold a container load (2000 cases) to Jimmy Duggan, head of booze buying at Tesco. Duggan shared Pearman's enthusiasm and they were both right.

The target market did not have many choices when they accompa-

---

* It is astonishing that, 40 years on, so few marketeers have learned this simple lesson. In a Pavlovian fashion they research the new product or advertising and launch it only if it does well. As a direct consequence, most fail.

nied their husbands to pubs. Wine had not yet arrived. What made us very uncomfortable was that they mixed Baileys with lemonade just like they made 'Snowballs' from Bols Advocaat. Bols should have withdrawn their approval. When Baileys knocked Bols Advocaat out of the market, the Dutch were very good about it. They were unlucky because the competition with the Snowball proved to be temporary.

Mac was unhappy with the stability of Baileys. After a few months on shelf, lumps of cream tended to coagulate. He solved the problem by changing the (natural) stability additive but that meant that Baileys curdled when lemonade (or any acid) was mixed in. It looked truly dreadful. Reluctantly, we had no choice. We did not have to tell consumers to stop mixing it with lemonade; they found out soon enough. And one could no longer make ice cream by just pouring Baileys into a freezer tray. My sympathies lay with the ladies who wrote in to complain that the lumps of cream, the best part in their view, had been removed.

But this too proved to be fortunate as Baileys' competitors cracked homogenisation but not the additive. And our patents and relationship with Express Dairies were further barriers to competition.

Beyond making people aware of the new brand and encouraging sampling, Baileys' initial advertising was not a driver. As with Smirnoff and Croft Original before, we wasted too much time on the differences and not enough promoting the essence of the brand. To be fair, that takes time to emerge from a new brand but it turned out to be something like personal luxury. A definitive ad (not one of mine) had a Persian cat lapping from a saucer. You were not intended to think it was drinking Baileys* but you were supposed to feel the luxury and the contented purring.

The UK launch was hugely successful: the brand reached 300,000 cases a year, a lot for a liqueur, in no time. The big worry then was whether it was a flash in the pan. Heublein had launched, coincidentally, 'Malcolm Hereford's Cows' despite being a cheap and rather nasty alcoholised milk shake, raced up to 1M cases a year in the US before crashing down. When Baileys plateaued, we kept the foot on the accelerator with more and better advertising and, after stuttering awhile, sales moved on upwards.

In parallel with the UK launch, David Dand rolled the brand around the world, starting in Ireland and the Netherlands. The prob-

---

* We had no complaints from the RSPCA.

lem was the big one, the USA. With all his charm and skills, none of the big import companies would have it. Our good friend and otherwise market savvy Abe Rosenberg pronounced, 'That shit will never sell.'

Dand and I did a double act with our Heublein partners. Charlie Herbert and Bill Elliott, Sales and Marketing Vice Presidents respectively, were the two key decision-makers. We persuaded them to drop in on York Gate on their way to the Grand National. Breakfast must have been good as they were in expansive form. Dand did his pitch and it was impressive. We poured generous samples. An hour later, the bottle was empty, we hadn't touched a drop, and they were in even more expansive form. Then they solemnly assured us that nobody, but nobody, would drink it. Dreadful stuff. When Elliott became a close friend, we never discussed this meeting.

Eventually Dand got Austin Nicholls to take the brand but then the company was sold to Pernod Ricard at the same time as we bought the sister companies, Paddington and Carillon. IDV had to rescue Baileys and a legal fight ensued. Amazing how much the French valued a brand they did not want.

It was not intentional but Baileys' success in the US owed a lot to 'scarcity marketing', i.e. building demand but not meeting it. We noticed, for example, that airline cabin crews were bringing Baileys back to the US and raving about it. Flight crews are the ideal ambassadors for a new drinks brand. Style is everything.

When the Irish did get stocks to Austin Nicholls, there were never enough to go round and the lucky retailers would advertise that they had a few bottles. Even better, the competitors sought to exploit the scarcity by – amazingly – advertising their brands as being 'nearly as good as Baileys'. Such flattery got Baileys everywhere.

Baileys went on to be brand leader in the US, UK and the world as a whole and, happily, there it remains.

The launch of Malibu, nice if you like coconuts, had some similar aspects but its genesis was quite different. One of the advantages of being an international company is the opportunity to 'Me One' the competition. It derives from the 'Me Too' practice of copying another brand launch if it looks like being successful. An international company sees success in country A and uses that experience to be the lead brand in country B. Sales forces and retailers like Me Too brands as they define the competitors and the retailers can use that to increase

James Ambler (1821-1857). In 1857, his father, also James, presented land to the Wesleyan Chapel in Manningham, Bradford, presumably in memory of his son. The street is named after him. The most prominent building there today is a mosque.

Grandfather Sydney Ambler (1875-1921) February 1914.

Grandfather Wilfred Swabey (1871-1939).

Grandmother Maud Swabey (1876-1955) in court presentation attire.

My father, Dennis, at Capri in February 1964.

Great aunt Amy marries Sir John Noble (St Margaret's 1902).

Returning from Malaya, 1940. These do not appear to be my mother Patricia's (far right) favourite dining companions.

But her other pets get on well enough.

Patricia, c.10 year later, fails to impress the
Macaw.

Naiad in Singapore 1952, the only horse I ever owned.

Barlow house prefects. Robert Walker (seated far left) became a Supreme Court Justice and Baron. Dudley Plunkett stands behind him. I'm seated right.

The officers and warrant officers of #6 Company, RASC, Singapore 1956. Major Boyldue between our two captains. CSM James is seated far right and my sergeant stands behind me, as he always did.

Basic training: bull. 1955.

A slimmer Tim parades with his troops. HMS Simbang, 1956.

An English class, Lublin, 1958. Krystyna is far left, later to marry Christopher Stevenson (at the back). The Modesta (Moda) is the dark haired beauty, second from right.

Success!

The 1960 Oxford University Expedition to Eastern Europe grinds to a halt in Niş, the Yugoslavia. The brakes were buggered.

John Brackenbury. My first IDV boss.

The Molony sisters: Mary (left) and Angela.

Martin Wells, my flatmate and then Mary's husband.

Flatmates James Wiltshire (centre) and Julian Cotton with Penny, subsequently his wife, who created the Model agency "Penny Personal Management", originally known as 'Pennys'. She ran it for 30 years.

Katie in Elba 1965.

Katie 40+ years later.

This was supposed to cross the Thames at Mortlake. It didn't.

Our wedding Eaton Square 4th June 1966.

The Accountant.

The Librarian.

It's a tough life, the wine trade. George Bull is on the left.

IDV vs. Watneys, c.1977. The four on my left are James Espey, Stephen Lewis, Arthur "Scoop" Hopkins and Geoffrey Butler, Personnel Director, in the hat.

Explaining cricket, or maybe cigars, to Ian Botham, 1980.

Jerez c.1979.

Flamenco that evening.

Miss USA with Old Grandad. c.1974.

Miss France and protectors. c.1974.

Allan Bell and I signposted in Namibia, c.1980.

Ambler family c.1980.

Uruguayan gaucho c.1985.

Nigerian off licence c.1982. Women dominate commerce in Nigeria, or did then.

Emir of Kano c.1982. Kano has been the capital of indigo dying for centuries. This does not do justice to the magnificent blue of his robes.

Kano palace guard.

Chinese spaghetti on the Silk Route. 1992.

Rafting on the Zambesi, 2000. I'm on the far right.

Gus and Viola's wedding.

Helmut Arntzen, Viola's father.

Golf is such an active sport.

Freddy soon to be the destroyer of rabbits.

Our bridge four 1999-2013. Taken at Nigel Jenney's (on the right) French farmhouse, near Mirepoix, SW France. The elegance of the bridge is only matched by the elegance of the shirts. Richard Jefferson is far left and Rupert Travis is next to him.

Gus's family 2013.

Wine tasting of Ch Latour 45 with some younger friends. 2011.

Jayne May-Sysum, a wonderful soprano.

Martin Baker, Master of Music, Westminster Cathedral.

margins. Our scorn for such copying may not have been wholly right as many brand leaders today were originally Me Too brands.* Pioneers tend to get killed; if the Me Too is a better product and backed by more resources it may win through. But then we never had more resources.

De Kuyper's CocoRibe had achieved great success in the US and was used in many ways but primarily for making Pina Coladas. With a white bottle and brown lettering, it communicated coconut very well. No other major market was selling it. The ever-creative Peter Fleck was our Marketing Director in South Africa. Sleeping with the competition can provide valuable market intelligence, or so I have been told. On this occasion it did. Fleck discovered across the shared pillow that CocoRibe was due to be launched the following month.

He had the Me One 'Coco Rico' out on the streets in a couple of weeks and De Kuyper withheld their launch. It cost him a girlfriend and I am still astonished De Kuyper did not sue for passing off. The match was very close but, of course, the South African consumers had never seen CocoRibe.

Following the South African success, we launched the UK Me One but with a different name. The South Africans may have got away with it but 'Coco Rico' was too close. We had been considering 'Malibu' for something else and that seemed just the ticket especially with more differentiated packaging.

The research was not bad enough to be encouraging and we were more excited at the time by Primavera, a sort of alcoholic marmalade. We launched them simultaneously and most of the betting favoured Primavera. Inevitably perhaps, Primavera bombed and Malibu soared. With hindsight, a large part of the reason was that Malibu was bland whereas Primavera was too strongly flavoured – more Oxford marmalade than Golden Shred. We should have learned from Smirnoff that, in mass marketing foods and drinks, bland is good and blander is better, at least initially. Marmite has an unending struggle with that. 'Blander is better' is not true in the long run, Johnnie Walker tops J&B Rare for example. But you have to get to the long run in the first place.

I have often wondered if one should gradually strengthen the flavour of a new brand once it has become successful but I never tried it.

---

* Perhaps because it is such a big branded market, the US is the HQ of Me-Too marketing. Gillette razors were a Me-Too brand.

Malibu rolled out successfully worldwide and overtook poor old Coco Rico in the USA. Part of that success was due to the uncertainty about where it fitted. Rum provides the base but it is not really rum and the strength is too low to be a liqueur.

Archers Peach Schnapps, later, was an almost identical story albeit not as successful as Malibu. We noticed the rapid growth in US Peach Schnapps sales, used in 'Fuzzy Navel' cocktails mixed with orange juice, and Me One'd it in the UK, Canada and, latterly, internationally. It took a while to get going in the UK and, in my international role, I had a chat with the then UK MD:

Me: 'Archers has to have some advertising to raise awareness.'

MD: 'We can't afford it. And especially not the cost of a TV ad. That would be at least £250,000.'

Me (thinking that Hugh Burkitt, who had the account, was going to kill me): 'I'll get you a perfectly good TV ad for £30,000. And the packaging needs improvement too.'

MD: 'I don't know about that. Tell you what, when sales pick up, we'll improve the pack.'

Some people are born marketeers and some are not. Eventually he gave way and it all worked out fine.

Baileys, Malibu and Archers all used their relatively low strengths to fatten margins and thus were on the side of the angels when the anti-alcohol lobbyists started beating their tambourines. Malibu production was moved to Barbados which seemed to some people a more authentic source for rum and coconuts than Harlow, Essex. When Seagrams was broken up, Diageo acquired Captain Morgan Spiced Rum which the competition authorities deemed too close to Malibu for comfort, so the latter was sold to Allied Domecq for £560m ($800m) in 2002 and later to Pernod Ricard who moved production to Canada. No shortage of coconuts on the Rockies.

The third new brand to add impetus to UK profits was Le Piat d'Or. IDV had been trying to come up with a mass market table wine brand since our success with Croft Original in the 1960s. The Croft-like guiding principle was that consumers admired red wine for being posher than white but they actually still liked things to be sweet. Over the 50 years since then the public palate has dried out but remember this was then.

The first effort was Doçura, a red wine from Portugal. This flopped deservedly as it was too sweet, too heavy and too tannic. In short it was revolting, but those of us who said so were told we were not representative of the target market. It did not do too badly in research which was another lesson: sweetness researches better than it sells – as Pepsi and Coke testify.

Our second effort was St Stefan, slightly more agreeable red wine from Hungary but it was not posh enough and there was still too much tannin. It did marginally better than Doçura but not a lot.

By the mid 70s, we had concluded that the wine had to be French and two streams of development were in hand. Tom Jago's team had got the prior messages and were going, in essence, for a red Blue Nun (the brand leading German wine) i.e. light, bland and with minimal if any tannin. My approach, with Louis Vialard of French Wine Farmers, was to go for something where we could claim superior quality but it would also be virtually tannin free and not too sweet.

There are four wine grades in the EU (EEC then): quality wines have two, Appellation Controlée and VDQS, and the lower grades have Vin de Pays and Vin de Table (to use the French nomenclature). Wines cannot be sweetened by using anything other than unfermented grape juice and that only with restrictions. In France it was allowed only for the lowest category, Vin de Table. Vialard thought that we could persuade French authorities to permit sweetening for our Vin de Pays wines, giving us a unique value proposition.

Tom Jago's team took the smart packaging of Le Piat de Beaujolais and we accepted some not glamorous enough labelling for 'Pierre Picard'. We launched them side by side in the UK in 1978, in our usual low cost fashion with the understanding that serious money would be put behind the winner. Pierre Picard did OK but Piat d'Or did far better. The quality wine classifications have since been made so wide that Vin de Pays has never made the impact it should. The trade at least was impressed we got the rules changed: it had been considered impossible. Significantly, Le Piat d'Or was blander than Pierre Picard.

The two brands that had largely built the mass market UK wine business, after Blue Nun and Mateus Rosé, were Charbonnier (Reckitt and Colman) and Hirondelle (Hedges & Butler a.k.a. Bass Charrington Vintners). They were cheap and cheerful plonk*. Our brand was to be premium. Two problems sank Hirondelle: the labels claimed the wine was Austrian but the brand became so successful

---

* A 1930s term derived from 'plink plonk' a Woosterish way of saying Vin Blanc.

that it was selling more than Austria's total wine exports. The wine was really from Hungary. It then emerged that the Hungarians were smoothing off the 'finish' of the wine by adding the anti-freeze more usually found in cars.

Le Piat d'Or found space in the market and, with excellent advertising by Winston Fletcher and his team, sales rocketed up to a million cases a year. Needless to say, middle class wine drinkers considered it truly naff, an offence to wine lovers and that we should be ashamed of ourselves. My response was that we were trying to keep the price of claret down by directing the public elsewhere.

One campaign was along the lines of After Eight chocolates, for example a young man would arrive very late for dinner but all was well when he produced a bottle of Le Piat d'Or. My favourite claimed, with an alluring French accent, 'The French Adore Le Piat d'Or.' A few pompous Brits complained about that:

'I've summered man and boy in France for 40 years and never seen the stuff.'

The Advertising Standards Authority required proof of our claim and we satisfied them by showing that Le Piat d'Or was indeed one of the highest selling wine brands in France. They were happy and we did not wish to trouble them with the detail that over 90% of sales were in the French channel ports, i.e. bought by Brits returning home.

The formula we developed for brand launches still works. It differs greatly from the standard brand manager model of high advertising and promotional expenditure to gain attention. The first thing is to make sure the product is right and customers will return. You may need some advertising for awareness but not much. Sampling is far more important and can be conducted via pubs and bars for spirits or shops and supermarkets for low strength products. Gain distribution first and only then pile on the advertising. There is no point in advertising if no one knows what it is or where to find it.

My days as a hands-on marketeer had their ups and downs but they were happy ones for me. I was doing what I most enjoyed doing. As the next chapter will show, promotion has its advantages but watching other people do the marketing was never as satisfying. Marketeers do not much care for advice.

# Chapter 8

# Life International

*This chapter begins with promotion to the main board and becoming CEO of IDV UK. International assignments were added progressively and a great deal of time was spent on airplanes. Specifically it covers:*

- *Anthony Tennant*
  - *The Christie's scandal*
  - *Working for Tennant*
  - *His first US Takeover Coup: Paddington and Carillon*
  - *His second US coup*
  - *Tennant moves to Guinness*
- *Allen Sheppard*
  - *IDV Retail goes to the wall*
  - *Taking charities seriously*
  - *Sheppard becomes GrandMet Chairman*
- *IDV Home Trade MD*
  - *Management development*
  - *Horses and golf*
  - *The unions*
- *IDV South Africa*
  - *The Rembrandt Relationship*
  - *Breaking the apartheid laws*
  - *Country baronies*
  - *Finding Allan Bell's successor*
  - *Trouble with Mrs Bell*
  - *Au revoir to South Africa*
- *International Distillers' Developments*
  - *Kenya*
  - *Malawi and Botswana*
  - *Mauritius*
  - *Sri Lanka*
  - *Nigeria*
  - *Nigerian Postscript*

Original IDV colleagues such as George Bull aside, the main new players for GrandMet were Allen Sheppard and Anthony Tennant, both good to me in their different ways and, before delving briefly into my time as UK CEO, this chapter begins with a short account of each of them.

Following the acquisition of Watneys in 1972 and the near collapse of GrandMet the following year, the Watney and Truman brewing interests were scrambled together by the few survivors of the Watney top management, Robin Soames being one, and the board of the smaller, Truman, group.

Anthony Tennant (1931–2011) joined the Truman brewing group as Marketing Director from Mather & Crowther, IDV's advertising agency in the 1960s. For whatever reasons, the GrandMet team decided not to give Tennant the top brewing job even though he was the obvious and outstanding talent. Rumour had it that Joseph and his lieutenants did not feel confident with Tennant's patrician style (Eton, Trinity Cambridge and Scots Guards) but it is more likely that they felt a rough and tough East End accountant was needed. Anthony did, after all, shoot with the beerage.

Allen Sheppard got the job (son of a railway man and LSE) in 1975 and Tennant was switched to the Green Shield stamps, namely IDV, in 1976 – although the appointment was announced a year sooner with Geoffrey Palau being appointed to cover the transition. Both appointments were well judged as the brewing and IDV sides needed an accountant and a marketeer respectively.

From Day 1 Tennant made it clear that he was interested in brands and not especially with ranges of products to support IDV's wholesaling and retail activities. We had a struggle to protect, for example, our rather ordinary range of Gilbey Vintners sherries – even though they were highly profitable.

Tennant was a wonderful boss in a number of respects. Making a mistake never landed one in trouble. He was only interested in why it happened and how we could avoid it happening again. His Cambridge education had taught him the Socratic method of constantly asking 'why?' and never supplying the answers. It could be very irritating.

As well as being supportive through thick and thin, he and his long-suffering secretary (Alice for most of the time) ran an amazing filing and brought forward system to the point that I did not need one at all. If we agreed I'd report back in four weeks, Alice would be on the phone after three asking where my report was. And she would have all the necessary papers. As I was convinced that the EEC inspectors would, sooner or later, raid our offices, I made a point of never filing anything. They didn't but as subsequent events showed, it was a realistic concern.

Tennant's career ended with the famous Christie's and Sotheby's price fixing scandal of 2000. The facts are undisputed: as Chairman of Christie's, Tennant had had a conversation about rates of auctioneers' commissions with his opposite number at Sotheby's, an American. In US competition law, these discussions were illegal and the Sotheby's Chairman, as US citizen, went to gaol. Under English law*, they may have been ethically dubious but they were legal, furthermore they took place in London, not in the US – Christie's is a British company and Tennant a British citizen. He was not prosecuted in the UK as he had no case to answer. The main witness was the Christie's MD, Christopher Davidge, who had been a protégé of Tennant's and some say he was protecting his own situation by sabotaging Tennant's, although I am sure that cannot be true.

In their usual Lex Americana = Lex Mundi way, the US authorities wanted Tennant extradited and, if Blair's extradition arrangements had then been in place, he would have been. As it was, the US extradition treaties made Tennant vulnerable in almost every country except the UK. So his final years were sadder than they should have been.

Reverting to the happier days of the 1970s and 1980s, Tennant was obviously a great supporter of advertising budgets and he did not seek involvement in the detail. Restraint must have been his middle name. Although he was fun and funny, mischievous and even misbehaved off duty, depending on the company, he was deadly serious between 9 and 5 and that included business lunches. On more than one occasion, I was taken on one side and told off about making jokes over lunch. My protest that we needed to lighten the atmosphere cut little ice.

New brands and brand building aside, his first coup was persuading GrandMet to buy the Liggett Group (tobacco) in 1980. GrandMet had no interest in tobacco but Liggett owned three valuable US branded drink import businesses: Paddington (the importer of J&B Rare), Carillon and Austin Nichols. Abe Rosenberg was 67 in 1976

---

* My understanding of English law is that executives from competing companies may talk about the market and pricing in general terms but not reach any agreement, e.g. if you do X, we will do Y.

and looking for retirement when he sold out to Liggett. He virtually owned Paddington and Carillon but I don't know the origin of Austin Nichols. I doubt it ever occurred to Abe to sell to GrandMet but, even if it did, money was still tight following the near collapse of the shares in 1973.

Buying Liggett was contentious. Their main tobacco business was doing poorly and shares were below $40. GrandMet bid $50 (i.e. $400m or so, a cheap deal by modern standards). US businesses hate being acquired and especially by Brits, or maybe any non-Americans. Apart from throwing a mass of lawyers and lawsuits into the fray, Liggett persuaded Pernod Ricard, in their usual helpful way, to buy Austin Nichols at 40x earnings. This was supposed to scupper the GrandMet bid but it actually made it more attractive: we did not need three import companies.

Tennant played the Liggett cards again with Heublein, IDV's main US partner. This had two stages. The Smirnoff contracts were due to expire in 1994 and IDV would have been in pretty poor shape if they were not renewed much sooner. One's bargaining position deteriorates as the terminal date approaches. From 1980 to 1982, Paul Doyle, CEO of Gilbeys Canada, and I, on and off, negotiated a long extension. Our main adversary was a nice and very clever man called Len Blado. Quite understandably, Heublein was in no hurry and the negotiation was not helped by the hostility of their Chairman, Stuart Watson. He was one of the team Max Joseph tossed out of his office in the 1970s.

Hicks Waldren was the CEO, and something of a Boy Scout,* when we had a stroke of luck. An asset stripper called General Cinema had bid for Heublein which made them nervous. A top team came over to ask how we could help. After one of those interminable meetings which got nowhere, Tennant saw them out in his usual courtly fashion and, in the car park, said to Waldren something like, 'Renewing the Smirnoff contracts will bind us closer together and make Heublein less attractive for General Cinema.'

'Good thinking. I'll talk with our people.'

Soon thereafter, the contracts were renewed, much to Blado's disgust.

Heublein then found a white knight in RJR Nabisco (part of Reynolds Tobacco) which acquired them for $1.3bn in 1982. They sold Heublein's Kentucky Fried Chicken business to Nabisco for

---

* He did actually have some senior role in the US Boy Scouts movement.

$840m, kept the A1 Sauce and the rest of Heublein's, admittedly small, foods business and, in 1987, sold the wine and spirit side to GrandMet for $1.2bn. A 50% profit is not bad.

But we were lucky there too. In 1985, Jack Powers, Chairman of Heublein after Watson, had flown over with his RJR boss, Ross Johnson, in one of their huge corporate jets to suggest Heublein merged with IDV. With their usual Big American world view, they assumed Heublein was much bigger and therefore merger was a polite word for takeover. Rather sweetly we said that it was an excellent idea and the shares of the joint company would be issued pro rata to RJR and GrandMet on the basis of the present value of the profit streams. Powers had not done his homework and was astonished to discover that IDV's, assisted by the Smirnoff contract renewals, was bigger than Heublein's. We would have been buying them. The deal was off.

In late 1986, the tom toms indicated that RJR was negotiating to sell Heublein's drinks business to Seagram. That would make Seagram far the biggest wine and spirit business globally but why had they not approached us, at least to get an auction going? They knew our numbers by now and that GrandMet could afford it. They may not have trusted us to keep Heublein's top management in place but then, why would they trust Seagram? I believe it was the same US superiority complex that gave us so much trouble with Liggett: it is OK for US companies to take over British companies but not vice versa. BP had the same problem 20 years later.

Anyway, Tennant held an emergency lunch at York Gate with our investment bank, Warburg. The home team were Stanley Grinstead, by then Chairman of GrandMet, George Bull and me. Warburg's advice was not to mess around but for Grinstead to phone his RJR opposite number and fix an urgent meeting at which Grinstead would produce a simple letter offering, subject to contract, to buy Heublein for $X. It was good advice and we talked about what X should be. We agreed it should be our top price, and therefore non-negotiable, as it had to be as high as possible to knock Seagram out. This was no time for chiselling. So $1.2bn it was. Never, before or since, have I come across an offer agreed with less hassle. Half an hour over lunch was enough. The accountants were left to stew on it.

This duly took place and the RJR Chairman was flabbergasted. He had never even thought of GrandMet as a buyer. The trouble was that the Seagram deal, albeit lower, was already agreed subject to contract and they were due to exchange contracts the following Saturday.

Johnson and Powers were brought in and went along with our proposal. Powers also stipulated that I should be excluded from the discussions, and they would keep Blado out, as we would otherwise spend too much time scoring points off each other. The GrandMet team would be Bull, leading, with the GrandMet strategy executive, the admirable Peter Cawdron. I wasn't sure whether to be pleased or insulted to be singled out in this way. Tennant tried to persuade me of the former and it certainly saved yet another trip to the US.

George and Peter did the business, the deal was signed Friday evening (16th January 1987) and Seagram never knew what hit them. They were not pleased. The deal included Almaden Vineyards which Heublein had purchased only two weeks earlier.

In March 1987, Tennant went on to succeed Ernest Saunders, the clever but dodgy CEO who had put together Guinness, Bell's whisky and then, in 1986 for £2.7bn, the Distillers Company Limited. Apparently Tennant had applied for the job six years earlier but been bested by Saunders. Saunders is a fine marketing strategist and had begun the process of straightening out the DCL's confused portfolio. He also made promises he did not keep (like moving the HQ to Edinburgh) and he arranged to have the Guinness share price boosted to flatter his bid. This had been sort of nearly legal a few years earlier but it certainly wasn't then and he went to gaol for it. The sentence was five years but it was only 10 months in the Ford Open Prison before he convinced everyone he had 'pre-senile dementia' and was released. But he was, as I said, a creative marketeer and he invented this new malady which, as far as I know, nobody else has ever suffered from.

More remarkably, he made an instant recovery as I can testify personally. The then IDV UK Marketing Director, Tony Scouller, used to work for him and the two of us were in a restaurant when Saunders entered and spotted him. All his neurons were definitely firing as he recalled more than I knew about Tony.

Tennant built on the start Saunders had made and did a great job as Guinness Chairman, not least because of his friendship with the boss of LVMH, Bernard Arnault. Tennant stepped down, aged 62 and full of vim and vigour, in 1992. Three more Saunders vignettes before turning to the Allen Sheppard side of the story.

Saunders was not the ideal boss as David Sandys Renton, the Guinness Marketing Director, rapidly discovered. Saunders rated himself, correctly, as a better marketeer than Sandys Renton who was perfectly competent and a nice man. He'd previously rescued Taunton Cider from obscurity. Saunders dived into marketing decision-making and Sandys Renton discovered, from a journalist, that their main advertising agency had been sacked. It was time to get on his bicycle.

On the other side, the Guinness family were the largest shareholders but rather disdainful of their hired hand. Soon after his arrival, Saunders was invited to a big family wedding in Dublin. As CEO of the company and a celebrity in his own right, he naturally expected to be on the top table. Not a bit of it: he was on the table for the family retainers, butler, cook, chauffeurs and so on.

Finally he was also unpopular with the beerage. Having no tied pubs as the other big beer brands did, he complained, over dinner one night, to his neighbour, Gordon Borrie, the head of the Office of Fair Trading who, also being no friend of the beerage, instituted the major review of beer distribution which virtually destroyed the British beer industry. To cap it all, Lord Young, the relevant Secretary of State at the time (1989), announced that he was 'minded to approve' the report without, so we were told, bothering to read it, still less the dissenting but much more credible opinions which it contained. Borrie, since knighted, is an honest and well intentioned man but prejudices were prevailing over reason.

As noted above, Sheppard* grew up on the other side of the tracks from Tennant but despite their huge differences, they got along well enough and, from a GrandMet point of view, were complementary. Joseph liked to say that Sheppard had made sense of his Watney acquisition and he was a man of robust commercial know how. In that, he was supported by Ian Martin and Clive Strowger, two more accountants. I got on well with both but some saw Strowger as being a tad sharp. I never found him so. City folk used to describe Sheppard and Strowger, wittily they thought, as: 'Sheppard and his crook'.

Sensibly, Sheppard retained Robin Soames, a senior member of the beerage from Watneys and universally popular, to do the ambassadorial stuff.

Sheppard and Strowger came from the car industry, not a great source of managerial, still less marketing, talent, but they were clear

---

* Born on Christmas Day 1932 and, yes, he always did believe in Santa Claus.

eyed. Sir Donald (later Lord) Stokes, then Chairman of the British Motor Corporation, asked Sheppard to sort out the production of Landrovers. Amongst other things, production was slow and customers had long waits for delivery. Sheppard did as he was bid and reported back that customer waiting times had been slashed from 10 weeks to two. He waited for a pat on the back but not a bit of it:

'Sheppard, you have destroyed the Landrover business. The order book is decimated. Get out of my office.'

And this was the man our Minister for Trade, Tony Benn, had put in charge of the UK's entire car manufacturing business.

Sheppard's team of accountants did a fine job of rationalising the business. They had acquired Fosters, the Australian lager, and that did well as did Holsten, the Hamburg lager, and Budweiser, but I think that owed as much to the brand owners as GrandMet since the group's own brands failed to improve.

Lord Young's beer orders did not help but Sheppard's efforts at squeezing more money from tenants – the 'Inntrepreneur' scheme – was too clever and alienated them. Over the 15 years since acquisition the brewery side had done OK, maybe on the bottom line, but not in terms of brand equity, i.e. its underlying strength. Nevertheless they had acquired, partly thanks to David Tagg, Sheppard's talented consigliere and Group HR Director, a great team of managers. Marketing was poor and the decision, when Diageo was formed with the merger of Guinness, to sell off everything bar the Guinness beer, wines and spirits businesses, tells its own story.

That said, Sheppard was fun to be with and to work for. He has a strong sense of humour. He set unreasonable targets but took it in good part if one had done one's best but missed them. GrandMet's 'Values' displayed everywhere ('Balls on Walls') declared that eccentricity was welcome and by Sheppard it was, but not by the rest of his team. He regarded long-term vision as no excuse for short-term failure: 'The long term is merely a sequence of short-terms added together.'

IDV Retail was a good example of false management professionalism. Sheppard was trying to make sense of the GrandMet miscellany of businesses he inherited from Grinstead and decided to split retail, which was seen as its own specialism, from brands. Not a bad idea on the face of it except that, in a specialist retailing business, it is quite a good idea to understand the products being sold and the nature of the specialism.

The GrandMet appointee came crashing in and made the spectacularly facile discovery that 80% of the sales came from 20% of the portfolio. So the slow moving 80% of the portfolio was removed and the business collapsed within six months. Because IDV was seen as a bunch of amateurs, our advice was spurned.

There are quite a few reasons why it was stupid. There is a limit as to the number of facings any one product needs, even if it is the hottest ticket in the shop. The only defence a specialist retailer has against the supermarkets is that it is indeed specialist, in other words it carries lines the supermarkets do not, and has the expertise to explain them. All that was blown away.

Sheppard's contributions were far more positive than some of the comments above may imply and included major charitable works helping the unemployed into work. This was no cynical PR exercise but a serious long-term, and productive, commitment.

This work overlapped some of the Prince of Wales's charitable efforts and they became quite close. Honours for most business people stem from some government department but Sheppard's KCVO (later upgraded to a peerage) correctly implies Royal connections. Sheppard, together with his deputy, Keith Holloway, was responsible for the Duchy of Cornwall range of groceries, itself a charity fundraiser. IDV provided Chris Nadin, the marketeer who got it started, initially just with biscuits.

One vignette of his association with the Prince of Wales before moving on. One morning I had a call from Brenda, Sheppard's PA, to say that he had sat next to the Prince at dinner the night before and got a bit carried away by the occasion. It cannot have been the drink as he was abstemious. According to Brenda, he could not recall how it came about but he seemed to have agreed to sponsor the next Covent Garden production of *Die Walkure*.

'Allen says you know about these things. Is it likely to be expensive?'

'Yes, very.'

'How much?'

'I don't know but at least a quarter of a million, maybe half a million. Can he get out of it?'

'No. That's not possible. Allen knows it is an opera but that's all he knows. Can you help him?'

'That's easy. I'll send a set of CDs.'

Two days later, Brenda was on the line again.

'Allen says it's the worst thing he has ever heard and wonders if you would be so kind as to take his place. I think you only have to turn up.'

Which is how Katie and I, with our good friends Michael and Valerie Jackaman, had the best four seats in the house for the first performance and dined in the Queen's private dining room just behind the Royal Box. The staff were splendidly obsequious. For us, one of the best nights ever at Covent Garden. Michael was chairman of Allied Brewers at the time, so there were brownie points there and we had the use of his Rolls Royce.

As with Grinstead and Sharpe before them, Tennant and Sheppard were racing neck and neck for the Chairmanship when Grinstead retired. It cannot have been an easy decision but it was gracefully done and Anthony bowed out. As he bowed straight into an equally good job as Chairman of Guinness, neither was the loser. Sheppard deserved the credit he got for his part in constructing GrandMet.

He handed over the Chairmanship to George, later Sir George, Bull in 1996 who merged the company, very successfully as it turned out, with Guinness to form Diageo in 1997. As I had left by then, it is not part of my story.

In about 1979, Bull was needed to sort out IDV Europe and I was promoted to take his place and join the IDV board. My time as CEO of IDV UK was relatively mundane compared with the international assignments that followed. The ever delightful Stephen Lewis replaced me as Marketing Director. He came from Trumans, prompted of course by Tennant, but I hired him gladly. And he inherited the wonderful Bineke as I inherited, as secretary, Jean Crossley from Bull.

Lewis had been on the ad agency side of the business and that gave him fresh insights and many valuable contacts. He was, and remains, amiable and popular.

Jean was between husbands and coping splendidly with two teenage children, singing with the Harlow choir, a busy social life and managing the Managing Director. It helped that she was well informed about, and able to transmit, what was going on in the company. After a while she expressed a wish for progression and became a very able #2 in our PR team of two. Arfer 'Opkins*, known as Scoop, was in charge and a far cry from the usual smooth PR person. He had grown up as a true East End cockney and a successful light-

---

* Arthur Hopkins, of course.

weight boxer. When he hung up his gloves he became a pugnacious reporter for the beer trade daily paper, the *Morning Advertiser*. We hired him because we were fed up with the smoothies. He was no respecter of persons and everyone loved him for it, even the French aristocrats.

Being CEO gave me, I thought, licence to interfere in all areas. One was wine buying and I expressed the view that Peter Dominic should be more entrepreneurial and not keep buying the same old things with which our customers were bored. They were persuaded, with huge reluctance, to buy a bulk container of Argentine red wine. It disappeared. I told them to buy another one and then both arrived together. We now had enough Argentine red wine, they told me, to last 10 years.

'Never mind,' said I, 'we'll mount a big promotion.'

And so we did. The banners unfurled across all our 500 shops on Friday 2nd April 1982. The date was unforgettable because the Argentines had decided to give prominence to our promotion by invading the Falklands that very day.

All the banners came down and we waited for victory and re-ran the promotion as a celebration. Wrong again. The wine was excellent value for money and it improved as it matured. We were drinking it at home for a very long time.

*Perhaps three things summarise this period: management development, racing and dealing with the unions.*

Geoffrey Palau provided the best insight on the transition: 'You may think your job is still about building brands but it isn't. Leave that to Stephen. The MD's job is management development. That and only that.'

Of course the MD of a public company has share prices and other things to worry about but at the subsidiary level, he was right. We had adopted the fashionable management by objectives system by which the boss and each subordinate discuss what the subordinate should achieve by the end of the period, usually six months or a year. When the time is up, they review the results together and set fresh objectives. Some companies tied performance to bonuses and salaries but at least we had the wit to avoid that. By the time government discovered this idea, as 'targets', in the early part of this century, business had mostly abandoned it.

More effective, if little more popular, was the callover system. In addition to the monthly executive meetings which every company has, each boss and subordinate sat together, or rather across the desk, and each month went through the subordinates 'to do' list. If you think that's a great idea, try doing it at home with your spouse. The system should be driven bottom up but, mindful of the army's 'never volunteer' maxim, it rarely was.

If I was starting again, I wouldn't bother with Management by Objectives: achieving annual goals is a team, not an individual, thing. I would keep the callover system though because one does not wish to embarrass even the idle at executive meetings. It is much better to move things, and people, along in private.

Being a CEO is about getting the best from one's current stock of managers and that includes giving them experience in different areas. We did quite a bit of that, with the most extreme example being the talented Colin Gordon. He had come in as HR Director and was the first we had ever had who knew the rule book from cover to cover. He had been a consultant and had a strong track record. He was an excellent HR Director but some of the company wits referred to him as 'Neutron' after the newly invented neutron bomb which destroyed all living creatures but left the buildings intact. The dome of his prematurely bald head may have been responsible for the joke.

Those who knew him, liked and admired him and knew perfectly well that the nickname was inappropriate. Gordon was ambitious, but amiably so, and always up for a challenge. After a bit of thought, he accepted the job of Finance Director, taking a short course at London Business School to equip him with the essential skills.

This in turn allowed Ian Ritchie, our Finance Director and as tight with the pennies as the Scots can be, to become CEO of IDV Retail where penny watching was crucial. His predecessor, Barry Sutton, went off to be CEO of the Wine Society which he did with great success until he retired. We missed Ritchie as Finance Director in one way especially. With the possible exception of Fred Bushell at Lotus, I never met anyone even half as good at bamboozling the auditors.

Following the disastrous start to our distribution operations at Harlow we had many years where our stocks did not reconcile, not even close. They were out by millions and a good proportion of our total profits. Ian decided what he thought the stocks should be, not least to produce the profit we needed, and that was what went in the books.

The auditors did, of course, notice the discrepancies and visited

Ritchie's office for explanations. They would emerge with glazed looks and strongly disinclined to repeat the experience. Each year we had a fresh set of young auditors so they never learned from experience. We could not tell errors in book-keeping from thieving and when we eventually got it sorted, the auditors had never escalated the matter as they should have done* – but Ritchie's estimates, overall, turned out to be about right. And we had pleasingly smoothed the profit growth line meanwhile.

Directors and shareholders love smooth progressions as jagged lines cause trouble. So any sensible CEO who gets to the year end making, by some miracle, more profit than expected, should hide the surplus away for a rainy day. The techniques for so doing are quite simple and still work.

As well as improving the existing stock of managers, one has to recruit new ones. That was particularly important for marketeers, who could be seen as the yeast in the dough, as the best and brightest tended not to want to work in Harlow. We had set up a graduate scheme back when Geoffrey Butler was Personnel Director and by now it was flowering. It was always important to refresh the culture with some new talent but we were now growing our own.

One recruit was Graeme Christie, a talented marketeer from Harveys. The interview had echoes of Joseph's with Grinling. I was in the Bristol area and agreed to meet him there. Recognising my own and Harlow's untrendiness, I thought a fashionable wine bar should be the setting. The decibels were at Heathrow levels. Neither of us could hear a word the other said. Back out on the pavement, I told him he had the job. Surprisingly, he turned up.

He told me later that trendiness had never entered his mind but it was easily the most eccentric interview he had ever had. My favourite graduate hire followed a few years after recruiting Claire Watson – one of the most successful. We needed another in a bit of a hurry so I asked Claire if she had a sister. She had.

'Is she like you?'

'I suppose so.'

'Is she looking for a job?'

'Funnily enough, yes she is.'

'Tell her she now has one starting Monday.'

Claire being a bit conventional told me I couldn't do that and what

---

* I don't think they wanted to reveal their own confusion.

would HR say and weren't we supposed to advertise vacancies .... One of the privileges of being a CEO is being able to break the rules. Claire's sister was also a great success.

Lest I give the impression this was all wine and roses, I should recall a disaster. The 13th/18th Royal Hussars were stationed at Debden and Katie and I became good friends of the Colonel and his wife. In the course of conversation we speculated what would happen to his officers when they had served their time. The military pyramid means that most leave quite young. We needed that kind of talent so we agreed that a representative group would come to lunch at Harlow and I would ensure it was suitably liquid.

We wined and dined them and told them about the booze business. They pretty quickly twigged what was afoot and fell about laughing. 'Surely,' their spokesman said, 'you cannot imagine we would be seeking employment, any kind of employment, when we have our family estates to manage in Yorkshire.' The Colonel, who had been drafted in from a less smart regiment, was as embarrassed as I was but we all enjoyed the port.

One break from the daily grind of meetings was provided by triumvirate outings. Our two biggest customers, but also competitors, were Hedges & Butler and Saccone & Speed, the wines and spirits sides of the big brewers, Bass Charrington and Courage. Brian Stark and Anthony Ainslie were MDs of Hedges & Butler and Saccone & Speed respectively. Luckily, we and the wives (Meribah Stark and Maria Ainslie, a splendid Spanish aristocrat) got on exceedingly well. It is important to wine and dine one's best customers and take care of their social needs and we did our best.

Stark had been in the Royal Navy until he joined the booze trade and he knew how to run a tight ship. Ainslie could give the impression, and did, of being a dour lowland Scot but behind that lurked a tremendous sense of humour.

The six of us felt we needed a few tours together to check out our suppliers in Italy, France and Spain (Jerez). The competition authorities might not have liked it but no one told them. Our visit to Jerez coincided with their Feria del Caballo, when beautiful people, magnificently attired, ride their horses around town with their girls draped across the hindquarters. Our hosts never seemed to go to bed at all. Fino was poured from breakfast until dinner at about 3am the next morning. Admittedly it is not as strong as sherry in Britain but when it is the only type of liquid on offer, it gets to you.

Meribah Stark has a cut-glass English accent which cuts through Spanish chatter. When someone offered her the 34th Fino of the day she lost it:

'Oh God. Will someone get me a gin and tonic?'

The Jerezanos were stunned. The shock horror was that of a Bateman cartoon.

Her husband achieved a similar coup on our way back. Stark is usually suited by Savile Row, shirted by Jermyn Street and the very model of the Royal Naval Captain he was. Jerez had undermined him and by the time we got to the Ritz in Madrid, he was almost dishevelled. As we entered, a doorman blocked his path and explained in his best Spanish that Stark was barred: no tie = no entry. I suspect this was the first time it had ever happened to him and he was banjaxed.

We had hired a limo which turned out to be the kind of 1930s American juggernaut used by Al Capone. The driver was out of the same movie. As the rest of us headed for the bar, Stark negotiated with the driver for his tie and appeared shortly in the most awful, grease-stained, plastic horror the world has ever seen. It cost him $20.

The other type of break involved horses. The Hennessys in particular, approved of horses and golf, so Katie and I needed to show the flag.

The annual Hennessy Gold Cup in late November at Newbury is an important part of the racing calendar. The reason the sponsorship paid off was that Hennessy had established the race in its own name and established it over 30 years. I don't believe that the Johnny Come Latelys who sponsor, say, the Grand National for a couple of years get their money back.

It was the main occasion when we entertained our customers. James Gulliver who was Chairman of the Fine Fare chain of supermarkets at the time and probably our favourite customer. His Finance Director was Martin Sorrell, later to become CEO of WPP, the largest global ad agency group, via Saatchi and Saatchi. Gulliver was a lovely man, funny, eccentric and a keen consumer. By the end of racing he would be completely legless. But he was not to be underestimated. Clifford Lloyd Richards, then IDV UK's Sales Director, could be a bit starchy and had a complete sense of humour failure when he discovered that Gulliver was sleeping with his secretary. One may lay down one's wife for one's friends but laying down one's secretary for a customer was, in his view, taking things too far. In the event, the two married and Lloyd Richards was pacified.

One of the joys of racing, and especially steeple-chasing, is that everyone is on more or less the same level from the Queen Mother and the Hennessys at one end of the social scale to our publicans at the other. Scoop was in his element. One problem with this universal bonhomie was that we attracted many, too many, gatecrashers. Put a name like Hennessy over a marquee and an amazing number of people find themselves in need of a drink. Short of getting heavy handed, we did not know what to do about it as none of us knew all of our guests.

By chance George Bull and I found ourselves at the big autumn Newmarket meeting a month before the Hennessy. SKF Ballbearings were the main sponsors and had a marquee just like ours.

'Let's test their security,' I suggested, 'and we might learn something.' The communist youth festivals years before had honed my gatecrashing skills.

'You mean we should gatecrash this marquee?'

'Yes. There's nothing to it. Just march in past the doorman like we own the place, grab glasses of champagne and mingle with the crowd.'

Our two wives opted out of this experience saying it was a business matter and Bull also expressed his disquiet. He is, after all, an officer and a gentleman and he was wearing his Coldstream Guards blazer which has the regimental brass buttons set out in a strange pattern only permitted for Coldstreamers.

'George, we are not doing this for ourselves but for our company. It will be a doddle. If a host-like person approaches just shake the hand warmly and say how nice it is to see him again. No sales director ever insults a prospective customer by refusing to recognise him. Just start talking with the other people in the crowd.'

Bull squares his shoulders and in we go. The doorman is no trouble but then we discover the marquee is completely empty apart from one host who is looking vaguely puzzled. I shake him warmly by the hand and say how nice it is to see him again. He looks even more puzzled but gives us a glass of champagne each. After minimal small talk, we make our escape.

'There you are. No problem.'

'Don't ever ask me to do that again.'

The Hennessy marquee door staff that year received strong guidance on checking credentials.

Hennessy also sponsored Ryder Cup golf, which I liked, and show jumping which quickly becomes very boring indeed. The latter gives one a small intimation of what it is to be royal. Apart from having to be gracious with everyone who comes by, one has to sit for hours watching horses lolloping around knocking poles off gates. Polite interest is hard to maintain.

The golf had the perk that we could play the same course after the professionals. The remaining crowds in the stands may not have been too impressed but it must have been interesting for them. Especially when Scoop managed to bounce his ball off the surface of the lake outside the Bellfry clubhouse and have it land safely on the fairway on the far side.

Katie and I had many happy days at Ascot, Sandown, Cheltenham and Epsom. Thanks to television, it is quite unnecessary to leave the box, or the lunch table, so long as there is a runner to place the bets. Mecca Bookmakers, our sister company in GrandMet, were especially hospitable.

Perhaps the happiest were at Goodwood. It is a beautiful course and setting but a long way from Essex and Eddie, our wonderful Irish driver, regularly got lost. You could tell he was in trouble: his neck turned pink, then red and then, if we were seriously lost, purple. Nothing was said and it was best not to ask. Eddie was a widower with a son in the Essex police which explained, we all thought, his lack of speeding tickets. In their maturer years, Eddie and Carla, our Italian cook, were married and very romantic that was.

Joseph was a reluctant racegoer but, being the clever man he was, he researched the runners and placed just one bet a day, a big one, on the most likely winner. He usually left even richer. Grinstead was far more involved as, thanks to his daughter, he had a stud in Kent. When I met him at one Goodwood he advised me not to bet on his runner and he was right, but only just. It came fourth.

The most memorable Goodwood day was sponsored in style by Lanson champagne. One neighbour at lunch was simply delightful in every possible way. To gain her ear one had to shelter under her magnificent summer hat. I fear I may have ignored my other neighbour but the object of my fascination had Robin Kernick, my erstwhile boss, on her other side. I could see no reason why she should waste time on him.

Needless to say, my enthusiasm had not gone unnoticed. After lunch my host said:

'Do you realise who you were sitting next to?'

'No, but she is wonderful so thank you.'

'That is Katie Rabbett. I thought you might be pleased to sit next to her.' The penny then dropped. She was the society beauty of her day and ex-girlfriend of the Duke of York. Despite all the wit and charm I must have displayed, she evinced no desire to sit next to me for tea. I can only assume her man must have been jealous. Katie, on the other hand, was quite nice about it.

The other memorable racing outing was our sole Grand National. By then, Seagrams had bought Martell cognac which was sponsoring the race. No expense spared, our helicopter took off from Battersea and landed in the middle of the racecourse. Well actually one expense had been spared. There was no car to meet the six of us and we had to trudge all the way to the grandstand. Ed McDonnell, the Seagram International chief, was a good friend and I was glad when Edgar Bronfman Jr treated him generously in retirement.

The hospitality, as one might expect, was unstinting. After that, we never felt the urge to visit Aintree again. How could that experience be topped? I do still have a small yearning for Goodwood.

Harlow equates with difficult labour relations. The Gilbey workers had always been pretty stroppy and their move to Harlow had not helped matters. In reality, the benevolent Gilbeys had paid them too well – especially the drivers – but that had not dulled their enthusiasm for more. The union was well entrenched and we had our first strike the day our first professional head of HR started, although that must have been coincidence.

By the time I got to be UK MD, something had to be done. The problems were not just ours: the 1970s were the worst of times for industrial unrest. We won, but probably not by much, two skirmishes.

First we announced that, as conflicts always resolved themselves eventually but often long after the due dates for pay rises, we would no longer apply the increases to the original due date if they went on strike. Backdating would only take place if no days were lost to industrial action. It seemed to work.

Second, as the drivers were the most militant, we collected quotations from potential outside contractors and details of what they paid their drivers. We shared all that with the drivers themselves and there was no more trouble.

The underlying problem was a basic distrust of management

fomented by the trade union people. The solution was to cut out the union reps as the main source of information for the workforce and substitute the first level of management. The main cause of industrial unrest is the company's own HR function and its readiness to talk with the unions. As a result the union reps usually know more than junior managers about what is actually happening in the company, and therefore become more trusted.

We dealt with that in three ways. First we formalised communications up and down the hierarchy with weekly time allocated specifically to discussing what was happening and what should. One always likes to imagine that boss to subordinate communications are open and good but one has to make sure they truly are.

Secondly we set up a works council which was fashionable at the time but not in GrandMet. IDV top management did not give a damn but GrandMet regarded it as subversive socialist weakness and were worried it might contaminate other parts of the group. I was summoned by a panel of GrandMet directors and they reluctantly withdrew their ban, if not their disapproval. It worked well and the interchanges with the workforce representatives were thoroughly refreshing. The union reps were not allowed to attend and we made sure that management were fully aware of the content before they were.

Thirdly and crucially, we cut off all communications with the union and their reps except what was formally required for wage negotiations. This made them very unhappy and the senior shop steward used to waylay me at the top of the office stairs. Whenever I felt sorry for him, and he was a good man, I remembered the trouble he was inadvertently causing by knowing too much. Union membership and unrest declined.

Tennant decided I needed international experience and should look after South Africa as it was the most similar business to the Home Trade. It had manufacturing, importing, wholesaling and bottle stores (shops). It also had a few awful hotels that had come with the bottle stores. Smirnoff was the main profit earner.

The business had been set up in Pietermaritz in 1951 to make Gilbeys gin. It was managed by John Handford, the son-in-law of the toughest family member, Alec Gold. By the time I encountered Gold at a bridge table in the Bath Club in the 1960s he was retired and seemed mild and charming but, I was told, that was not always so.

As I was to discover, it is not easy setting up a booze business in a distant country and Handford had made a hash of it. The on-site Customs Officer, Allan Bell, saw the opportunity and persuaded London to let him take charge. By all accounts he had been an entrepreneurial Customs man and some things don't change. By the time I arrived, supposedly as his boss, 30 years later, he should have been preparing for retirement but he wasn't. He was a wily old bird and York Gate was convinced he was, as often as not, up to no good.

The company had nearly bankrupted itself a few years earlier but Stanley Lee and Allan Bell had stitched up an excellent deal with the Rembrandt Group (Anton Rupert). Stanley showed great determination. He set up camp in Stellenbosch (by then Gilbey's HQ) and refused to go home until the deal was done. Rather unusually the conclusion was a 50/50 equity split, with refinancing by Rembrandt. They promised not to interfere in the day-to-day running of the business, much to Bell's relief. In Afrikaans South Africa, their backing of an otherwise English business was important.

In 1948 Rembrandt had been created by two Afrikaners, Rupert and Dirk Hertzog. For 40 years Rupert garnered all the publicity whilst Hertzog worked quietly in the background. Both were cracking good marketeers. In keeping with his low key style, Hertzog's office was not in the Rembrandt HQ but the first floor of a traditional home. Their half share of Gilbey South Africa was in Hertzog's charge.

The IDV director visiting South Africa, and therefore Hertzog, would be offered a cup of tea. Hertzog would suck at his pipe and not say much. I was briefed not to raise any business matters but conversation would begin to flow well enough about life in general. After a while, he would indicate that he wanted to tell a story. This appeared to be an old Afrikaner tale of no great interest but you needed to listen carefully. He never spelled it out but there was always a moral: it was always relevant and important for the business. One would be ushered out soon after and left to figure out what the hell he was talking about. The routine was always the same and I admired the man for his wisdom and restraint.

Allan Bell and the Gilbeys company bravely breached apartheid laws. The sales force was hired from all races – black, white and coloured. As a result sales conferences had to be held outside South Africa. We went to Botswana and Swaziland amongst others. At these events, the South Africans liked to show their independence by tossing the visiting UK director fully dressed into the swimming pool. The word was out so one dressed accordingly and there are worse ways to be made fun of.

Bottle stores were legally required to have a separate section for non-whites with the result that 80% of the business was done from a rather nasty 20% of the premises. The Gilbeys stores operated under the name 'Rebel' and rebel they did, albeit quietly, by opening the whole of each store to all-comers. They did get some complaints but these stores were not that profitable and the policy was not entirely altruistic: mixed race stores were more profitable. If a community made a big fuss, it was cheaper to close the store altogether and let the locals get the point.

The CEO of the bottle stores was Christopher Pearman's brother, Trevor, who told me that his promotion to the job was in the Joseph Grinstead mould. He had been summoned on a Saturday to meet Allan and feared he was in trouble. They had a few drinks together and he returned home none the wiser. It was only when others started congratulating him that he discovered he was now CEO.

The company was a fine group of people and they deserved to do better but they were only 10–15% of the market and South Africans play hardball. Whenever South African Brewers' market share dropped below 97%, and it wasn't often, they tended to panic and crush everything in sight. On one occasion they literally did crush everything. A soft drinks competitor started up with rather smart branded bottles. Bottles were returnable in that market so SAB swept them all up, had them crushed and the competitor retired – or so the story goes.

IDV SA's main commercial problem was the overheads, not helped by building a fancy new office building. Bell was resistant to the very suggestion that our two supposedly similar businesses should learn from one another and adopt the better practices of the other. Bell was, in fact, the very model of what we then called a 'Country Baron'. Each country's CEO regarded it as his personal fiefdom: he might, very rarely, import a practice from elsewhere but only when he discovered it himself. The other popular term for this was NIH*. It is less prevalent today but it was a huge problem then.

The irony, of course, was that I was a Country Baron myself. For years Heublein suggested that Smirnoff advertising be harmonised internationally. We would research their ads against ours and never

---

* Not Invented Here, i.e. if the country had not itself come up with it, it would not work in that country.

once did theirs win. The score was about 10–0. There are three possible explanations: ours really were always better, we were researching the familiar against the unfamiliar and the market research agency knew who was paying the bill. Probably all three applied.

The UK team, in turn, thought it ridiculous that a small market like Ireland also insisted on running its own Smirnoff campaign, with all the extra production costs, when they had a dramatically successful campaign on their doorstep. It was NIH but it is a hard habit to crack when country CEOs have full responsibility and have been in place for anything up to 30 years. From Bell's perspective, he did not have to worry about the current London director as another one would be along very soon.

We all have our quirks and one of his was a fondness, when in Natal, for curry – but drinking its natural partner, beer, was a sackable offence. Gilbeys did not sell beer and therefore staff consumption was prohibited. Every visit to Durban involved driving 30 miles up the coast to an undeniably excellent curry house where the food never seemed to arrive but the wine did. It was like Sunday tiffin in Malaya. You might order your food at noon but it would not arrive until 3pm and maybe 4pm. The restaurateur and the Natal team knew the form and, after the first experience, the visitor knew to have a good breakfast. It was no use looking at one's watch. Some business was discussed during these long hours but not a lot. But there is also not a lot wrong with sitting on a Durban beach, in the sunshine, with some good people and a never emptying glass of Twee Jongegezellan.

Bell, once one got to know him, was an amiable old stick and a very likeable man. Business aside he was mad on horses and a senior member of the South African Jockey Club which gave him reciprocal rights all over the world. If you wanted to know the source of trouble it was *cherchez la femme*. Bell's second wife, Diana, took a keen interest in the business, too keen. She was hospitable and kind but she also knew what was best for the company and that meant Allan staying CEO.

Although they were supposedly seeking Bell's successor, no candidates seemed to appear. When pressed, Bell eventually pronounced that his Finance Director, James Botha, should take over. Botha was a cuddly family man who was hired from the auditors largely, in my view, because he did not make the kind of trouble that auditors should. He was also very much an Afrikaaner, a balance the company badly needed. He was a competent Finance Director and although he would not have refused promotion, he would not have been comfortable with it.

London took over the hunt for the successor with Bell's full involvement and we all agreed that Bill Husband was the man. A strike against him was that he was English but he and his wife, also Diana, had lived in South Africa for many years and were well liked by both the white tribes.

Husband was still in a transitional role when the trouble started. Bill's wife being so pretty and also called Diana did not help. Mrs Bell set out to destroy them and thereby keep her husband in place. The only thing going for the Husbands was that everyone in Stellenbosch was aware what was happening so there was some rallying around. The team did not care for Diana Bell that much but they were terrified of her. We in England, of course, were unaware of this and just glad that Bell, with our assistance, had finally found a successor.

By my next visit things had come to a head and Bell and I had a frank discussion about what to do.

'Allan, Diana must stop this. It is undermining the company. Please make her back off.'

'You know Diana. What makes you think I have any influence on her? Why don't you talk to her?' Bell could be something of a wimp.

It seemed there was no alternative but I was terrified too. Indeed my interview with Diana Bell was one of the bravest things I have ever done. It proved not to be as bad as I expected. Diana expressed astonishment that anyone thought she had not been supportive to the sweet new couple. We got over that eventually and she promised to reform, to accept Bell's retirement and to stop meddling in the company. That was the drift. I cannot say the reform was total but it worked.

Husband did a fine job in the circumstances but some malcontents grumbled. I don't know what would have happened in the longer term if he had not fallen sick with motor neurone disease. That is a horrible wasting disease. His wife tended him like a saint and everyone was stricken by his death. I am glad to say that, a few years later, she married happily again.

Peter Fleck, the Marketing Director, was appointed country CEO and maybe should have had the job in the first place. He was a little wild, and perhaps not just a little, as later events were to show, but he was the right man for then. He had grown up in the business and bridged the two white tribes. When South Africans are good at marketing, they are very good and Peter is a fine example.

My last visit to South Africa, in June 1997, was to give a marketing course to senior executives of South African Breweries. Even then it had still not become the hugely successful international marketing group it is today. Then it subsisted on 97% of the South African beer market. As noted above, if their share ever dipped a fraction, they crushed the competitor. To their executives, marketing seemed pointless: why worry about competitors when you do not have any?

Since I had last been there, South Africa had become dangerous. Even in Sandton, the posh suburb of Johannesburg, everyone I met had been carjacked at least once. An alluring divorcee greeted me at the airport and informed me she was my bodyguard and I should consider us joined at the hip for my stay. It was an attractive prospect but she went off duty when she delivered me back to my hotel each evening at 6pm prompt. She was hopping mad when she discovered I had been out to dinner with friends the previous evening.

The remainder of this chapter addresses the other parts of Africa and the Indian Ocean for which I was given responsibility and where our small businesses had been collected together under the title International Distillers Developments, mostly under the charge of David Eaton. Previously Allan Bell had responsibility for all Africa and was none too pleased when IDV took the other territories back under HQ's wing.

Eaton was the third of the able executives hired and developed by Bell – James Espey and Peter Fleck being the other two – and probably the least amenable to normal business practice. I think he owned a suit but he rarely wore it and was happiest out of top management's line of vision. At the same time, I do not know anyone else who could have created and built distilling businesses in the third world so successfully with minimal resources.

Mike Fogden* was MD of the Kenya company which had cunningly stitched up a monopoly. Some years earlier, the government had fussed about that but their anxieties were quelled by giving 30% or so of the action to KWAL, the government's agency business which also involved Saccone & Speed. The details escape me but the bottom

---

* Son of the Chairman of Gilbey Canada. Tom Fogden had started with Gilbey Canada soon after it opened in Toronto in 1933. Presumably aiming to meet the demand from Prohibition USA.

line was that it was a nice cosy little business.

Despite the temptations that monopoly can offer, the company was well run, lean and efficient. And very profitable of course. Glad handing aside, there was little for the visiting director to do except enjoy the Norfolk Hotel (until GrandMet bought the Intercontinental and we moved there), the Muthaiga Club and, just once, the Mount Kenya Club, still the glamorous place created in 1959 by William Holden and a couple of Hollywood film stars. Today it is owned by the Fairmont hotel chain which has doubtless destroyed its character as they have with the Savoy in London.

The Kenya company came up with enterprising ventures including sachets of spirits. Most working Africans could not afford bottles of spirits. They bought tobacco by the cigarette, not the packet. The answer was to supply gin and vodka in small sachets. It worked fine until about 2010 when they ran into trouble with the health lobby. Inevitably perhaps, the packs were too easy for minors to buy.

Malawi and Botswana even less justified visits. They rolled along quite happily when left to themselves. For some historical reason, Malawi sold Malawi Gin, not Gilbeys. Hastings Banda was still in charge, as he was for over 30 years to 1994. The country was poor, poorer and less healthy than it should have been, but otherwise stable enough. Previously 'Nyasaland', it was famous for a naval engagement in the first world war. The Germans and the British each had a boat on the lake armed with a small gun. Supposedly the British heard about the outbreak of war first, trundled over to the other side and sank the German one. They considered that unsporting.

That story is not, however, correct but the authentic one is just as good. A year after the outbreak of war, 28 men commanded by Geoffrey Spicer-Simson, the oldest Lieutenant Commander in the Royal Navy and already court martialled, took two gunboats to the lake via South Africa, a train to the Congo and, using steam engines and mules, through the jungle to the lake. They captured one German gunboat and used it to sink the second. The third, more heavily armed, was later scuttled after a land attack by Belgian and British troops. It has since resurfaced and still trundles round the lake as MV *Liemba*.*

Botswana was also a backwater. The company's performance mirrored that of the farming community. When it rained, it made money

---

* Giles Foden (2004). *Mimi and Toutou Go Forth: The Bizarre Battle for Lake Tanganyika*, London: Michael Joseph

but not if it didn't. My visits to bars, stores and officials could have been written by Alexander McCall Smith.*

A visit to the British High Commissioner reinforced my prejudices about British diplomats overseas. Whatever we wanted seemed important at the time and a meeting was booked for mid-morning. We settled down with cups of tea and outlined the problem to the clearly bored FCO man who kept looking at his watch. Sooner than politeness required, he said he had an urgent meeting to get to and bowled out without agreeing to what we requested.

My colleague and I agreed it had been a waste of our time too. As we now had an hour to kill before our next meeting we stopped off at the golf club for a quick gin and tonic, or rather to check our brands in the bar. There on the first tee was none other than His Excellency – playing alone.

In the course of my international travels with IDV and then with London Business School, he was the worst example. Others were good. We got some good help from the Paris Embassy when we needed help with Martell and our man in Korea was the best – but most of the FCO overseas people I dealt with were hopeless.

IDV's involvement in Mauritius was classic. For 20 years, the Jago team pursued the idea of rivalling Bacardi, then the #1 spirit brand in the world. Around 1970, they identified an island with lots of sugar cane and no distillery, namely Mauritius. It looked like a green island, so the Green Island rum brand was born. They went to the IDV board for approval.

'Well, Tom, that all looks very good but how will you transport the rum for bottling in the UK? You tell us there are no bottling facilities on the island and we have very little direct trade.'

'I am suggesting we buy a small tanker to transport the bulk liquid.'

This scheme had a number of problems. One shipload would be enough for 10 years even if the brand took off. What would the tanker do the rest of the time and, indeed, transport back to Mauritius? IDV had no experience of running a ship. Half the board were unsure of the location of Mauritius was and assumed it was in the West Indies. The tanker idea was scrapped.

Incredible as it may seem, the distillery was half built by then and

---

* *No.1 Ladies' Detective Agency* novels

they decided to persevere regardless. We then had a distillery in the middle of the Indian Ocean with no way to get the rum off the island. Enter David Eaton who liked problems like that.

In no time he built a bottling line and started exporting Green Island in cases. Exports did not take off and they started selling it on the island where it did. It didn't seem to me, then or now, that being a me-too to Bacardi with no pedigree or rationale was ever going to work. David Gluckman's next white rum effort, Stubbs 20 years later, stood a better chance, being premium to and tasting better than Bacardi. It had a good Queensland story but that failed as well. By the time I took over, Eaton had built, on Mauritius, a thriving domestic wines and spirits business on the back of burgeoning tourism.

I am not disparaging Tom Jago's new brand development team. They were far more successful than any before or since. The economics are important. Failures in new brand launches, if you did them our way, cost very little. Successes make a great deal. So one could afford any number of failures: the two important things were to keep building expertise (by finding out what went wrong) and to keep trying.

Eaton had also built the most efficient sales and distribution team. UK sales people averaged 12 calls a day whereas he was claiming 60, including making the deliveries.

'David, I don't believe it.'

'Come and see for yourself' – so I did.

Mauritius is a small island and the stores and bars are crowded together, which helps. The salesman rode in the delivery lorry with the driver and his mate. In the UK, when a salesman drops by he waits for the customer to finish his business before engaging with the shop or pub manager/owner. Not in Mauritius. The mate would immediately start delivering what the salesman thought would be needed whilst the latter checked the outlet's stocks. This would get the manager/owner's immediate attention. Farce would then develop with the manager/owner waving his arms to prevent more cases coming in and the salesman now getting into negotiation mode. Any outlet customers had to wait. Finally the salesman would collect the cash for what had been delivered. Terrific but no chance of getting the Brits to match it. And yes, it was 50 to 60 drops a day.

Mauritius was a great place to tack on a few days holiday and I did, once with Katie. On one flight back to Nairobi, I happened to sit next to the Kenyan Finance Minister. He was friendly and we saw each other a few times, once at home in St John's Wood. Unfortunately one of our cats insisted on sitting on his lap but he took it in good part. I mention this only because of the lovely story he told of his own foreign travel.

Thanks to apartheid South Africa was, at that time, a pariah in the view of other African countries. Nonetheless there was a conference of African finance ministers in Johannesburg and almost all showed up including Kenya's. About half way through he ran out of cash and took his travellers' cheques to the bank. The cashier, refusing to accept them, pointed to a stamp on the back: 'Valid in all countries of the world except South Africa, by order of the Finance Minister, Kenya.'

'But I am the Finance Minister and I say it's OK.'

'Sorry, but I can only go by what the cheques say.'

I have no recollection of the logic, if any, of building another green island distillery, this time in Sri Lanka in the 1980s. The first had been trouble enough. The market opportunity was seen as the gap between the domestic spirits market, mostly arrack, and imported western brands. Sri Lanka is the world's largest manufacturer of arrack which is distilled toddy, the fermented sap from unopened coconut flowers. It is easy for westerners to be snooty about arrack but it is the Sri Lankan national spirit and they are as proud of it as the Scots are about Scotch. I don't think we quite understood that.

As Sri Lanka has plenty of sugar cane in the south around Galle, Eaton and the technical team built the distillery there. It wasn't a major problem but it was 100 miles from the company HQ and bottling plant at Kaduwela, 10 miles east of Colombo.

All things considered Eaton did well but we had underestimated the problem. Consumers were quite happy with arrack and did not want Western brands. The market was dominated by the government-owned Distilleries Company, since privatised. They were not going to make life easy for an intruder. And the tax on 'foreign liquor' was 20% higher than arrack. It would have been cheaper to redistill arrack as we discovered for Nigeria next but we did not think of that then and it wasn't really the problem.

Ever flexible, Eaton switched to making premium arrack part of the portfolio. If you cannot beat them, join them. When Christopher Pearman took over from me, bringing more professional sales management, sales rose to 10-15% of the market, a perfectly adequate return on our investment. When I last looked, International Distillers was still in operation in Sri Lanka with the same market share. Merely surviving over 20 years in a market like that is a success.

My last involvement with a new distillery was in Nigeria. Gilbey's man covering Black Africa, Adrian Houghton, had previously worked for Guinness Cameroon. I first came across him at a Home Trade vs. York Gate cricket match in Harlow. We had use of the main ground which was Essex county standard but not much used.

Houghton announced over lunch that, as an international player, he should bat #3 for York Gate. I kept quiet about the new salesman, David Surridge, we had hired when he retired from opening the bowling for Gloucestershire. He had a Cambridge blue (1979) and played part time for his native Hertfordshire while he was with IDV. I instructed him to bowl at half pace off a short run. The York Gate team would cry 'ringer' if they knew who he was.

I was standing umpire as Surridge came in to bowl. He may have been half pace but it looked very quick to me and Houghton never saw it at all. The stumps were demolished.

'Not out.' We never allowed players to be out first ball. The other umpire repaired the wicket. The next ball was identical with the same result.

At tea I asked, 'Adrian, I thought you said you were an international player.'

'I was. I played for the Cameroon but the French don't play cricket.'

At a callover soon after, Tennant said:

'Have you considered Nigeria as our next country development?'

I provided a long list of reasons why Nigeria was a really bad idea. A few days later by phone:

'Tim, have you considered Nigeria as our next country development?'

Tennant tended not to take 'no' for an answer and he always asked questions rather than issue instructions so I got the message and summoned Eaton who listed all the objections I had already made.

Out of the blue, Houghton surfaced saying he had heard we were interested in Nigeria. Could he help? It was part of his Gilbey territory and he had contacts there. Some time later, it transpired that Houghton had decided that IDV should enter that market and phoned the Chairman of Guinness to ask him to suggest it to Tennant. Guinness, of course, had a huge and very successful brewery in Nigeria. The locals believe the black stuff was highly beneficial for night time activities. Tennant was flattered, if puzzled, by the call but never admitted the source of his enthusiasm to me.

Eaton reconnoitred the market and came back with a great wheeze. As the excise taxes on western liquors were prohibitive, they were smuggled in for the black market. The only alternative was locally distilled under primitive conditions. It went under different names such as kai kai, but around Lagos it was called ogogoro. Our technical people analysed a sample and pronounced it lethal but if it was as lethal as all that, the population of Nigeria would have been falling, not rising. I limited myself to a sip and it was pretty disgusting.

Since they could not lock up all the local distillers even if they could find them, the Nigerian government pronounced that these locally distilled spirits need pay no duty, i.e. they were 'duty paid'. If we distilled spirits from scratch, we would have had to pay full duty but if, and this was the wheeze, we were merely rectifying spirits that were already duty paid, we would have no further duty to pay.

This would require formal government approval. Houghton introduced us to one of his contacts, the splendid Chief Dotun Okubanjo who lived in Lagos but headed a tribe a dozen miles north in Ikeja. Okubanjo knew everyone, or claimed to. Certainly any visit to his club was just a trail of glad-handing. We put a presentation together to explain why giving us a licence would be good for Nigeria and good for the Nigerian economy. In particular, it would help reduce the smuggling, a matter of great irritation to the government. We spent hours sitting in corridors waiting to meet ministers and senior civil servants. Eventually we got our licence.

The other issue was funding the new company. The currency, the naira, looked a little dodgy and indeed proved so. In 1980 US$1= 0.55 naira. By the late 1990s, US$1 = 22 naira. The trick therefore was to finance the enterprise entirely in naira, thus eliminating the sterling risk in London and ensuring that the percent return on investment would be unaffected by the changing value of the naira. Financing would therefore have to be a combination of local equity and bank loans.*

Okubanjo produced various candidates as local investors and one day phoned in a great state of excitement.

'We may have just the investor we need.'

---

* The banks wanted London guarantees on the loans but they were glad to make them as Nigeria was in recession (part of our rationale for a licence) and demand for loans was low. If London had to make good the guarantee, it would have been in naira at the then rate so this was still an all naira deal.

'Who is that?'

'The Emir of Kano.'

'Dotun, you must be joking. He is not just head of state, he is the head of the Muslim faith in that part of the world and this is alcohol.'

'He is the third most important man in Nigeria and could be hugely influential for us. He has just invested in a pig farm but he does not eat pork so where is the problem?'

After further enquiries with his people, it emerged that the Emir would indeed be interested and would visit us when next in London. Soon thereafter we were informed he would join us for lunch on a certain Sunday and the only day he was free. He was happy to come to York Gate with two or three staff. We were briefed on protocol:

'Obviously you will not be serving wine with lunch and please would you also remove any bottles from sight?'

'He does realise International Distillers and Vintners is in the wine and spirit business?'

'Of course, that is why we are meeting you. It is just a matter of discretion. Oh, and by the way, strict Muslims do not like to be associated with tobacco either.'

'Now you are going too far. If I want a cigar after lunch in my own house, I shall have one.'

'Harrumph.'

The staff accepted Sunday working well enough and we were all intrigued by the situation. Lunch got off to a theatrical start with the Emir's consigliere leaping to his feet and accusing us of serving pork.

'I think you will find it is smoked turkey.'

He had been baleful since they arrived and thankfully we did not hear from him again. When the cigars arrived, the Emir accepted one with much pleasure.

Alhaji Dr. Ado Abdullahi Bayero, to give him his full title, is an impressive man, born 1930 and therefore 53 at the time of this account. He rivals the Queen in that he has reigned since 1963. He has had to balance the modernism he personally favours with respect for tradition and for the Muslim faith in particular. He has tried hard to keep the peace between Christians and Muslims and between north and south. He is very bright, charming and good company.

No business was discussed during lunch but we were invited to visit him in Kano when next in Nigeria. He would have an answer for us then. Okubanjo and I therefore made an appointment and attended the Emir's audience. He sat on the throne and the petitioners sat cross-legged on the floor. We, mercifully, were given chairs. I doubt if Okubanjo would have stood any more chance of crossing his legs than I did. Hausa country (Kano was the historical capital but had been replaced) was as foreign to a Yoruba like Okubanjo as it was to me. Kano is 460 miles north of Lagos.

The whole palace set up was medieval. We may sometimes think time has stopped in our royal palaces but there it truly had. Petitions were heard and answers handed down until it got to our turn. Most of the locals were flummoxed by this as their English was about as good as my Hausa. Unlike in York Gate, the conversation was stilted and formal. We made our proposal, and the Emir appeared to consider it. I cannot remember if the answer came from him or the dreaded consigliere but after much flowery language, the answer was 'no'. The Emir hoped the venture would be successful and would be happy to help behind the scenes. He also hoped we would be his guests at the next Durbar. These events are spectacular and I am still sorry we never took it up. Katie might not have enjoyed Nigeria in general but she would certainly have enjoyed that and indeed Kano. We saw them dyeing cloths in pits as they had for hundreds of years with the famous indigo blue (it denotes wealth in that part of Africa) and I believe they still do.*

Whether he really was helpful in getting government approval, I have no means of knowing, but with government approval and funding in place we could begin work on the factory on, guess what, land from Okubanjo's home village. In my travels around the world, Okubanjo stands out as one of my favourite people. Like so many Yoruba men, he was interested in talking, socialising and having fun. Work was a four letter word and its practice could safely be left to the ladies, as could money-making with the exception of web-based fraud, a Nigerian male speciality. Almost all village level commerce, and especially smuggling, was done by the women and so was agriculture, household chores, shopping and bringing up children. One of the reasons that the discovery of oil proved such a blight on Nigeria was that it destroyed agriculture; money, albeit in the east, now came out of the ground with much less effort. It did not take much for Yoruba men to hang up their spades. We noted that when we socialised and it was Okubanjo's turn to pay, it was always his wife Elizabeth who did so.

---

* Kriger, Colleen E. & Connah, Graham (2006). *Cloth in West African History.* Rowman Altamira.

Okubanjo almost always wore his flamboyant national costume and this was undoubtedly a plus with westerners. The only time I saw him in a European suit was when we were meeting in a hotel lobby and I did not recognise him.

Amazingly (in Nigeria) the factory got built, went into production and selling began more or less on time. Eaton was getting good at this. The issue of managerial staff was more tricky, not least for the reasons above and of trust. Those of us with access to the web know how creative Nigerians can be in financial matters. We employed three Brits and about 50 locals. The problem centred around Okubanjo's relatives not all of whom performed, shall we say, as desired. Moving them on was difficult but ultimately achieved and the business did well, if not as superbly as we hoped.

Perhaps the most memorable part of the adventure was a Sanders of the River* experience. I asked to visit an ogogoro distillery. As discussed above, local distillation was not really illegal, and the products were freely on sale, but it wasn't legal either. It is a bit like prostitution in England: selling one's services is not illegal but owning a brothel is. So the distilleries were hidden in the bush.

We drove out of Lagos and stopped in the middle of nowhere which looked like every other part of nowhere. It turned out to be a short walk to a river where a flotilla of canoes awaited us. These were the most primitive canoes I had ever encountered, simply hollowed out tree trunks. Each could only take one passenger before the water pouring in through the knot holes sank the boat.

It was idyllic, not unlike the Cherwell on a sunny day. After a few twists and turns we found what we were looking for: a large pool with bubbling vats on wood fires with copper pipes in all directions. The water came up into the vats without any filtration, sterilisation or purification. The distillation itself was supposed to take care of that. The water was clean enough for the half dozen naked girls jumping into it and splashing around. They were about 15 or 16 and delighted to have an attentive audience.

The head distiller told me proudly that they understood the importance of passing distillations through copper (he was right on that). The copper pipes were a home heating kit bought in an English DIY

---

* *Sanders of the River* is a 1911 Edgar Wallace story of a British Commissioner in the colonial Nigeria which was turned into a 1935 film. It includes the splendid briefing: 'Don't expect any recognition in this post. The only decorations you will get here are mosquito bites.'

store and smuggled back. I had a small taster and congratulated him knowing that it would soon be cleaned up and become 'Eagle Schnapps' from Ikeja. The place was a Garden of Eden and there were no reptilian Excise Officers to spoil the fun.

I cannot now recall why Eaton started with Eagle Schnapps but it went well enough and was joined in 1987 by Chelsea Gin. The managers of Smirnoff and Gilbeys refused to grant licences and that was understandable.

Twenty years later, I was indignant to discover that, as a consequence of the merger, Diageo had passed on International Distillers Nigeria to a 100% national company, Intercontinental Distillers Ltd., who claimed, in splendid Nigerian fashion, 'The Genesis of our company dates back to more than two and half centuries ago precisely in 1749 when two Italians, Justerini and Brooks, came together to form a wine and spirit business which they called J & B.'*

Intercontinental Distillers introduced Bull London Dry Gin and Bull Dark Rum, no doubt in gratitude to Sir George, Chairman of Diageo when they acquired the business.

I was told that the Nigerian government had claimed malpractice and London believed they were correct. The company was accused of not paying duty on the local spirits sold. That, of course, was the very thing the company was licensed to do as the files would have reminded both Diageo and the government. My indignation arose from the apparent acceptance of the accusation of malpractice. The terms of the licence had been negotiated in the full light of day as anyone could have checked. Secondly nobody consulted me. I was actually rather proud of what we achieved. The company had made money all along and never cost London a penny.

On reflection, Diageo was right to do as they did. Apparently the Nigerian government was threatening Guinness' huge, and very profitable, brewing interests in the country and it would have been unwise to challenge their version of events. Furthermore, they were entitled at any time to change Nigerian law and make the ogogoro deal illegal. We had been dependent on goodwill and International Distillers Nigeria was, in the scheme of things, a minnow.

For an account of the rest of my time with IDV, the story returns to York Gate, our new home in St John's Wood and the Americas.

---

* http://www.idlng.com/aboutcompany.html.

# Chapter 9

# Global Marketeer

*This chapter is one of transition. First it is farewell to the comfortable life of IDV UK and Debden. It covers:*
- *Our new home in St John's Wood*
  - *Katie gets a job*
  - *Gus gets a job too*
  - *Jury Service*
  - *Jason gets another wife*
  - *And then yet another*
- *Global Marketing Director: Everything and nothing*
  - *Counter alcohol terrorism*
  - *Acquisitions*
  - *Martell*
  - *A Seagram Postscript*
- *IDV in the Americas*
  - *Gilbey Canada*
  - *Carillon, USA*
  - *Paddington, USA*
  - *Uruguay*
  - *Heublein, USA*
- *Goodbye to GrandMet*
  - *Organisational issues*
  - *Annual planning*
  - *Time to say 'goodbye'*

I had been happily IDV UK's MD for three or four years when Tennant asked me to dinner. A Scot buying dinner should have alerted suspicion but, naively, I did not twig his motive. He inquired about my career aspirations, I said I was quite happy where I was and we went on to other matters. The next week, James Espey, who he had imported from South Africa to be Global Marketing Director, and I were advised that we were switching jobs. Espey was also on the IDV board and in terms of status pay and perks the jobs were the same – but I was not pleased. I was switching a country barony for advising other country barons.

With the benefit of hindsight, Tennant was quite right and I would have done the same. I was getting stale in Harlow and the senior team were resenting my stream of helpfulness. Espey took a much more cheerful and relaxed approach. And the life international, as discussed in the previous chapter, was full of interest.

The Saffron Walden to Regent's Park commute was a pain. The mornings were fine but flogging back through Liverpool Street and never knowing which train one would catch was grim. Katie generously (she loved Debden) agreed we should live within walking distance of York Gate. That meant walking across Regent's Park but Primrose Hill was a bit steep, the east side was mostly grotty so we settled for St John's Wood.

I saw our home-to-be on a beautiful summer's day, usually a mistake. The main room was originally two and french windows at the back opened onto a charming garden which in turn backed onto all the large gardens of Hamilton Terrace. The house was early Victorian with the right number of rooms and bathrooms on three floors: lower and upper ground and first. The owner was playing, rather well, a grand piano by the french windows. Breezes wafted through. Despite the noisy road in front, I fell in love with it at once. Round the corner in Hamilton Terrace would have been better but twice the price.

Today it does not bear thinking about but armed with nothing more than a spade, I opened up the rather dark kitchen living room by digging down three feet of garden and moving the horrible London clay to the far end to form a terrace along with stone pillars, timber rafters and lighting for night-time eating. With a black iron staircase down from the drawing room and my new brick staircase up from the kitchen, I reckoned it all looked *House and Garden*. The stone pillars were erected by Katie and Gus with much complaint but someone has to supervise these things.

Unusually for any part of London, we had a capacious garage and also space, just, for two cars to park in front. The delightful little Victorian front garden, much admired by passers by, is now gone. Being just 100 yards from Lord's we were not surprised, at Test Match time, by the good friends we did not know we had enquiring sweetly if space might be available for their motors.

Moving to London was no reason to abandon our autumn bonfires – christened 'bonks' by Gus when three. Clouds of smoke drifting across a main highway was a bad idea but only one couple, American again, ever objected. Parents should embarrass children and I did manage to do so to Gus when he joined us with a girlfriend for supper one evening and, during a lull in the conversation, I said,

'Lovely afternoon yesterday. Your mother and I had a bonk in the back garden.'

I thought the girl looked at me with new respect.

Most importantly, our two Debden cats, Paisley* and Steffie, took to St John's Wood as if they were returning home. They could, and did, forage far up Hamilton Terrace and their social life improved markedly.

They also enjoyed weekends in Cley. Even in winter the cottage warmed up in 30 minutes which was about as long as it took them to impose their authority on the local cats. After that amount of time yowling and hissing, peace would break out and they would return to the cottage looking smug.

Two of the most hospitable locals were, and indeed still are, Patricia and John Glasswell who live(d) round the corner in Hamilton Terrace. Drinks and supper parties apart, they gave an annual Victorian evening at which most, if not everyone, was supposed to do a turn. I have a weakness for these things and my enthusiasm is only matched by my incompetence. One occasion was just saved when the famous musician and conductor, Sir Charles Mackerras, a friend of the Glaswells, left just before my turn to stand up and sing 'Caro mio ben'. Not my finest hour. As one of the audience put it:

'I used to like that song.'

Patricia is a good water colourist and John is highly placed in the world of fencing. Like many other Yorkshire people, Patricia is fun but determined. She is prepared to organise one's life whether one wants that or not. Maybe my own Yorkshire genes are to blame but I regard that as helpfulness rather than bossiness. One can always say 'no'. Anyway, she decided to manage Katie's and it was a great success.

Thanks to her introduction, Katie was employed as an apprentice picture restorer in Landseer's old studio just down the road. It was a very old-fashioned business under the care of Charlie Butcher and his

---

* An Orange tom named after the Revd. Ian Paisley. We were told all orange cats are male so called the other, rather shy, kitten Zephaniah (the Lord hideth away) but rebranded her Steffie when she turned out to be female.

two sons, Ray and David. Most of the pictures were Victorian oils brought along by the dealers. Over the 10 years she was there, they trained her to a high professional standard and, when she came to Norfolk, she practised on her own account until she became too irritated by ignorant clients to continue.

A fellow apprentice, Laura Hoskins, was a year ahead and became a lifelong friend. She was Mike's second wife and they met when she was cabin crew with PanAm. No surprise that as she is always very lively and competent in many areas, notably in golf and as a magistrate. She was Ladies Captain at Highgate Golf Club where Mike had also been Captain. Sadly for us, he announced that, after 20 years or so in London, it was his turn to retire to his native America. They picked a lovely spot, with British-type seasons in the hills of North Carolina.

Gus was pleased when we moved from Debden. He was 14 by then and fancied the bright lights. We were delighted to forsake sitting outside kids' parties until midnight at which time we were permitted to ferry them home. Black cabs are marvellous.

By this time we had acquired a holiday cottage in Cley, in Gus's name for tax reasons, and he had moved on to Downside. That proved a disaster. All the things that were lucky for me were unlucky for him. The headmaster turned all academic matters over to a dim-witted Head of Studies. What is the point of a headmaster who is not a headmaster? Gus's housemaster, Dom James, was just learning the job and, albeit a lovely and talented man, had not yet acquired the necessary skills. In short, Gus neither enjoyed it nor profited from it.

Patricia, who lived closer, entered into the spirit of things. She began by asking 'this young monk' where she would find the Abbot. 'I am the Abbot.'

He was fortunate enough to be given the benefit of Patricia's views on matters monastic and thereafter asked to be warned when she was visiting so that he could go into hiding.

Gus's teenage arrived in his twenties, just when we thought we had escaped. It struck during university vacations and was not immediately obvious because Gus would be asleep when we were up and vice versa. Irritating but tolerable. Clearly a job would be a good idea. I helped get him a job with IBM for one vacation. They were kind to him, too kind, and gave him an alarm clock as his leaving present. After copious, according to Gus, searches, he announced there were no vacation jobs.

'The estate agent down the road has an ad in the window asking for help. Try that.'

He did and it worked quite well. His hair at that time stuck out about a 30cms in all directions. He said his manager did not mind so why should we? When we met the manager over drinks a while later, he told us that Gus said: 'My parents don't mind so why should you?'

Normal hair was resumed.

Being an estate agent was not for Gus but it did get him started in the property world. A master's degree at Cass (City) Business School in property followed and a job with Murley Wood – it was just the three of them plus a secretary – safely guided him through the Chartered Surveyor exams. We even made a few small property investments together.

Then he moved into one of the world's biggest commercial property firms for a dozen years, DTZ.* Even better, we helped him buy a house in Battersea from Ian Hislop, Editor, *Private Eye*. He was a delight to do business with. Gus's lodgers, some quite decorative, paid the mortgage. We'll pick up his story towards the end of the book.

All previous summonses for jury service had been escaped by nipping off to visit the colonies but this one arrived with menaces. I knew the form and rocked up at Southwark Crown Courts in my best suit, old school tie and a *Financial Times* under the arm. The officer allocating juries to cases knew the form too and, with a wink, said he'd send me home once the defence counsel had objected to my inclusion. Amazingly he didn't but the officer assured me it would be a short one and I could go after that.

It turned out, as many others have found, to be an interesting experience, if tedious. Time and again the usher corralled us in the jury room whilst the judge discussed matters with counsel. The courtroom with the robed and bewigged judge on high was, though modern,

---

* Their website: 'DTZ, a UGL company, is a global leader in property services. We provide occupiers and investors with industry leading, end to end property solutions comprised of leasing agency and brokerage, integrated property and facilities management, capital markets, investment and asset management, valuation, building consultancy and project management.

DTZ has 47,000 employees including sub-contractors, operating across 208 offices in 52 countries.'

most impressive. During one of these intermissions, I mentioned that it was Derby day and we should have a sweep on the big race, £1 per head. Some grumbling but it was agreed.

'What about including the judge?'

'Don't be ridiculous!'

Back in the court, I scribbled a note, folded it over and beckoned the usher.

'Please give this to the judge.'

Deeply suspicious and dying to know what was in it, he did as asked. The judge took one look at it and swept out.

My fellow jurors were not impressed. 'Now you've done it.' 'What exactly is Contempt of Court?'

A court official whispered in the ears of the two counsel and they too swept out. Three minutes later they were all back in place and the judge pronounced:

'I have received a communication from the jury. On the understanding that the offer is available also to counsel, it is accepted. Now can we get on with our business.'

By this time the usher, still ignorant of the note's content, was beside himself. Ushers like to know what is going on. By the afternoon he had relaxed. He had discovered that the judge, highly amused, had read the note to his fellow judges over lunch. It read: 'Your Honour, it is Derby day and we are having a sweep on the big race. If you'd like to come in on it, we will trust you for the £1.' In the event it was won by the Prosecuting Counsel and it may have been some small consolation for losing the case.

In the jury room we quickly agreed that the defendant probably was guilty but we couldn't give that verdict because the Counsel had so messed up her case that she had failed to make the charges stick. We agreed that any one of us could have done a better job. I hope she bought a nice bottle of wine with the winnings.

Jason is so keen on monogamy that he keeps doing it – four times thus far. His second wife, Eve, and their children, Felicity and Nicholas, went with him to France when he became the French manager for a smart German accessories business – but things did not work out well for the marriage or the business and Eve took the children back to Australia.

Soon after, Jason suggested a drink when I'm next in Paris and we met in the rather gloomy downstairs bar at the Intercontinental where I was staying. He was with a very pretty 17-year-old who did not say much on account of the fact that she did not speak English. I can understand Jason's French quite well but French people have not acquired his ways with the language. It emerged that they were engaged, soon to be married. My congratulations were a bit perfunctory as the age gap was worrying – Jason was over 40 by then. In the light of day, my age worries eased.

She is not just pretty but funny and charming and her family own a block of exceptionally handsome flats in the VIIth arrondissement. Jason and Joelle were given free use of one of them. Her family is from Bordeaux. It was a quiet wedding with the big celebrations reserved for the christening of their child, Sophie.

Katie's brother Roger, otherwise known as Biggles, had the bright idea of flying me down in a light aircraft borrowed for the occasion and Katie back. We told all concerned but not that it would take two days, unlike the hour and a half that BA takes. The first sign of trouble at Biggin Hill was that, after numerous delays, our plane was still not back from France so we took a Piper Cub, still in its WWII camouflage.

We had hair-raising landings at Deauville and Arromanches – where he capitalized on some Normandy landings celebrations – and by the time we got to Bordeaux, the families were hysterical and demanding to know why we had not phoned. Explaining that we were having such a good time we forgot, did not seem wise. We were (just) in time for the christening which was just as well as Katie was godmother to little Sophie. Katie had a less fraught return once they identified which part of Sussex they were flying over (it was Roedean).

I returned to find our front door knocked in. It being St John's Wood, no one had noticed it to the point of informing the police. This burglar got away with all our silver. The next burglar was not so lucky. I had greased the drainpipes and installed barbed wire which is illegal. The PC told me that Health and Safety did not allow the potential risk to burglars. But we had no more burglars and the police did not prosecute. Katie said it was time to leave.

Jason was responsible for his break up with Joelle. He was now the agent for various brands of upmarket women's clothing: 'travelling in frocks' did not amuse. German suppliers were more expensive but the clothes were more fashionable and the right goods appeared at the right time. None of these things were true of his British suppliers.

Katie regarded this marriage break-up as one too many and she was especially upset for her goddaughter. Sophie is nearly 30 now (2013) and has weathered it all very well thanks to her mother and step-father Richard, perhaps, but she is on good terms with, and close to, her father. Jason is much loved by his children.

Not long after I joined London Business School, Jason called. There was someone he wanted me to meet. Where have I heard this before? We had drinks at the Landmark Hotel and I was introduced to Roshini, an attractive and charming Sri Lankan woman. Wedding bells could be heard in the distance. I suggested to Jason that he might want to visit the men's room.

'Does she know about the other ones?'

'Er, yes, up to a point.'

This marriage too had its ups and downs and, at the time of writing, Jason is on his own again but I am not betting that it will be for long.

A multinational group has, relative to a single country business, considerable extra cost from the corporate HQ and international travel. In theory that is more than offset by the ability of the countries to share expertise, to learn from what works and what doesn't, to share research and advertising production costs and so on. In short the benefits of sharing should outweigh the costs of the global overhead.

A global group made up of country barons and, worse still, global brand managers insisting they know best, has the worst of all worlds. Our executives were intelligent people who could see the problem but *amour propre* did not allow that understanding to be converted to practice. Conferences helped chip away at NIH* and it was more effective when the global managers were persuaded to lay aside their own splendid ideas and simply market one country's successes elsewhere. Learning from failure is potentially far more valuable but few executives admit to it.

So the whole *raison d'être* of a Group Marketing Director was dubious at that time. The walls did crumble eventually and today it more or less works as it should. In between trying to demolish country ramparts, life was filled with responding to the unprincipled anti-alcohol lobby and new acquisitions.

The anti-alcohol lobby are terrorists because they are unscrupu-

---

* 'Not Invented Here.'

lous in their own methods but cry 'foul' the moment the industry slips up.

But these are good well-intentioned people. We disarmed much of the antagonism by attending their events and buying them booze at the bar. No amount of alcohol is excessive for an anti-alcohol lobbyist. We assured them, as was the truth, that we were just as interested in the health of our customers as they were. 'Dead customers ring no tills' was my expression of that at the time.

One could get a bit pious about all this. In one of my very few TV appearances, I was challenged about young people going into off-licences and buying for their parents, or so they claimed. 'Outrageous,' says I, 'that is illegal and the law must be upheld.' You can guess what happens next. I got home and told Gus, then aged 14:

'I've had a heavy day. Just nip round to Mr Patel and get me a couple of beers.'

'Dad, I've just seen you on TV ...'

Having a convenience store as a neighbour was indeed very convenient and the Patels were a lovely family. They took Katie up to see their new, bright and shiny Hindu Neasden Temple constructed in 1992/5 following 'ancient Vedic architectural texts – using no structural steel whatsoever.' (website)[*] Mr Patel tended to become hysterical at any mention of immigrants.

'What are these people doing? We do not want them here.'

'But Mr Patel you and all your family are immigrants.'

'Not at all. We are British.'

In addition to bandying research, defending alcohol advertising (the code we devised in the 1970s did not need much revision) we took three strategic initiatives. Firstly we set up a library and information service[†] covering this whole field but impartially (unlike the terrorists). Once it was seen to be robust and capable of meeting hostile media enquiries, the plan was to open it up from the trade only to all comers. When the time came, my trade colleagues chickened out so the whole enterprise lost its rationale, at least for a time. It seems to have survived but I am not sure how its role has changed

---

[*] 2820 tonnes of Bulgarian limestone and 2000 tonnes of Italian Carrara marble were shipped to India, carved by over 1500 craftsmen and reshipped to London. In all, 26,300 carved pieces were assembled like a giant jigsaw puzzle in less than 3 years

[†] According to the web, the Centre For Information On Beverage Alcohol was incorporated on 28 Mar 1988, but it got going operationally earlier than that.

and how it now relates to the International Center for Alcohol Policies since set up by the same companies in Washington DC.*

Secondly, I thought we should be seen to be marketing adult drinks in much the same way but with one difference: they would not be alcoholic. So Callitheke was born with an intended range of five drinks although we stopped after three. Dexter's was an isotonic (revitalising) after-sports drink, up market of Lucozade Sport launched just before. The Americans also launched isotonic drinks at this time but theirs tasted horrid whereas the British ones were enjoyable. We got Dexter's into the target markets like Hurlingham but it did no more than wash its face.

Aqua Libra was another matter. It was conceived as a white wine substitute for ladies who lunch. Harrods took it at once and the brand charged away; we could not keep up. In an effort for authenticity – one has to justify a premium price somehow – we claimed it was a Swiss formula. Technically this was true but the formula came from, with a little prompting, the Swiss aunt of one of our marketing team. Success has its dangers, not least from competitors, and Aqua Libra was too hot, too soon. The *Daily Mail* ran a double page spread exposing the brand's background. That did us no good at all. I think we could have fixed the problem with the right advertising in the right quantity but by then GrandMet's enthusiasm, such as it ever had for the strategy, had worn off.

That was a pity because the third brand, Purdey's, was a slow burner but much the most successful. It was a precursor of Red Bull and similarly aimed at clubbers; Damiana was one of the herbs and that would keep you going. The package looked like a hand grenade and was very effective. Purdeys, the long established sporting gunmaker, grumbled about the name but right was on our side.

Sadly Callitheke was sold off and the brands then mismanaged. I reckon it as a small success, too small, rather than a failure and Claire Watson, one of our first graduate intake in the 1970s, did a fine job launching the company and its brands. Happily she went on to grander things in GrandMet and then Director General of the Marketing Society. She now runs her own consulting business.

Thirdly, we created a public face for the industry, first in the UK, the Portman Group, and then a similar operation in the USA, the Century Council. Both countries had separate trade associations for

---

* http://www.icap.org

the different types of alcoholic drinks, beer, wine etc., but neither had a common front to defend all such drinks against the terrorists. Sometimes these trade associations warred against each other and you would have thought it obvious that cooperation was essential.

The UK got going first. The idea was to have a body to promote responsible behaviour by the industry, i.e. not doing anything to damage the health of our customers. Second, the body would publicise that responsibility, point to the inconsistencies and errors in the claims made by the terrorists and be whiter than white in dealings with the government and media.

The chairmen of the two largest UK brewers managed to block the universal agreement by everyone else for maybe five years. They never made a coherent objection, just a veto. I presume it was NIH: brewers regard themselves as the kingpins and don't like being told what to do by wine and spirit people. When they retired, the Portman Group was formed in 1989 with John Rae, previously headmaster of Westminster, in charge. He did an excellent job.

Peter Mitchell, then with Guinness, who had been part of the team setting up Portman, proposed the trade did the same in the USA. He called it the California Project. The main antagonists in the US were the Mothers Against Drunk Driving (MADD) but there was a mass of others, many of whom thought that although they could vote and fight for their country at 18, no alcohol should pass their lips before they were 21. It was a modified form of prohibition and makes little sense to Europeans. The minimum drinking age, as distinct from the minimum age for purchasing alcohol, in the UK is five.

The logic for what became the Century Council was the same and getting it going took several years for similar reasons. The dominant brand in wine was Gallo and the other winemakers tended to take their lead on these matters from the Gallo CEO, Ernest Gallo. Similarly, beer companies took their lead from the Anheuser-Busch (Budweiser) CEO August Busch III, and spirits from Edgar Bronfmann Sr. (Seagram). The trouble was not just differences between the sectors so much as these three families hating each other for historical and personal reasons. Furthermore, each was used to having his own way.

I was contracted, somewhat reluctantly, by GrandMet to set up the California project and Seagram's insisted on having their man bird-dog me. In fact Steve Herbits was very valuable and we worked well together. Herbits had had various powerful offices including being the Special Assistant to Secretary of Defense Donald Rumsfeld from

1976-7. When we joined up he had just become Seageam's Executive Vice President, External Affairs and Corporate Policy and served a total of eight years in that role. The Americans decided it would be good to have an ex-ambassador be CEO of the Century Council as such a person would carry weight with government and the anti-alcohol lobby and be seen as independent of the beverage alcohol business. Herbits found John Gavin who had retired from a five-year spell as Ambassador to Mexico in 1986. He was a Hollywood actor and good friend of Ronald Reagan who appointed him. It was a *bona fide* inside track.

Gavin was a handsome man, a joy to work with, and as civilised as grand Americans can be.* He was married to another handsome and charming Hollywood star, Connie Towers.† If Gavin had a weakness, and one cannot belittle him and his achievements, it was that he had no commercial experience. Luckily, his friend Peter Dailey, ex US Ambassador to Ireland, backed him up and filled any gaps.

There were times when Herbits and I seemed to be the two organ grinders' monkeys but Gavin and Dailey were doing what we asked them to do: getting the big guns on our side and facing outwards. The initial Advisory Board was a truly impressive set of top US people and it was a privilege to meet quite a few of them. The four of us got it going in 1991 and Gavin and Dailey passed it on to a new team in 1994. Gavin was 63 by then and looking to retire to Ireland.

But before that the monkeys had to get the trade to sign in because Gavin and Dailey, for all their charm and people skills, did not talk the language. Seagrams had already bought in, of course, and I forget who persuaded Busch to join up. I was left to deal with the wine side with some help from a long-standing California wine veteran and good friend, Jack Welch. The wine people took the view, and rather unhelpfully published it, that wine was good for you but beer and spirits were not. Why then contaminate wine by joining up with the enemy? The Ambassadors and I made a trip up the Napa Valley and to other wine centres. We were royally entertained but made no converts.

Jack Welch acquired invitations from Ernest Gallo to lunch at his

---

* He was recruited for the Bond role in Diamonds are Forever in 1971 but was ousted when Sean Connery returned. Jack got the money though.

† Wikipedia: 'She played Anna Leonowens opposite Yul Brynner in a revival of The King and I on Broadway (1977-8).'

home one Sunday. It was memorable. A beautiful Californian day and we lunched outside. Ernest (March 18, 1909 – March 6, 2007) had a fearsome reputation and the circumstances of his parents' deaths in 1933, nearly at the end of prohibition, were never finally resolved. The two older sons certainly had every reason to hate their father. The consequence was that Ernest and his younger brother Julio took over the business. Ernest, just turned 83 when I met him, was still running the business day-to-day and not a man to be crossed.

He could not have been nicer to me, no doubt due to Jack Welch's pre-selling. Gallo was not unlike Francis Showering, both small and softly spoken but with a look which said 'don't step out of line'. Conversation was general and complicated by Gallo taking care of his wife who had dementia; he could not have been kinder and I was struck by his wish to include her in everything. Eventually he wanted to know why I was there, although he must have been briefed by Welch. I was pretty relieved when he agreed to consider joining the Century Council and, if he did, he would encourage the rest of the US wine trade to do likewise. He also agreed to come to an industry meeting in New York where the issues would be debated. At 83 he did not do meetings, still less 3000 miles away.

The chairman of the meeting messed it up in a number of ways but chiefly in failing to defer to Gallo and make much of his position and generosity in flying over. Gallo did not say anything but looked, and was, furious. 'Respect' is an important consideration in high-level Italian culture – ask the Agnellis – and he had been denied it. The wheels had come off the whole deal but after a great deal of grovelling and soft soap, he came around to it. He was, after all, a highly intelligent man.

Gavin and Dailey took off from there and the Century Council, after 20 years has done, and is doing, all we hoped.

The final part of the Group Marketing Director story concerns acquisitions and, much the same, major contract negotiations like those already recounted for Smirnoff Vodka. We were trying to expand from the old Gilbey colonial multinational to a global company. Tennant and Sheppard were keen on acquisitions because we could save their overheads and add their remaining profit straight to our bottom line. The stockmarket analysts always forgot about our capital investments and just rejoiced in our escalating bottom line. Magic! I never understood how they could be so stupid and get paid for it but so much of business is deferring to presumed expertise whether or not there is any.

Acquisitions were really helpful to me at planning time. GrandMet required five-year plans with profits increasing steadily at 15%. Even in those days that was unrealistic. Sheppard knew it was but pretended he didn't in order to drive his executives on. It was never a problem for me: we would add up the profits from all the subsidiaries once we had talked them as far up as they would reasonably go and I would add the missing figures to make up the 15%, labelling them 'acquisitions'.

'What acquisitions are these?' the GrandMet planners would ask with some scepticism.

'Can't tell you yet. Early days, so very confidential but you can rely on something like that.'

Of course, they did not exist. The 'acquisitions' were just plug numbers to make the totals acceptable. Five years is a long time and, luckily, with a little massaging, the numbers always did turn up. I am not sure one can still do it but part of the trick was to inflate the purchase price, which went straight to the balance sheet, with a good wodge of negative items, knowing that things were unlikely to prove as negative as all that. That would allow profits to be judiciously increased to meet Sheppard's targets. He couldn't complain, if he ever found out, as he played the same game and nearly got into serious trouble for so doing.

As recounted earlier, George Bull and Peter Cawdron landed the big fish, Heublein, and Stanley Grinstead had secured Paddington and Carillon, *via* Liggett Tobacco in 1983. My contributions were mostly USA oriented and included Rumple Minze – a 100° peppermint schnapps – from Bill Elliott (ex Heublein Marketing VP), Sambuca Romana from Harvey Stone, renegotiating Amaretto di Saronno* and Gilbey's Gin for the US, and a part share of Cinzano which was 50/50 owned by the Cinzano family and the Agnellis.

Colin Gordon negotiated with Spiros Metaxas† for his family business, both an international brand (Greece and Germany) and the domestic distribution business. Spiros was the original Greek bearing

---

* A singularly sweet and sticky liqueur based on almonds from north of Milan. In the UK it does well in East Anglia and is mostly used for cooking. Very profitable in the US.

† The Greeks do not pronounce the final 's'

gifts and although he struck a tough deal, he was a generous man. We told him that providing a personal Mercedes as a gift to Gordon and each of his team would not be acceptable. It would have to be a small token. When they returned from Switzerland, his colleagues skipped through Customs but Gordon, ever the white man, declared his 'small token'. The watch, according to HM Customs was worth £5000 and they dunned him accordingly.

The big one was Martell. The IDV relationship with Hennessy Cognac went back over a century thanks to George Bull, his cousins and his forebears. In the late 1980s, Colin Campbell, one of the industry's best marketeers and Moet Hennessy's chief guru, approached us with a deal to merge distribution around the world. They were stronger in the Far East but we were stronger in North America. On paper it made sense but there was a catch which he mentioned rather diffidently. They'd be 50/50 except Moet Hennessy would have control. He knew I would reject it out of hand so he approached George Bull.

When George said 'no thanks' as gently as he could, Campbell took his brand away and stitched up a deal* in 1987 with Tennant at Guinness reinforcing the relationship Tennant already had with Campbell's boss, the Moet Hennessy CEO, Bernard Arnault. The following year Guinness and LVMH[†] each bought shares in the other. It was a complex deal but 14% each way was about the level, at a cost of $390M each (23 times earnings).

But before all that, we were now left without a cognac and Martell seemed the obvious choice. As we did not think we were French enough, we had already hired a French ex-ambassador to the United States, Bernard Vernier-Palliez, known as 'Sonny'. Sonny was a large, lovely, warm man and bright with it. He had served as an artillery spotter flying Piper Cubs just like the one Roger and I took to Bordeaux. He loved that story. He owed his life, he said, to German fighter gunfire missing because they could never believe he was going that slowly. He did a great job for IDV on a variety of fronts.

In June 1987, we had picked up a rumour that Seagram were going to bid for Martell, so we thought we should bring this to their atten-

---

* It was similar to the one he proposed to us but, no doubt learning from our reaction, less dominated by Moet-Hennessy and therefore acceptable to Guinness.

[†] Louis Vuitton and Moet-Hennessy merged in June 1987 to form LVMH. It was a $4 billion deal keeping Arnault on top.

tion as soon as possible. They were rattled by the news and we sat down together to devise a defence for them. We were, we said, happy to make a friendly bid but they said they did not want that; they preferred independence. So in July we agreed a Campbell-style mutual distribution agreement under which we would market each other's brands as and when they could be freed from existing contracts. Critically we signed it and it proved watertight. That, of course, diminished the attraction of Martell to any hostile bidder.

Things then went ominously quiet and our calls were not returned. Edgar Bronfman Jr did a terrific job in turning Martell's top management around. He spoke French very well (I do not speak it at all), he wheeled in the Canadian ambassador claiming that Seagrams was Canadian if not Quebecois and Vernier-Palliez was trashed on the grounds that he had been appointed ambassador by a socialist government and might even be a socialist himself. We had never asked. Furthermore, perfidious Albion, and me especially, was not to be trusted.

Then they all went on holiday. In September we got a message back to say they would see George Bull, he being of good cognac stock and a gentleman, but not me. Seagram were now their best friends, and I had, apparently, swindled them in making the distribution deal. George returned from Paris to say it was all over, the Martells had done a final and irrevocable deal with Seagram and they only asked to see him to be polite.

Sheppard did not take kindly to that. We did not see how the Martell management could deprive the widespread family shareholders of a better price from us. In October we went to court in Paris, supported, for a nice change, by our ambassador there, Sir Ewan Fergusson. Even more surprisingly, the court found in our favour and an auction ensued.

We bought 20% of the equity with our first offer which was about FF1800 a share. I'm working from memory and not at all sure of these numbers but they give a flavour of what transpired. Fresh from the Irish Distillers debacle, I was told to pitch it as high as we could go and FF1800 was it. Seagrams promptly retaliated with about FF2000. Sheppard phoned to say, 'Surely you can do better than that?' It wasn't a question nor was it useful to point to our last bid as the maximum.

Before returning to the auction, we need a few words about Edgar Bronfman Jr., the grandson of Sam the founder of Seagrams in Canada in 1924 during US prohibition. Edgar Jr. was chosen, in 1971 when Sam was dying, to be his successor. He was only 16. That is not a good thing to do to a 16-year-old, unless he is Alexander the Great.

In 1982, his father, Edgar Sr.*, decided to bring him into the business in some lowly position so he could learn the business. Edgar Jr. therefore started at the bottom which, in his case, was head of Europe, under Ed McDonnell's, the international chief's, tutelage. As we have seen, Tennant always believed in being friends with the competition and wasted no time in inviting Bronfman to lunch. He remained grateful to Tennant for being a kindly father figure when most of the trade was a bit frosty. Edgar Sr. progressively moved over to be a leader of international Judaism leaving Junior in charge of the spirits business worldwide in 1984 and the whole group in 1994. Through poor judgement and, doubtless, bad luck, the Seagram group destroyed itself over the next seven years. The Martell story was a harbinger of that.

In January 1987 we bested them over Heublein and they were clearly still smarting from that when the Martell opportunity came up in the summer. Bronfman persuaded Martell that we had invented the rumours that got our foot in the door but we hadn't. Seagrams' security had been weak. This time he was determined to win.

Our internal acquisitions team was John Hall and myself. Grand-Met and IDV finance management sprinkled holy water on our numbers but they did not get involved. George Bull, IDV Chairman since Tennant's departure in March, was on the line with Sheppard and Peter Cawdron. Hall had an early micro computer (PC). It was heavy to lug around but powerful enough for churning out impressive spreadsheets of 10 year projected profit and loss accounts to justify acquisitions.

When Sheppard demanded justification for a higher bid, and we did not just do this for Martell, I would always expostulate that we had covered everything and more was impossible. I would then be told, again, to go do it and I would say, 'Well, I'll see what we can do.' Half an hour later we would have adjusted a few figures, especially the terminal values on the far right of the Excel sheets. No one ever looked at terminal values. Ten years off were too far to worry

---

* The Bronfmans are an unusual family. In 1973, Edgar Sr's second wife was Lady Carolyn Townshend but it only lasted a week and was annulled on the grounds that she refused to sleep with him.   There must have been more to it than that.

about and few knew what terminal values were anyway.

To go back that same day was too quick and would have implied a lack of exertion. John Hall and I would wait a couple of days before, wiping sweat from our brows, we returned with the hoped-for justification. I cannot recall it ever being challenged.

After a few more bids and counter-bids, we returned to say FF2800 was more than Martell was worth but could, just about, be justified. Seagrams countered again with FF3,000 or so within a couple of days. By now this story was all over the financial press with some pundits backing us and some Seagrams. Sheppard was not about to give up.

'We can only justify going higher, e.g. FF3300, if we are sure they are crazy enough to top it. Then we make even more money on our 20% or so holding and we would financially cripple a major competitor.'

We took the risk and Seagrams did which was a mighty relief for me. On 1st February 1988 Seagrams agreed to pay FF3475 a share and GrandMet bowed out. The two weeks between our final bid and theirs were nerve-wracking. At 38 times earnings the $920M for the outstanding shares ($1.2bn in total) was a dreadful investment and it got worse for them.

When the dust settled, we pointed out that we had a distribution agreement with Martell and we intended to enforce it. Seagrams told us we must be joking and we said, 'Far from it.' My friend, Ed McDonnell and I had a long and acrimonious negotiation, fortunately on our own, and we settled that they would pay us $50M over three years if we tore the agreement up. It may have looked like failure but we had made about $100M on the escalation of our 20% equity holding so this $150M was for nothing except some fees. And our competitor was stuck with an investment that would never pay back.

Of course we still did not have a cognac. We had protracted but amiable discussions with Remy Martin but they came to nothing. In any case, cognac is, even in China, no longer the crucial part of the portfolio it once was.

For reasons which remained mysterious, Bronfman said he wanted very private discussions with George and me about cooperation – so private that they would be at his home. I had business in New York that day so I took the Concorde as I did quite often in those days. Colin Marshall, British Airways CEO, was on the GrandMet board so we had the minor perk of flying Concorde at first class prices, still not cheap.

Concorde was the last airline where smoking was permitted and they even handed out good cigars, albeit Jamaican to avoid ruffling US feathers. As few others smoked, that kept me well stocked for some years. The other thing one needed to know was that sitting in the rear cabin was naff. Serious people always rode up front.

This particular morning Robert Maxwell, the bouncing Czech, strode aboard shouting into his mobile phone. The crew asked him several times to sit down and switch it off but he ignored them. He did sit down when we started taxiing but continued his mobile rant. Quite soon we are out of range; he shakes his mobile and then puts it in his pocket and looks around to see what other trouble he can make.

I'm sitting about four rows back with a white-faced elderly chap, breathing badly with a couple of oxygen cylinders and not looking like he'll complete the journey. Maxwell spots him, walks down and claps him on the shoulder. My friend shudders.

Maxwell says: 'Goodness, I haven't seen you in ages. How are you?'

'You can see how I am.'

'I've missed you. We were such chums.'

'I haven't missed you.'

'We used to do so much business together. Why did we stop?'

'Because you are a crook, Robert.'

'Funnily enough I could have something here that would interest you.' He produces a grand royal blue prospectus with zloties and a great number of zeroes on the front.

'I doubt it.'

Maxwell glares at me for eavesdropping:

'I think we'd better discuss this in the back.' There's nobody that matters back there. He drags my neighbour, now looking rather perkier and as he starts to frogmarch him towards the back, I chip in:

'Would you like me to hold your cheque book while you are gone?' Two baleful looks.

By the time my neighbour gets back, even closer to death, they have indeed done a deal. Amazing.

The dinner with Bronfman proved hard work. Staff glided in with the best of wines and *cuisine nouvelle*. The lights were low. Conversation was sticky. To lighten the gloom, I told an abbreviated version of the Maxwell story above. Big mistake. Neither Bull nor Bronfman thought it was in the slightest amusing, or in good taste, or appropriate. There were a few desultory discussions of how we might cooperate before George and I sloped off into the night, none the wiser. I do not know if it was a consequence of this dinner but we did cooperate to create the Century Council.

Acquisitions and negotiations have their moments but I never really warmed to them especially where staff were involved. In my view staff are stakeholders in any business and ought to have the right of veto on any takeover of their business. Acquirers have to make things right for shareholders and they could do the same for employees, or at least those with some length of service.

The appointment to run our American interests, then Paddington, Carillon and Gilbey Canada, was more rewarding in many ways but it provided less to recount. If all is going well, the IDV visiting director has little to do except tell the troops to carry on and keep up the good work. Watching other people do business is a little like watching paint dry. Just be patient and do not touch it to see if is dry yet.

Gilbey Canada was a good example. Based in Toronto, they were still doing what they had always done since the 1930s. Retailing is mostly done by the provinces but it is immensely complicated with differing regulations from province to province. The provincial liquor boards change slowly too and that puts a premium on long-term relationships. I realise I am in no position to comment on anyone's weight but you could calculate the length of service of a Gilbey Canada salesman from his waist measurement. It was like counting rings on trees.

The thing that defines a Canadian is that he is not an American. How else could a provinces have quite major differences, especially Quebec, but, by and large, they are proud of their mutual distinction from the US. That means that they cannot run any US ads even where the US ones are far better. It means Absolut vodka is premium south of the border and a cheap brand north. I'm not sure how much good I achieved, if any, trying to open Gilbey Canada doors to the rest of the world and better practices but at least they were nice about it.

I had just one major problem and very disagreeable it was. Paul Doyle, the CEO, was not getting along well with his team and the profits were flat-lining. It was disagreeable because Doyle was by now quite a close friend. We had worked together for some years, on and off, on the Smirnoff renegotiation. Tennant had selected him, apart from his talents, because most of the negotiations would take place on that side of the Atlantic and that Gilbey Canada's Black Velvet was a reciprocal deal with Heublein, i.e. they marketed it in the USA on a contract that matched Smirnoff's. Smirnoff was far bigger than Black Velvet, a Canadian whisky, but the reciprocity helped.

Doyle was born and brought up in Dublin where he also became a Chartered Accountant before emigrating to Canada. Being both Catholics, about the same age and having some Irish blood myself, we had a fair amount in common except he had had the benefit of being liberally flogged by the Christian Brothers. Downside could not match that. He was good company and still is, I am sure. He had a sensible wife and unruly children.

Many of our meetings took place in New York and we had the evenings to ourselves. This typically involved some of the bars along 3rd Avenue. The better ones were, and probably still are, run and frequented by Irish Americans. They would be routinely astonished that an Irishman and an Englishman would be out drinking together. Irish issues would arise and I would invariably be in a minority of one but it was all light-hearted except for one night. A middle-aged man was not just biased – they were all that – but downright offensive. I was really angry and, as he was smaller than me, my fist went back with a view to planting it on his face. I had had a few beers by then. The bar-tender's quiet brogue broke the silence:

'I wouldn't do that if I were you. He's a Captain of Police.'

That seemed good advice. The Captain was hugely amused and bought the next round. By now we were best buddies and after a couple more beers, the Captain looks at his watch and says he has to go home but he'll show us around town first. His car was parked illegally, naturally, beside the fire hydrant just outside. We pile in and he asks what we would like to see at that time of night.

'Maybe some jazz?'

'No problem. Harlem is the place for that.' With which he clamps the flashing light on the roof and we sweep off at speed. Harlem is fine now but in the early 1980s was still rough. We screech to a halt outside a bar and walk in.

'These are my friends. I want you to look after them and get them a cab when they are ready to leave.'

'Yes, Captain. We'll take good care of them.'

The jazz was bluesy and gentle and, so far as I could judge by then, high-class stuff. In due course the taxi whisked us back to the hotel.

I think we paid for that.

So the boardroom brawl I faced a few years later in Toronto was the last thing I needed. Trust and relationships had broken down and promises of change were not fulfilled. After considerable angst, Paul left. I still think we should have been able to work it through but we didn't. Gilbey Canada was not an easy company to run in the last two decades of the 20th century. Doyle's successors did no better.

Doyle himself went on to good things. Although we have lost touch now, we remained good friends.

Michel Roux was Carillon's CEO but before that he had been a French paratrooper in Algeria, very likely participating in unspeakable atrocities, or so we thought. He had an air of menace so one did not ask. He then trained as a chef and came to the US, maybe in pursuit of a girl. He was married even more times than Jason. I do not recall how he came to run Carillon, Abe Rosenberg's #2 company, but his chef training never deserted him. He was even more Gordon Ramsey than Gordon Ramsey. In any restaurant one might otherwise be enjoying he would find some fault, throw down his napkin and storm into the kitchen to tell them what they needed to know.

Along with the menace, there was charm and technical knowledge so that he was loved and respected as well as slightly feared. And he was no respecter of rank.

The main brand was Absolut vodka, owned by the Swedish liquor monopoly and stylishly launched in San Francisco to the gay community. Roux, ably assisted by his Marketing VP Dick McEvoy, was (is) a terrific marketeer. He has no Harvard MBA or training with Procter & Gamble – it is intuitive. The packaging was just a clear surgical bottle, like the drip-feed source, with the name and legal requirements stencilled on. Heublein dismissed it as a no-hoper but they were wrong. It was premium-priced and, with the Swedish heritage, it communicated purity. By the time I arrived, it was romping away driven largely by great advertising from TBWA.

Every year it out-performed plan so, at the end of each year, Roux and TBWA could tuck funds out of sight from London and the auditors to get the new year off to a flying start.

The Grand Marnier brand was small but very profitable. The main use was Crêpes Suzettes where Roux's culinary skills came in useful. So did being French.

Bombay Gin was the other important brand. The convincing

British Empire packaging, with its picture of Queen Victoria, is entirely fictional.* The brand and sketched design were invented in a Chicago nightclub around 2a.m. one morning in the 1970s. My friends at G & J Greenall (Warrington, Cheshire) made and packaged the brand under licence from Carillon.

Sales were respectable but no more than that so, in 1987, Roux, McEvoy and TBWA created Bombay Sapphire at a still more premium price. Using blue was a stroke of genius as it had never been used in the industry before,† as blue bottles were associated with poison. That may have helped in fact. A selling point was the extra botanicals and listing them on the pack was also a first. Sales zoomed away.

Roux used his air of menace to great effect with distributors. They did not mess him about. And he used his charm on media space salespeople. Overlooked by everyone else, these sales people are bright and creative but have rather pedestrian jobs. Roux told them that he would be much more likely to buy space from anyone who came up with a good promotional concept for one of Carillon's brands. He did not need, as was the convention, a promotions agency; he had a top class one for nothing.

Basically, all that the London director could do for Roux and Carillon was to applaud.

Abe Rosenberg bowed out of Paddington when Liggett sold it to GrandMet in 1983. His chosen successor seemed fine but, by the time I arrived, there were rumblings, notably from Roux who thought his opposite number in Paddington was useless. Many in York Gate thought otherwise and were impressed. I was unimpressed when I discovered he had to get to a Paddington sales conference, at some very expensive resort, two days early so that, when he opened the conference, his suit would have been freshly pressed. There were no mobiles or WiFi in those days: if you were out of the office, you were out.

Paddington was putting on a pretty good front, that being an example, but business was not as good as it should have been. Mar-

---

* Wikipedia says 'Its name originates from the gin's popularity in India during the British Raj and the sapphire in question is the Star of Bombay on display at the Smithsonian Institution.' Only the last part of that is correct. I presume they got their information from Bacardi who purchased the brand from GrandMet at its merger with Guinness as the competition authorities required one of the gins to be offloaded. It is a pity they did not buy the authentic history with it.

† Allied Domecq subsequently (in 1994) used blue bottles for Harvey's Bristol Cream and Babycham. Allied was then wiped out in the Great Implosion when it and Seagram went to Pernod and Diageo.

keting was unprofessional and sales were weak. The main brands were J&B Rare and Baileys Irish Cream and they had just taken on Malibu.

J&B sales were sliding and the dreadful advertising was partly the reason though it was hard to blame the CEO for that. It had been poor from the beginning. The current campaign was dreadful because it emphasised J&B's strategic flaw, namely that it was seen as weak. Being bland and light in colour was an advantage in the early days of Scotch in the USA but now that Americans had got the hang of it, they wanted a bang for their buck. Johnnie Walker was growing fast. Unfortunately both branches of York Gate, top management and J&B export, had blessed the new agency and the campaign so the Paddington CEO could not be the scapegoat.

I was slow to act and cannot really blame my London colleagues for being so. When I told the CEO that Peter Thompson was joining as COO, he asked when the other shoe was going to drop. I should have said, 'Today.'

Thompson was Australian but educated in England, including Oxford. He had been working in the US for some time and become an American citizen. Apart from not knowing the US drinks trade, he had all the right credentials. A slight irritation for me, but welcomed elsewhere, was that he was (is) very handsome. Sitting next to him on an airplane meant getting no attention from the female cabin crew at all.

When Thompson, I and a few others visited one of the famous cat houses* in Nevada, his impact was even more annoying. We had gone, you will understand, just to check the brands used in the bar and not for any of the other delights. As one walks in, a bell goes and the girls line up for selection. The price depends on how much they fancy you. In my case, dalliance was going to be expensive but less so for my younger colleagues. In Thompson's case it was not just free but they considered paying him. They were exceedingly annoyed when he left intactum.

I advised Thompson to learn from Roux but, although they were friendly, I doubt he did. One has to be tough in the US drinks business, then anyway. If Thompson has a fault it was that he was too nice. The business became altogether more professional but we still could not crack the J&B advertising problem and sales only steadied

---

* Brothels, of course.

at best. Overall the business was considerably improved. Thompson was never really happy at Paddington and, when he got a much better offer, he took it.

Luckily, Heublein had just joined us and their International VP, Bill Seawright, who was tiring of constant travel, fitted the role just perfectly. Bill is a wonderful, exuberant, outgoing leader with the wine and spirit business running through his veins. It was a happy time both for Paddington and for Bill and Anne* Seawright. His son, Bill Jr, is now in the business.

We had North America reasonably covered but, before Heublein joined with its big company in Brazil, we had nothing in Central or South America. I approached both Tennant and Grinstead with this issue and neither were much interested. I suggested we started with Uruguay on the grounds that we were bound to mess up our first entry and, as one of the smallest but most European of countries, it would be the least risk whilst providing valuable learning. The minimal interest waned further but I had the go ahead.

I started Spanish lessons most mornings before work. The first Berlitz woman was very pretty but we got nowhere, in any sense. I was transferred to a solid middle-aged woman who proved to be very good. Unfortunately she was dealing with a non-linguist. I could manage the basics when travelling around but my one effort with a prepared speech, and unprepared stammer, was such a disaster that I was advised not to try it again.

Cinzano had a thriving business in Argentina and a small, not-so-thriving business in Uruguay. They were worryingly keen to off-load it but with our better portfolio and marketing skills it should have been a doddle. By this time we had 50% of 50% of the Cinzano Group in Switzerland and thereby management control. It was all very affable as were our new partners in Montevideo, a Sephardic Jewish family called Zeinal. They already represented some IDV brands so we were able to put the parcel together.

Nothing, you might think, could go wrong and nothing did. But nothing went right either. Uruguay brings new levels of conservatism to conservatism. Absolutely nothing changed and, I suspect, still hasn't. Driving illustrates the point. Argentines drive like Italians only more so. Uruguayans not only drive at 20mph but do so very badly. They rarely drive into each other as they are not going fast enough to

---

* Bill's Swedish wife.

do so. Argentines rarely drive into each other because they know each others' reactions and are very skilful. When the Argentines drive over for the summer holidays at Punta de l'Este, or wherever, prangs were everywhere as the two driving cultures clashed. I am told it is better now but my point is that the Uruguayan drinks market was impervious to innovation. The steaks were good though and so was the polo club.

As discussed earlier, the acquisition of Heublein proved remarkably straightforward. The consequential relationship was anything but. Heublein had been given, or so they claimed, various assurances some of which were true, some uncertain and some simply assumed by them. One example of the last category was that they had been acquired by GrandMet, not IDV, and therefore would report only to GrandMet side by side with sibling IDV. It took a while to get rid of that notion.

Heublein's Chairman, Jack Powers, remained in place, and joined the IDV board. We understood that to be a non-executive, advisory role with the Heublein CEO, Bob Furek reporting to me as London director. They saw Powers as fully executive with Furek answering only to Powers and my role as being advisory at best and probably unnecessary. The latter was closer to what happened.

George Bull was anxious to keep the peace and not rock the boat.

The truth of the matter was that Heublein was a good sales company but a poor marketing company and with excessive overhead. Having the top executives on a separate, rather grand, top floor of their HQ did not help their internal communications. I dare say there were many things we should have learned from them but they were too busy making sure they did not learn anything from us.

None of this was as clear at the time as it is now and we muddled along. Powers and I had a few dust ups but we got along well enough personally and he resolved the dust ups by promising to do things he never did. He was a big strong man and rejoiced in his Friesian ancestry. The other Dutch can be obstinate but they consider Friesian obstinacy in the way other Scots consider Aberdonians tight with their money.

When Bill Seawright went to Paddington, Denis Malamatinas took over as global brand manager for Smirnoff operating, as a concession, out of Heublein's HQ, not IDV's. This should have been an example of beneficial mutual exchange. The Paddington side worked well enough but Heublein executives were poisonous to Malamatinas, as he was not a Heublein man. We had hired him from Pepsico to run Metaxa. He did a first-class job there and was altogether a fine drinks executive. With Smirnoff he not only got the ad agency to come up with the best campaign yet but got it accepted by all the major countries worldwide. This was a first.

He went on from there to run Burger King and was in the running to become CEO of Diageo when the wheels came off in a big way. The winner was Paul Walsh who has done a wonderful job so no one else will grumble about the choice. Part of Denis's problem at Burger King, where he did not manage to fix the dreadful advertising, was that it is difficult to change the culture if you are not within it.

Bob Furek had come up the sales management route to become a loyal #2 to Powers. He started with Gallo and there was no tougher sales school than that. He is now retired but there is no question that he was, and is, a good man doing what was right in his perspective. But his perspective was not IDV's perspective. For example, although IDV was not above fixing the accounts in our own way, we strongly objected to loading up distributors in the last month of the financial year with stocks that should have gone through in the early months of the new year. It makes meeting plan in the following year doubly difficult as the Group's expectations are set by the old year but that has stripped away the chances of meeting those expectations. Those pursuing this approach have to load the trade even more the next time.

Worse than that, it cheapens the brand. The trade finds out it is not selling to expectation and they start running price promotions to get rid of the over-loaded stock. It was an example of why Heublein was good at sales and bad at marketing. It had not always been thus. Jack Martin who launched Smirnoff was a first-class marketeer and Chris Carriuolo who left after 11 years in 1981 was, or so I was told, also strong in that department. My old friend Bill Elliott could be but he was dominated by the Sales VP, Charlie Herbert.

Two chief grumbles from Heublein were that Furek should have been on the IDV board: they were probably right about that. The other was that Paddington and Carillon, being US companies, should have been integrated into Heublein. They were definitely wrong about that. They were much better run than Heublein with far fewer overheads. Heublein's portfolio was already overstretched and there would have been brand conflicts, notably in vodka, which the brand owners would never have accepted.

Furek had many strengths as he demonstrated when he left the company and sorted out the Connecticut education department and its schools. He did that very successfully and it must have strained even his sales skills.

In short, I may have done some good when I was nominally in charge of Heublein but I made mistakes and there were frustrations galore. It was no comfort to learn that the troubles continued for many years after I left.

There was one organisational issue which proved highly controversial. Back in the UK, I had concluded that it was quite easy to overload a sales force portfolio. Customers would only give a rep a short interview and so the rep would sell what was easy and/or what was best for the rep's commission. No problem with the latter as a commission system should be designed to harmonise the company's and the rep's priorities.

The solution, then quite fashionable, was to have the sales force and marketing people split into separate teams divided by portfolio. The rest of the structure was unaffected. We did this in the UK by creating Morgan Furze Agencies to run alongside Gilbey Vintners. Some customers will insist, supermarkets for example, on dealing with the company's portfolio as a whole, but that can be handled as can trade marketing. Over the years, the number of sales people has declined as a percentage of employees, partly because customers have merged. Paddington and Carillon were examples of this approach in the US although they did not combine back offices.

A second issue was GrandMet's decision to separate retail (shops and pubs) from manufacturing and brand owning. As a result, Peter Dominic was stripped out, as discussed earlier, with catastrophic results and IDV was awarded the breweries, an almost equally dumb idea. Although beer, wines and spirits all contain alcohol, that is where the similarities stop. Beer is about bulk and production costs. Yes, marketing is important but nothing like as important as it is to spirits. Wine falls somewhere in between. Wines and spirits are not bulk and, though saving money is always useful, the business is not primarily about manufacturing and distribution efficiencies. Jasper Grinling made that mistake in the 1960s.

A third issue was that IDV's reporting lines had become too complex and a fourth was that HR was trying to run the group. I think I was on my own on this last one. I referred to them collectively as the

KGB and Sovietised the name of their senior agent in IDV. I thought that quite amusing but no one else did. Christopher Pearman strongly advised me to desist. Flattery will get one almost everywhere in business; mockery has the opposite effect.

Annual plans for example had become tedious. We had the same ritual dances every year and spent far too much time and energy doing so. I am all for having a short, sharp annual planning session where you practise what you are going to do before you do it. Performance can be improved that way. Endless rounds of number-crunching have the opposite effect.

Having strategy plans followed by five-year plans, of which only the first year gets any attention, and then re-forecasting every two months is ludicrous. If you are spending more time planning than doing, the company has lost the plot.

And as a distinguished CEO of Whitbread showed, planning should begin only very shortly, six weeks at most, before the new financial year. With modern online methods, that could be two weeks.

When I had a managerial role subsequently at London Business School, I managed to get to the other extreme by not doing any plans at all. Two were expected from the Chair of Marketing, the financial plan, i.e. the budget, and the teaching plan, i.e. how the faculty would spend their time and how each would earn the required 100 points from teaching or other points rewarded activities. I did neither and sooner or later the phone would go:

'Professor, we have not had your plan yet. Why is that? Might it have gone astray?'

'No, no. I have not done it.'

'When can we expect it?'

'I don't know. Tell me: if I did this plan, you would find fault with it and have me correct it. True?'

'Probably yes.'

'So you know what is expected, what it should look like and therefore you should write the plan. Is that OK?'

'Well yes, it is actually easier for us. We'll send you a copy and you just sign it. OK?'

It very much was. I did not look at it but I did sign it.

One of our PhD students did her thesis on this topic and showed that fast moving and stable organisations got little benefit from planning at all. The middle speed ones, like GrandMet, did benefit but nothing like as much as they thought. A stable business like a university might as well dispense with them, just as I did.

20 years on, these planning and forecasting nonsenses still continue and may even be worse. The future is unknown and no amount of arithmetic makes it certain. At best a few possibilities can be ruled out but that is irrelevant. The issue is deciding what actions to take and what to avoid. Those decisions should not be made until they have to be. Yes, one should use state-of-the-art mathematics to predict the most likely, or least unlikely, outcomes of the action alternatives but, for most businesses, the horizon needed for these decisions is quite short, usually a year. In these circumstances, five year forecasting is a complete waste of resources.

As indicated above, I was getting restive. It was time for me to move on and a lot of GrandMet people agreed with that.

# Chapter 10

# Academic Grooves

*This chapter covers 20 years of academia and some of the remarkable people I met.*
- *London Business School, early years\**
  - *Two heads are better than one?*
  - *Beginnings with the School*
  - *Why micro-economic† theory is bunkum*
  - *Chris Styles my PhD student*
  - *What is academic 'research'?*
- *Columbia*
  - *Bob Guccione and Kathy Keeton, Penthouse Royalty*
  - *Bill Lyons, fighter ace*
- *London Business School, later years*
  - *What China can teach us about business*
  - *Advertising research and neuroscience*
  - *Metrics research*
  - *Ivory Tower?*
  - *Defending Advertising against the Political Correctness Police*
  - *Leaving the Marketing Area better than I found it*
  - *Dabbling in national politics*

First a few words on the man who suggested I join the School and to whom I am eternally grateful for that. Keith Holloway (13th May 1936 – 5th August 2003) had a gilded youth. Winning scholarships to Wolverhampton Grammar School and then Corpus Christi, Oxford, he read Greats and acquired blues for the Long and the Triple Jump.

I first came across him when he had been promoted to Deputy Chairman of Cadbury Schweppes, high flying for someone aged

---

\* The School is so regularly confused with the larger and older LSE, that the abbreviation LBS was banned. I doubt it made any difference.

† The study of business at the firm or product level. I have no problem with macro-economics, i.e. national level.

about 40, and jolly irritating that was. He wanted to create a soft drink that would team up with vodka like tonic did with gin. Although we were keen to cooperate in general, I do not recall being very helpful on the specifics. Nevertheless Russchian was born. A clever play on words, it did OK and it is still on the market.

In the 1980s, he was appointed Commercial Director of the GrandMet breweries and in 1987 moved on with Sheppard when he became Group Chairman.

Keith, being P&G trained, was what one might call a classical marketeer, so he and we did not always agree on technical matters. The difference was that between classical and guerrilla military commanders. He did not want to involve me, for example, in the launch of Prince Charles's Duchy Originals which he masterminded very well. He was right. On the other hand, I was sceptical of his approach to a small US beer import business that GrandMet acquired in the 1980s. Horses for courses.

Despite, or perhaps because of, these differences, we became good colleagues and friends and played golf together when we could because, thanks to his medical afflictions, he was almost as bad as me.

Paddy Barwise was Faculty Dean (HR Director, the job rotates around professors) at the time Keith suggested I join the faculty which was a lucky break as he was also Chair of the Marketing Area and open to ideas. He said, after conferring with colleagues, that appointing practitioners had always failed before but in view of my academic track record into MIT and success there, they would give it a go. I would need an initial five year contract in place of the customary three to give me a chance to catch up and I would be a Senior Research Fellow rather than an Associate Professor as I had no teaching experience.

Ken Simmonds told me later that we should have pushed for a full chair with tenure but, as it turned out, it did not matter and, thanks to my age, everyone treated me as a professor anyway. Ken and Tony Eccles were my sponsors in applying to the School as I had worked and grown friendly with them in the course of executive training.

Tony was, and is, a consummate organiser of executive education and that was his main role, along with MBA teaching, at the School where he was a long-standing faculty member. When the School decided to upgrade research and put far more emphasis on publication in the world's top journals, Tony opted out along with other

British faculty who were primarily teachers.

Tony is from Liverpool and wonderfully relaxing company. Ken has a string of initials after his name, including accounting, which gave him a strategic view of marketing, i.e. more competition than worrying about what is going on in the consumer's head. He is from New Zealand and seems to have been involved in every UK business school development as well as having a wide circle of contacts, many being ex-students.

His teaching style is challenging: the best students love it and him. The worst ones do not. Students at business schools are usually asked to grade their teachers 1 to 5 on various scales. It is an exercise of doubtful merit but one can understand why the bureaucrats, and the students themselves, want some indication of quality. Ken gets a uniquely large number of 1s and 5s with very little in between. He is therefore one of the best remembered teachers and, whether they like him or not, the best value for money for the students.

The Marketing Area when I joined London Business School was chaired by Paddy Barwise who did his best to keep the peace between the two seniors, Ken Simmonds and Andrew Ehrenberg, each of whom led distinct factions. They agreed about little or nothing. Simmonds was on the Senate of the Chartered Institute of Marketing, for example, and Ehrenberg was a Fellow of the competing Marketing Society. From the School's point of view, it was good to cover both bases but there was no cooperation.

Ehrenberg was as unusual as Simmonds. He had come over from Germany as a small child about 60 years earlier but his German accent sounded as if he had only just stepped off the plane. By training a statistician, he had a healthy scepticism of micro-economics* in general and econometrics (the main statistical tool of micro-economists) in particular. He was scornful of those who dressed superficial ideas up in scientific clothing. His term 'SONKing' referred to the Scientification Of Non-Knowledge.

The only thing they had in common was their failure to conform to one of the three US stereotypes for marketing academics: quantitative (econometricians mostly but anything with equations), buyer behaviour (drawing on psychology to explain why buyers act as they do) and, the least respected of the three, managerial (what marketeers

---

* The study of business at the firm or product level. I have no problem with macro-economics, i.e. national level.

do). There is surprisingly little crossover between these three and it is almost as if marketing had no theory of its own – just clothes borrowed from economics and psychology.

Ehrenberg had two Big Ideas which he pursued remorselessly. The first was pure logic/mathematics and based on one of marketing's very few laws: the Dirichlet model* links together a number of marketing metrics such as market share, penetration (% buying), loyalty (% repeat buying) etc. to show 'double jeopardy', i.e. if measure is small another is likely to be. This attacks the concept, for example, of niche markets where a few buyers are unusually loyal. Of course there are exceptions but overall it works remarkably well and Ehrenberg spent many happy years exploding marketing myths. Some major companies, like Procter & Gamble, listened to him but most academics did not

Dirichlet requires the market to be stable and, luckily for Ehrenberg, most markets (sizes and brand shares) are far more stable than companies, and especially young brand managers, think they are. It also gives too much importance to market share as the only metric that matters. To a true marketeer, relative price, i.e. the brand's price compared to the average price for all brands in the category, is at least as important. It is a key indicator of perceived quality which in turn drives both market share and profit.

Soon after I joined, he called me to his office and asked if I would like to know how to know, ahead of time, the steady state market share of a new brand. Would I like him to show me how to do that? Having launched a number of new brands without the least idea of their steady state sales volumes, I smelled a rat. I was right: first I had to tell him what the penetration would be and so on. The metrics are indeed mathematically linked so if you have some, Dirichlet will give you the others, or at least what they should be.

This use of some numbers to provide related ones is like the Texas methodology for weighing a pig. Texans consider guessing the weight of a pig to be unscientific. Instead they carefully balance a plank across a rock and then tie the pig to one end. The basket on the other end is now loaded with stones until the plank is exactly level. Then they guess the weight of the stones.

Apart from in South Bank University and South Australia, where

---

* A negative binomial distribution extended to account for brand choices.

he has a large number of loyal disciples and researchers, Ehrenberg never got the credit he deserved for these insights. They do provide a framework for identifying variations of brand behaviour from what should be expected and that in turn should inspire management learning and action.

His other Big Idea was about how advertising worked or, more often, didn't – and owed nothing to scientific method, still less statistics. It was, however, more helpful for practical marketeers. He concluded intuitively that advertising reinforces positive brand experience as distinct from persuading people to do something they did not already do. Of course there are exceptions but he was broadly right as neuroscience has since confirmed.

Given the lucky break, I then proceeded to do everything wrong. The School did not see me as a teacher but I reckoned I was. What else had I been doing trotting round the world and speechifying at sales conferences? No one was teaching International Marketing and that seemed the perfect slot for me. The School provided a short course for new faculty and I decided, wrongly as it turned out, that I was now ready to impart wisdom to MBAs.

It began well and the annual course was well attended and the students gave me surprisingly good grades. Emboldened by this I volunteered to do the basic marketing course for the Sloans. Like most business schools, London had three levels of master's degrees: the full-time two year course for those in their late 20s, a three year part-time course for those in their 30s and a one year Sloan Masters Programme for those in mid-career, and often changing career, in their early 40s.* The Sloan programme was originated by the MIT Sloan[†] School and then shared with Stanford and London when it got going at the end of the 1960s.

The Sloans were difficult to teach because they reckoned, with 20 years business experience, to know everything except the theory and they were hostile to marketing. All the marketing faculty had tried and failed with the Sloans. My colleagues thought my age and even

---

* Since then the part-time programme has been abbreviated to two years and a one year 'pre-experience' course added for those wanting to go straight on for undergraduate studies.

† Alfred P Sloan was the creator of General Motors and progenitor of MIT applying its scientific approach to business. The case study method is not noticeably scientific.

longer business experience would carry weight but it didn't. I took on a recent graduate from the Sloan programme as co-teacher and we both thought that would establish empathy. It didn't and they took against him even more than me so we had to retire him early on, leaving me to ride out the storm. The Programme Director gave me a bollocking and said he could not understand the problem:

'All you have to do is teach.' I have had more insightful reviews.

Part of the problem was that case studies were integral to the syllabus. I had never done case studies. I did not like them and chose MIT rather than Harvard to avoid them. Harvard Business School* is now trying to reduce dependency on case studies but that is 20 years on from my teaching experience. Most students love them as they give the illusion of reality and flatter students as making the big decisions instead of the grubby business of understanding consumers which marketing really is.

Thereafter we brought US professors over for this course who coped much better but, in my time, the Sloans still did not like marketing.

In parallel with this I was running executive marketing courses in GrandMet (no case studies). I was careful not to criticise the marketing developments in my old company. Some were good, such as standardising market research globally, and some not. Discretion was definitely the better part. These courses were popular partly because we found exotic places to hold them: being 'global' means going anywhere one likes.

Naturally those who had been pleased to see me go were unpleased that I was still around. My successor and I reached the crunch when IDV was implementing a new policy of concentrating only on the very biggest brands and creating new brands. Forgetting discretion, I asked how the new brands would get from being small to being big without becoming middle-sized on the way.

I turned this role over to our newly joined star teacher, Kent Grayson, who did it very well and continued to use my first book *Marketing from Advertising to Zen.*† It was fun writing that. It only took a couple of months and was modelled on Robert Townsend's irreverent *Up the Organisation*††. Townsend had been a no-nonsense CEO of Avis and was no fan of bureaucracy. He recommended, for

---

* Nitin Nohria, Dean of Harvard Business School, and previously at MIT, interviewed by Peter Day, BBC Radio 4, Sunday 12 May 2013.

† FT Pitman, last edition 1996.

†† Michael Joseph, 1970

example, getting rid of HR departments. In like mode, I recommended getting rid of internal market research departments and introduced the Chi of Life. The Greek letter Chi is like an X except the strokes are curved and flatten out at the top and bottom. Any marketeer, when things are going well (the up curve), needs to know there is an equal and opposite down curve going on somewhere and look for it. And vice versa. An example: as one ages, the proportion of the opposite sex one finds attractive increases. The proportion of the opposite sex who finds you attractive decreases.

Grayson had just secured his doctorate from Northwestern (Kellogg), arguably the best business school for marketing in the world. His doctoral supervisor was new to the game of securing appointments for one's protégés and we were lucky to nab him. Grayson proved a brilliant teacher and a fine researcher. Kellogg eventually wooed him back and gave him tenure.

Soon after this the country went into a mild recession and we had some problems recruiting the best talent and placing them when they graduated.

The then Dean agreed with my point about cobbler's children and suggested that, being a marketeer, I should sort out the School's marketing myself. Big mistake. I had not realised that the vast majority of the faculty were as ignorant of marketing as our incoming students. Very, very few business school faculty have MBAs or any business experience. They go straight from undergraduate studies to specialist doctorates to faculty. They were indifferent to my appointment to sort out 'marketing' as they thought that meant improving the advertising and running a few promotions, maybe.

When they discovered that the first job of a marketeer is to get the product right and then the price, they were up in arms. My efforts to explain the concept of 'brand equity' (loosely speaking the School's reputation) and the need to manage that to attract and place top students (and indeed top faculty) were derided by the economists and the finance faculty in particular. If one could not feel it or put numbers on it, they said, it did not exist. In any case, university teachers are as production-driven and resistant to change as any member of the CBI. It is much easier to give the same class as the year before, changing just a few slides to make it look topical. I was, in effect, challenging their *modus operandi*.

It did not help that I in turn had been mocking (micro-)economists and that the School's largest and most influential Areas were economics and finance. To cut a long story short, I came within a whisker of being sacked and the project was aborted. I had some satisfaction, a few years later, when I heard the very people who had derided the term using 'brand equity' in a well-informed manner. The penny had dropped. Perhaps I should explain why economists derailed the British economy and are inimical to marketing. Feel free to skip the next rant.

Adam Smith can be considered the father of modern economics and showed the need to balance supply with demand. Two of his followers got into a huge debate about whether supply or demand was the more important. Malthus (a country parson) argued for demand and Ricardo (a Cambridge academic) for supply. Perhaps understandably in the early 19th C when demand took care of anything that could be made, Ricardo won. It helped being part of the Cambridge mafia and they have had an important place in the UK's economic thinking ever since.

In the past 100 years, production has become ever simpler and the problem has switched to the generating and satisfaction of demand. Whilst micro-economists have still been tinkering with production and with costs in the belief that lower costs generate higher sales, marketeers have been generating demand and recognising that people are not computers but human beings looking for value, not necessarily the lowest price. As observed before, brand leaders are usually premium priced.

Micro-economists sought to get around this mismatch between theory and observed practice by inventing something called 'utility' – a fuzzy concept of unknown benefit. It is like the plug numbers used by accountants to make balance sheets balance rather than seek the causes of the errors.

The truth of the matter, confirmed by modern neuroscience, is that habit is the prime driver of what we buy followed by emotion (what feels right, social aspiration) and only rarely by logical analysis, conscious or unconscious.

The British car industry was brought to its knees by constant cheapening and lack of consumer-oriented innovation. The Japanese have shown that Britain can make cars so long as they do not have to market them.

Unfortunately economists are given priest-like reverence in this country and especially in government. When HM Treasury started to win all its arguments with other departments by deploying economists, the other departments hired their own, thus further miring the civil service in inertia and false analysis, wind farms being a current example. Economists spread throughout Whitehall in much the way the Grand Inquisitor's clerics infested the court of Philip II and are feared similarly.

Chris Styles (see below) and I tried to bring marketing theory and practice to the Department of Trade and Industry (as it was then) in respect of exports, the subject of Styles's PhD thesis which debunked conventional (micro-economic) wisdom in this area.* We showed one could not successfully select export markets using the market research and rational analysis the DTI recommended. As a trivial example, if no one buys air-conditioners in, say, Iceland, does that indicate a huge potential Icelandic market for air-conditioners (export there first) or a lack of demand (do not export there at all)?

Study of the origins of successful exporting, as well as more modern marketing theory, show that relationships are the key. Who you sit next to on the plane is likely to matter more than a formally constructed export plan.

Of course you cannot keep a rationalist down so the economists are now reinventing marketing and calling it 'behavioural economics' and labelling the findings of neuroscience 'neuro-economics' but this is no more than putting new clothing over what marketeers already knew.

Not only have micro-economists undermined British manufacturing, commerce and economy by replacing a sound understanding of marketing, brands and brand equity by false theory, they are largely responsible for the excessive regulation of business. As the next chapter will describe, I spent 10 years trying to stem the flow of regulations which gathered speed in the mid-nineties and has accelerated, both from Whitehall and Brussels, ever since. Bureaucrats use micro-economists to justify market intervention and distortion. This unholy alliance of micro-economists, consumerists and bureaucrats believe that they know what consumers want better than the consumers themselves do.

Of course markets need some regulation but, by and large, consumer choice should rule. Those who fail to understand marketing also fail to understand markets. My advice to businessmen, not just

---

* See our co-authored book *The SILK Road to International Marketing*, FT Prentice Hall, 2000.

marketeers, is to burn their micro-economic textbooks, except those by Adam Smith and the Revd. Thomas Malthus, and forget everything you ever knew about it.

In 1993, Chris Styles arrived from Procter & Gamble to do a PhD. He had been a marketeer in the entrepreneurial part of the group that deals with small countries, in his case mostly middle-eastern. An Australian from Perth, he had been based in Switzerland. He was interested in export marketing and was assigned for me to supervise as the only internationalist in the Marketing Area and, as practitioners, we spoke the same language. He just wanted to get his doctorate in the minimum time and get on with the rest of his career. Four years is the allotted span, and some take longer, but he did it in three.

We were equally sceptical of the international marketing textbooks' approach to opening up new markets in particular. They all said much the same, citing each other, but we had done it in practice and we knew their approach did not work. Their approach was micro-economic analysis; our experience was that a new market worked or failed according to the competence of the importer and the quality of the exporter-importer relationship.* As it happened, 'relationship marketing' was just becoming a hot topic at that time, initially in Scandinavia and Australia and subsequently in the US.

To keep a long story short there are only three ways (so far) in which marketing can be understood: 4Ps (Product, Price, Promotion, Place), strategy and relationships. Since the fifties[†], the 4Ps had been the dominant ideology and most marketing plans are still written that way. The 4Ps are production driven, i.e. supplier, not consumer, oriented.

In the 1970s, Harvard's Professor Michael Porter pointed this out and proposed strategy as the dominant philosophy, i.e. it is not what you do that matters, being seen by the consumer as better than your competitor is the key. The old story which illustrates the point is the

---

* There was also some work before ours on a simpler but more rudimentary concept namely 'psychic distance' which says that the two export and import parties are more likely to be successful if the two parties are more alike, e.g. culturally. But that proved to be wrong – Barbara Stöttinger, Bodo B. Schlegelmilch, (1998) 'Explaining export development through psychic distance: enlightening or elusive?' International Marketing Review, 15(5), 357-72.

† Peter Drucker has been dubbed (by Philip Kotler) the grandfather of marketing and saw it not only as the distinguishing feature of any business but, with innovation, the only part that mattered. Most thoughtful marketeers still subscribe to his views. See (1954) *The Practice of Management*, New York: Harper & Brothers.

one about the grizzly chasing two hunters. You do not need to be faster than the bear, just faster than the other hunter. In this paradigm, market share is the key performance metric. The Marketing Science Institute (MSI, founded 1961) published research by Bradley Gale* showing that market share was the pathway to profit. It was a load of rubbish and Gale, generously, recanted later but the theory remains pervasive.

In the 1990s, relationship marketing re-established the customer's, or consumer's, perspective as crucial. Never mind the numbers, does the consumer love the brand? How can that love be increased?

We had some silly simplistic talk of it being impossible to have a relationship with an inanimate object like a brand but that has now died away. Those who use plug numbers like 'utilities' are, in my view, in no position to mock.

We approached the DTI for financial support and data and they were initially helpful on both counts. Their serried ranks of micro-economists, and other worshippers at the Temple of Baal, discovered they were being undermined. We were no match for their established positions and politics. I was even banned from one meeting on export marketing on the grounds that I did not have a doctorate in economics. And these people were criticising trade unions for restrictive practices.

We published a few papers together, one notably in IJRM, one of the Big Five marketing journals. His thesis won a prize from MSI and he returned to Australia, living in Sydney with delightful wife and children. Initially he joined the University of New South Wales, gaining rapid promotion, and then transferring to the University of Sydney with a full professorship. We stayed friends and I saw him when I visited Australia, but time and distance have had their effect.

One last warning to new PhDs: Chris was rightly pleased with his new title of Doctor and checked into Quantas as such. Halfway through the first leg, he was approached by the cabin crew. A passenger had fallen seriously ill and could he come and deal with her. It took a long while, including the production of a copy of his thesis, to persuade them he was not a medical doctor.

It took me a while to figure out that research in academia does not mean research in the conventional sense of making new discoveries, it means getting articles, with your name on, published by the top

---

* B.T. Gale 'Market share and rate of return,' The Review of Economics and Statistics, 1972, JSTOR

journals for your discipline. Novelty helps but proving a weak theory by replication does not. Proper sciences aside, disproving published work is a complete no-no as the editor will start by sending your paper for review by the authors of the paper you are criticising and they will find all manner of reasons for rejecting yours. On the other hand, joining the new bandwagon with some little tweak, no matter how small, is a winner. No top marketing journal would publish anything on relationship marketing in the 1980s but ten years later they were falling over themselves to do so. It had become fashionable.

Cross-disciplinary work is also a problem. It is welcomed in theory and it should be good for knowledge transfer but editors have a problem in practice finding reviewers outside the set defined by the journal. We hit rocks trying to get our cross-over neuroscience-cum-marketing work accepted by marketing journals. The regular reviewers thought they knew about neuroscience but didn't and our papers were rejected for spurious reasons. The neuroscience editors were far easier: their reviewers were aware that they knew little of marketing but did not care.

None of this is true today in the hard sciences, such as physics. Criticism and cross-disciplinary work is welcomed.

Be all that as it may, the fact remained that, when contract renegotiation time came around near the end of my first one, I was in trouble. I had not expected to survive at the School so I had not paid much attention to the word 'research' but I was now enjoying my time there and I had also had a good time at Columbia, see below. The whole business of renegotiating a contract had rather escaped my mind when I found myself, one afternoon, in the office of the new Marketing Area Chair, a top professor from a top US school, with Paddy Barwise trying to help but looking a little uncomfortable. As it turned out, the rather liquid lunch I had just enjoyed proved useful.

The Area Chair explained why we were meeting and asked, quite politely, why my contract as a Senior Research Fellow should be extended when I hadn't done any research. At that point, my best publications were all in the future, and my articles in the lower grade journals did not count. When I asked him for a list of the journals that would count, he wrote the top five on a napkin. Outsiders do not appreciate that the lead time on top journals is three, or even four, years. My teaching did not count either as I was not supposed to be doing any teaching, still less setting up the Century Council in the US. I don't think he referred to my abortive attempt to sort out the

School's marketing which so alienated my senior colleagues. His points were irrefutable and he obviously hoped I would go quietly.

This was where the good lunch kicked in. Years of negotiating impossible business situations have taught me a bit about using emotion to defeat reason. I did use in my defence the work I had done on how ads work and export relationship marketing but there was little in print to show for it. They both looked increasingly uncomfortable and the next day I have to admit to feeling a tad guilty. The upshot, after a couple of more genteel rounds, was that I could stay for another three years but I was at risk and, since I did not do any research, the word would be removed from my title leaving 'Senior Fellow'. I was delighted with that and I did get the message about doing some research. Four of his five top journals published my work.

Executive education had introduced me to James (but always known as 'Mac') Hulbert, a Columbia marketing professor. He was English but had been at Columbia for many years. He had a large house in Gloucestershire and liked to get back when he could, especially when his wife took up a position at the Henley College of Management. Mac was due a sabbatical but CBS was short of marketing faculty so he, and then they, suggested I be a Visiting Professor for a year and teach the starter MBA marketing course, alongside three of their own faculty.

Katie is not fond of the US. She agreed I should do it but was not going to join me. I was also concerned about further damaging my relationship with my School so we settled on half a year, i.e. the September to December semester. Everyone seemed happy with that.

It is probably just as bad for Americans coming to London but getting a bank account, finding somewhere to live, getting logged into the Columbia systems etc. are problems one cannot even begin to address until one has a Social Security number. Columbia is just south of Harlem and the Social Security office there was an eye-opener. The woman before me at the window was enraged that they had stopped paying her husband's social benefits. The clerk gently explained that the reason was that he had recently died. That did not seem a good reason to her.

I was just as bad. I remembered months later that I already had the Social Security number I needed when doing consultancy work at MIT 25 years earlier but by then I had my second one – something the US authorities claim is impossible. One wonders how many US citizens are drawing multiple benefits with multiple numbers.

Katie joined me for the recce in August to find an apartment and set up a bank account. We stayed at the stuffy but comfortable Yale Club (shades of Great Gatsby) and pounded the burning hot pavements. Luckily we found a beautiful third-floor apartment on Central Park South, looking over the trees, not too pricey and handy for everything.

Due to the proximity and a desire for social responsibility, CBS employed a number of Harlem denizens with no discernible secretarial skills or work ethos. I had a part share of Desiree, a charming and splendid woman in all other respects. I dare say London had spoiled me but it was self-help time. Colleagues kindly explained all I needed to know, well, most things, and Noel Capon, another Brit and the senior professor on the course, copied his materials for me.

It should have been a breeze. Just walk into class, talk to his slides and hand out copies to my two streams of about 60 students each. It turns out that, as everyone else knew, it is extremely difficult to use someone else's material. I didn't know what his slides meant and he had no time to explain. I had done more or less the same course myself at MIT but that was 25 years earlier and marketing moves on even though the main (Philip Kotler) textbook was still virtually the same. CBS, unfortunately, did not use Kotler.

It would all have gone well enough, despite these hazards, if I had not applied English standards of marking to CBS students. I knew US marking is more generous and I thought I had allowed for that but not enough. Part of the problem was that CBS is one of the top schools and to get there at all, students must have had straight As throughout their education. I doubled the percent of As from my usual 10% but that was not enough. All those, and especially the women, with less than an A started queuing up at my office to complain. There was no possibility in their minds that I might have been right, only that I must have made a mistake.

I had been warned to make sure my office door was wide open when female students were inside, although I am not sure I could have relied on Desiree as a witness. That proved not to be a problem once I made sure a good supply of Kleenex was on my desk. I never had a single weeping student in London, American or otherwise.

There were two upsides: my faculty colleagues and especially the Area Chair, Don Lehmann, a kind and generous man. They also had a retired practitioner with whom they thought I would get on and we did. He was helpful and hospitable but was only engaged to do occasional talks about his experience, not to do the standard class modules.

The second upside was that they were all putting money on my hitting problems with the political correctness police (PCP). I did terrible things like referring to the female students as 'girls' and making jokes that may have been acceptable at Sheringham Golf Club but not in 1990s USA. They were wrong. The students made allowance for the eccentricities of an elderly Englishman and New York is far more cosmopolitan than the US in general. I had discovered that when we ran the raunchy UK Haagen Daz ice cream advertising in the US. It was welcomed on both coasts but caused a storm in middle America.

Katie did not return after the August recce but sent over a stream of visitors to make sure I wasn't lonely which, of course, I wasn't. I had enough friends there but not necessarily people whose reports she could trust. As it is the thing to do in Central Park, I bought roller blades and a long-suffering teacher did her best to get me up to speed.

I swore my visitors to silence about the roller blading and they were very good about it.

I saw quite a bit of two New York couples both with stories eccentric enough to need recounting. Other good friends, such as Harvey and Sheila Stone, also had interesting tales to tell but space does not permit.

Bob and Kathy Guccione appeared earlier in these memoirs when they were in London and we had occasional encounters since then as IDV took advertising space in their magazines. Even though some of their titles were eminently respectable, some were not and few other drink brands took space. The PCP were, of course, outraged and even threatened Max Joseph, GrandMet Chairman, but, as I have mentioned before, he was not a man to threaten. In advertising terms the magazines provided the right target market and outstanding value for money.

In 1994 their empire was at the peak of its financial success. Bob and Kathy had, according to *New York* magazine*, one of the largest mansions in Manhattan, with 30 rooms, and costing $5M per annum in upkeep. They had had craftsmen from France and Italy over to build it. But this was nothing like Hugh Hefner's place and, more's the pity, there were no Great Gatsby type parties. Dinners there were

---

* Haden-Guest, Anthony (February 9, 2004). 'The Porn King in Winter', New York magazine.

sedate affairs with lively conversation, apart from Bob who rarely said much and disappeared into the kitchen to do the cooking. Kathy was the intellectual and interested in everything, especially everything scientific. Having Kathy on one side and one of their centre-fold models on the other made concentration difficult. I asked one of these girls once what her hobby was. She gave me a long smoldering look with her big brown eyes and just said, 'Beds.' It turned out she really was a collector of antique beds.

The most memorable guest was Tony Curtis, the Hollywood star, a most amusing conversationalist. But there were always interesting people to talk with.

The Gucciones were big art buyers, notably early 20th C masters such as Modigliani. Bob still saw himself, with justification, as an artist. He had a good eye and plenty of money. But even with 30 rooms, they ran out of space to put them. Kathy dragged me into one of the larger rooms on one occasion to ask my advice. Why she should have thought I knew anything about art of any kind, I have no idea. The walls were bare but ranged around the skirting board were a mass of pictures, about four deep.

'Which of these,' she demanded, 'should we hang in here?'

I guess she was just showing off their treasures but we moved round the room flipping over one stack and then the next. It was not difficult to express astonishment. When the empire collapsed after Kathy's death*, these works of art must have raised a tidy sum for the administrators.

Probably the kindest thing they did for me was to include me in their Thanksgiving celebration. In the US, that is primarily a family day, not a time to invite outsiders. Guessing that I would be on my own, they insisted I join them and I was the only non-family person there. The contrast between the wealthy, glamorous couple and their very ordinary cousins, nephews and nieces from New Jersey was remarkable but the mutual warmth was tangible.

Some years before all this, the Gucciones invited Katie and me for a weekend at their country mansion about 40 miles outside Manhattan, with a 55-acre estate overlooking the Hudson river. I did not know them so well then and, to be honest, it was fascinating but a bit scaly. The Willows's 16 rooms needed a houseful of guests but there

---

* Kathy was only 58 when she died. She launched a magazine called Longevity and wrote a book using the magazine contributions from scientists and others. Just shows you should not tempt fate.

were only two others, Bill and Carole Lyons.

Carole is an artist and they live nearby. Bill is now retired but he was a marketing consultant and never short of ideas he was trying to sell. That's a tough way to make a living as clients want to feel their own ideas are being developed, not those of the consultant. David Gluckman had the same problem which was why he stuck with IDV. New brand consultants do exist and some, like Craton, Lodge and Knight become successful but they are always working against the grain. As it happened, Don Knight, now sadly deceased, shared Mount Carmel Chambers with me and became a great friend of James Wiltshire.

Bill went to MIT after he was demobbed, a point in common he frequently mentioned, but the most remarkable thing about him is his war record.

They are both Jewish with such extremely right wing views we agreed some time ago never again to discuss Israel or the Middle East. In all other respects they are delightful. Long before America thought of joining WWII, Bill decided to do his bit against Hitler and signed up for the Air Force, partly inspired by a cousin who had done the same. Once trained, Bill, then known as 'Tiger', was stationed at Steeple Morden, Cambridge and flew Mustangs with 357th Fighter Sqdn/355th Fighter Group.

He flew the 300 mission limit by March 1945 and by then two-thirds of his colleagues had been killed. Only eight of the original 28 survived and Bill is now one of the most revered US fighter pilots ever. He is a very brave man and, amazingly, got through the war without a scratch.

Towards the end of the war, he was on his own over Belgium when he saw a German fighter he had never seen before. It was sleek and it was fast; it seemed twice as fast as anything Bill had seen before. It shot at Bill and missed because, presumably, of their different speeds. Bill retaliated with the same result, the enemy fighter peeled off for home and there was no point in following.

Returning to base, his colleagues were mostly amazed by Bill's story. Some thought he was hallucinating – too many missions. It turned out that this was the first combat involving a jet fighter. The Air Ministry had known for some time that the Germans were building them but decided not to brief the pilots that might have to fight them – another example of the Air Ministry incompetence shown in the years up to and through the war.

The Spitfire was built privately because, in the 1930s, the Air Ministry turned it down. In the event, the Spitfires and Hurricanes won the Battle of Britain. Jetsy Whittle, ex Royal Air Force himself, invented the jet engine but this too was rejected by the Air Ministry who considered it had so little value that they did not even classify the plans. The Germans collected them from the public record and the plane Bill met was the result. Some history books give Germany the credit for inventing the jet engine on the grounds that they actually built them first.

Bomber Harris, as my son's German father-in-law never fails to remind us, was a third example. The carpet bombing was not only inhumane but counter-productive as any analyst of the London Blitz should have known.

Returning to the School I buckled down to research of which the three main strands were international marketing (China), how advertising worked and how marketing performance should be measured. These did get enough top journal coverage to achieve some academic reputation. The brief descriptions below are according to those three topics and therefore not in chronological order.

I have mentioned the Chi effect before. As my research improved, my general marketing teaching deteriorated. Giving lectures on my research topics went well enough but my iconoclastic approach to marketing was poorly received by students. I now recognise that the iconoclasm was the problem. You cannot explain why X is wrong unless the class is familiar with what X is in the first place. So my lectures were better received by other faculty. It would be better not to teach the dubious traditional marketing in the first place – but that was too big a step.

In general, the School allowed me to do whatever I wanted with the exception of cigar smoking.

My office was next to the Dean's which might have been a problem but Dean Quelch turned a blind eye to the extent that he passed on any cigars he was given. He was followed by, we were told, a female economics professor from California, the lovely Laura Tyson. The view was that she must be a fully paid up member of the PCP herself. When I was introduced at the welcome party one thing was buzzing through my head: 'do not mention cigars'. This was not just my local difficulty but her close association with Bill Clinton as a member of his economic team. Younger readers may need to know that President Clinton was notorious, amongst other things, for using his cigars with young female staffers in unmentionable ways.

We smile, shake hands and I'm still thinking 'do not mention cigars'.

'So you are Tim Ambler. I expect you think I will mention your cigars.' It was uncanny.

'Well, I'm not sure about that.'

'Don't worry. My husband smokes them and I quite like the smell.'

'In that case you will like mine. I only smoke Havanas.'

In 1992 Katie and I took the train from Samarkand to Shanghai. The Chinese and Soviets had taken the two railway lines to within a mile of each other but then, because Stalin and Mao did not trust each other, not joined them up. The connection was made in 1991/2 but to different sides of the same platform as the gauges are different. Ours was, supposedly, only the second through service.

A well-known scandal at the time was that the one child family meant that boy babies were preserved but few girls made it past the cot. This was bound to cause problems 20 years later and it has. China had to put a stop to population expansion somehow and it did so. The policy is now relaxed, population is slightly shrinking and, in the absence of potential mothers, likely to shrink further.

The train was very late at scheduled stops, sometimes even a day late. Inconvenient tourists were shunted to one side to let goods trains rumble past. In Western China, then anyway, it was almost all single line track. I ran a book on how late we would be by Shanghai. The train supervisor was not amused and refused to take part. An old China hand bet on us being on time and we were – to the minute. The Chinese take punctuality very seriously.

A star member of the group was Hallard Croft, then the senior mathematics don at Peterhouse. He took his doctorate there 30 years earlier. When he wasn't doing sums and complaining about the wine at High Table, he was travelling the world. Great fun, he was always up for any unscheduled outing and we became good friends.

What took me back to China was the recognition that the relationships paradigm for marketing may be new in the West but it was how the Chinese had always seen it, in a word *guanxi*. Americans do business first and those relationships may lead to personal friendships: the Chinese make personal friendships first and those relationships may lead to business. Rather than re-invent the wheel, it seemed best to immerse myself in the Chinese market.

The late 1990s was a good time to go. Deng Xiaoping, arguably China's greatest modern leader, had not only opened business to private enterprise but created business schools* and instructed them to re-start the teaching of marketing. Translating Kotler's textbook into Chinese was easy enough (I'm not sure if he received any royalties at first but some accommodation was doubtless found) but where to get the teachers? Some were imported from the US but they did find two professors who had been teaching it pre-Mao, i.e. in the 1930s. Clearly elderly, they did pass on the basics to the new marketing PhDs, i.e. teachers to be. They financed one of these, Wang Xiucun, to spend a year with us.

The China Britain Trade Group was immensely helpful with contacts. I interviewed entrepreneurs and my interpreters were valuable as sources as well as translation. I did not need word for word translation so much as understanding their business models. *Guanxi* was indeed the name of the game.

Loaded up with all this stuff, it seemed a pity to waste it. Since my trip to China in 1992 I had been arguing that the School was too US-oriented. That was where the faculty had obtained their PhDs and that was where the case studies were located. Of course the top (theoretically international but really US) journals want US research but the School's MBA students are in their 20s. By middle age, Asia will be commercially dominant and China in particular will overtake the US. We should be teaching, I said, business in China.

Maybe I did not sell it right but, in 20 years, that made little or no impression. It did not help that one of our Deans had a Chinese wife who was totally Manhattan-oriented and pooh poohed the whole idea. Not did it help that there are so few Chinese who can teach Western MBA classes. Indians yes, Chinese no.

By chance a Canadian writer the School used, Morgen Witzel, knew a lot about China and was friendly with a number of China hands including a very good (ex-) ambassador (yes, they do exist). I never discovered the source of his knowledge but it was sound – a rare commodity then and maybe still.

'Why not practise what we preach?'

'Why not indeed.'

So we launched a 'Doing Business in China' elective course and got

---

* Largely from economics and production engineering departments of universities.

quite a good sign up, one-third Chinese. I asked why they were there. Some were ethnically Chinese but had no knowledge of China. In those days (since rectified) we had no one from the PRC. The students that did know about Chinese business methods wanted to compare the Western perspective (ours) with theirs.

Of the many speakers, the old hands were fine; but the journalists and economists included some duds who knew not whereof they spoke. Wang Xiucun attended for the year she was with us and that added credibility although that never proved to be a problem. The Chinese have immense respect for age which is a mixed blessing. So far as she was concerned, and many of her compatriots, everything I said was right simply because I was too old to be wrong. Much the same applied to her comments on our book but it was reassuring, none the less.

A couple of the China Britain Trade Group staff took the first course which was helpful in a number of ways. Overall the course was a success, as well as good learning for me. In 2000, the MBA students changed dramatically. According to them, the arrival of the Worldwide Web had altered everything. The business world was now global and there was no need for regional courses. A case study dated 1999 was already out of date. This was a whole new world.

Nothing we said made the slightest difference to this fixation until the shares in most digital companies crashed. That brought sanity back but the beliefs of the time were extraordinary. For example, one indication of business success, according to the mindset of the day, was the money burn rate: the faster a new business could spend money, the better it was doing. Our China course, along with the School's other regional courses, no longer drew students.

Witzel and I condensed our teaching materials into a primer for Westerners wanting to do business in China and it sold very well.* For the third edition we had the brainwave that a book on China might benefit from having a Chinese author so Chao Xi, a Hong Kong academic lawyer, joined the team. The publishers were excellent and it was a happy relationship from the start.

We also produced respectable journal articles to satisfy the UK's five yearly Research Assessment Exercise[†] – some with Wang Xiucun.

---

* *Doing Business in China*, Routledge, 3rd edition, 2009.

[†] The School's research is highly rated globally and the last RAE put it top for the UK: 55% of the School's research received the top 4* 'world-leading' rating. This was easily the highest percentage achieved by any UK higher education institution.

The ad research began when we hosted a 'how does advertising work?' seminar in early 1995. It all went well enough until someone at the back gently asked what he had heard that morning that he would not have heard 10 years earlier. It was an exceedingly good question. Plenty of journal articles were appearing on advertising, sometimes with new language and sometimes SONKing, but there was nothing new of substance.

This is partly a problem of age: a young brand manager, or ad agent, or marketing academic assumes that what is new to him or her, must be new to the world. And New is Good. The same still applies: read any issue of *Admap*.

Our response was to hold a rather longer seminar, at Peterhouse to give it respectability, which would make us really think. We invited three professors in related areas: Steven Rose, a molecular biologist and expert on memory and neuroscience, Igor Aleksander, an expert from Imperial College on machine 'brains' including how they dream, and Frank McKenna (Reading), a psychologist and expert on how propaganda works. The brief for all of them was not to talk about advertising but, in layman's language, about their own subjects, leaving us to draw the inferences.

Understandably, they were reluctant speakers but the venue helped. Steven left a message to ask if it was OK to bring his chimps as he used them in his experiments. I said 'yes, of course' and then spent a lot of time worrying about how to get Peterhouse to agree. Some of their undergraduates were uncouth but chimps? Should I discuss it with Hallard? I concluded that some things are best left until they have to be faced and was relieved to get a call from Steven to say he had decided not to bring his chicks after all. He hoped I had not been to any trouble on their account. The chimpanzees I had expected turned out to be one-day-old chicks which would have been no trouble at all.

Demetrios Vakratsas, a mathematician, had joined me from Texas for two years as a Post-Doctoral Fellow. When I could distract him from models of innovation diffusion, he applied his logical mind to advertising. It helped that he arrived with no preconceptions. We began with a literature review building on Simon Broadbent's 1992 synopsis of 456 studies of how advertising works, 122 of which were case histories. Simon, probably the most intelligent practicing market researcher of his day, promoted the Peterhouse seminar and was thoroughly helpful throughout.

Circulating the rather large literature review to those attending was a mistake. The general view was 'don't bother me with old stuff: what's new?' It was, however, invaluable for us as we were able to reduce these hundreds of studies down to a few simple models using Cognition (a term academia wrongly uses for thinking), Affect (feelings) and Experience of the brand. With encouragement from our then Area Chair, Tom Robertson, we sent it off to the *Journal of Marketing* which, after a struggle, made it the lead paper in that issue.*

Vakratsas went on to a successful academic career in Canada and marriage with a brilliant and beautiful doctor, also Greek, but not before unwisely visiting his home country. He had avoided national service by going to Texas for his higher education. Ten years later he thought they must have forgotten about that but they hadn't. He spent 18 months camping on the Macedonian border. Now a dozen years older than the others, he had nothing in common with them. They promptly made him a Sergeant Major and he did not like the responsibilities of that either. They compromised on Sergeant. He became brown, lean and fit. It did him a power of good.

The outcome from the seminar, JM paper aside, was that we should pursue neuroscience as the most likely avenue for the best understanding of how advertising works. Of course, different ads work in different ways according to context. This means that there are always exceptions and generalisations are dangerous. Nevertheless one can talk about which models are most often correct, or insightful, and which are, most often, misleading. The main 'persuasion' model is derived from the 19th century AIDA in which Attention drives Interest which in turn drives Desire leading to Action. It was originally a model of selling, not advertising, where it does work. Of course the 100 years since AIDA arrived have seen increased complexity in models of how advertising works as well as plenty of SONKing but the persuasion approach is still the holy grail in the US.

The main competitor was Ehrenberg's ATR model (Awareness leading to Trial leading to Reinforcement), the trial being a semi-random effect, e.g. from one's usual brand being out of stock, more often than choice induced by advertising. The key difference is that Ehrenberg saw habit dominating advertising as a predictor of choice and the persuasion advocates had it the other way around. Neither could

---

* Five years later it got a prize for the best JM paper of that year: 'How Advertising Works: What Do We Really Know?' Journal of Marketing, 63(1 January), 1999, 26-43.

be proved or disproved without knowing what is going on in people's heads.

Four enthusiastic supporters* funded the £40K Steven Rose needed for the neuroscience side of the research and we were off. We knew two things before we started:

1   Advertising cannot directly affect sales because ads are seen so long before sales that ads can only affect memory (brand equity) which later affects sales. Some research had already showed that ads 'warmed up' the memory of brand experience, e.g. those seeing ads after drinking Nescafe recalled Nescafe more favourably than those with the identical experience but without receiving Nescafe ads.

2   Thanks to pioneering work by Antonio Damasio,[†] we knew that reason plays little, if any, part in brand choice. Advertising a unique product advantage to persuade people to switch brands is therefore unlikely to work.

Steven wanted to use the top of the range MEG brain scanning equipment. The only one in Europe at that time was in a redundant A bomb plant in Germany. MEG machines need the lead lining to keep out external electromagnetic influences. The Germans were a bit stuffy about doping half our subjects to cut off their emotions so we had to split the research to the emotions bit in the UK and the brain scanning in Germany. It was, however, helpful that our chief, and very valuable, analyst, Sven Braeutigam, is himself German. He now has a MEG machine more or less dedicated to his use in Oxford.

The results were not inconsistent with our MAC model, i.e. Memory matters more than Affect which matters more than Cognition (or Cogitation). The German experiment scanned reactions to the ads. Part 2 (scanning as buying choices were being made) took us to a newer and cheaper (it was funded by the EU) machine in Helsinki. There are several now in the UK as well as improved machines using similar brain scanning techniques such as fMRI.

This round supported the findings in 1 and 2 above although the parts of the brain 'lighting up' when making a buying choice were not quite as Damasio proposed. We did find that male and female brain patterns differ (no comment) and the ways that brand choice varied

---

* They wanted to be anonymous as they were concerned about public animosity to major advertisers messing with their brains.

† Damasio, Antonio R. (1994), *Descartes' Error: Emotion, Reason and the Human Brain*. London: Papermac (Macmillan).

when the brands were, and were not, familiar. We may even have identified where (some) brand equity sits in the brain but such a claim would be premature.

Sadly, time, opportunities and research money ran out at that point and the team had to disband before we had taken the research to its logical conclusion. More papers came from it but the principal consequence was the *Handbook of Advertising*. The publishers, Sage, were keen I should take it on and Paddy Barwise agreed with them. Gerry Tellis* agreed to be co-editor and we found a terrific Australian researcher, Jane Scott. The process was long but painless and we were all happy with the result. At £90 ($150) a copy it was never going to be a big seller but it has done well enough.

In one of its periodic fits of trying to get attention for Marketing in the Boardroom, the half dozen or so senior marketeers in the UK, mostly knights of the realm, created the Marketing Council with John Stubbs, a senior Unilever marketeer, as the chief, and indeed only, executive. Before the knights rode off in all directions, thereby sabotaging the whole project, Stubbs approached me to conduct a study of how firms measured marketing performance. They weren't interested in theory, just what was actually done.

The Marketing Council provided enough funding to cover a Post Doc for two years. When another Greek, Flora Kokkinaki, arrived glammed up for the interview, the interview was over. Sadly, the glammed up version rarely reappeared; more often she was all in black looking like Electra at Agamemnon's tomb. Wonderfully Greek in fact. Unlike Vakratsas though, Kokkinaki arrived from UCL with plenty of preconceptions about everything. We had our ups and downs. But she is a talented person and it all worked out really well. She is now a successful academic in Greece.

Collecting data was the big obstacle. Measurement processes were in the dark ages even in the most famous marketing companies. They knew it and did not wish to admit to it. The focus on costs rather than profits meant that brand managers were more interested in spending their budgets, and not a penny more or less, than making profits. Market share was, unsurprisingly, the most frequent measure but otherwise financial measures dominated non-financial. Brand equity had only been popularised by David Aaker a few years earlier;

---

* University of Southern California, Los Angeles.

unsurprisingly also that had made almost no impact. I suspect that is still true as people continue to confuse the asset itself (brand equity) with the measures of that asset.

We called the topic 'marketing metrics' as the word 'metric' was not then in common use. The (US) Marketing Science Institute bought into the idea and our research very quickly.* Marketing Metrics remained their lead priority research area for the next 10 years. Journals, however, turned up their noses on the grounds that there was no theory. We cobbled together some theory but hit the 'no demand for that' response just like the corner shop refusing to take a new brand. How can there be a demand for something that has not previously existed? You might expect marketing academics to know about things like that but the reality is that they are just as production oriented as other academics.

Nevertheless there were strong findings from analysis of the data. Return on investment, much hyped as the holy grail, is actually a bad metric to use; it gives rise to under investment and misleading conclusions. Quite a few 'customer value' metrics are similarly false as are all forms of cash flow forecasts. Assessing marketing performance boils down to two sets of metrics: short term profits (easy) and the changes in brand equity (difficult).

Marketing metrics became a major topic for academia around the world. Philip Kotler in particular was a big fan and very supportive. He nominated the second edition of the book, *Marketing and the Bottom Line*, for the marketing book of the year award in the US and it would have won but for being pipped by Paddy Barwise's and Sean Meehan's book, *Simply Better*. It seems that it was.†

This research prompted many invitations from around the world. Most I rejected on the grounds that I had joined the School to avoid Heathrow and 747s. Those I accepted included Australia, New Zealand, Kiev, Reykjavik, Ireland, Athens, Cyprus, Beijing and, of course, the USA. The Australians, led by Roger James and Chris Styles, have been especially hospitable and generous. Both practitioners and consultants such as Kevin Luscombe have a more pragmatic approach to marketing than their UK equivalents.

---

* Tim Ambler and Flora Kokkinaki, Marketing Performance Assessment: Current Practice and the Role of Firm Orientation, 1999, Marketing Science Institute Working Paper #99-114.

† Its theme was that marketeers try too hard to create, and promote, difference when they should just be focusing on making the brand experience better.

One would have thought it blindingly obvious that academics would like to have their work make a difference in the real world and that practitioners would like to improve their knowledge and skills, and therefore need research to help them do so. The US have a body, the Marketing Science Institute (MSI) mentioned above, charged with exactly that. The large marketing companies pay for a small administration which publishes what the practitioners want to know and also the academic working papers that respond to those requests. It is not that tidy but that is the basis and it works very well. They also run seminars on those themes with a mix of academic and practitioner speakers to ensure that the ivory tower has transparent walls.

Like many others, I liked to publish with MSI as the review process is far less picky and the lead time is only half that of a top journal. Furthermore, publishing a working paper does not preclude top journal publication later.

The UK has nothing similar nor virtually any form of communication between the two groups beyond individual consultancy and a little executive education. The US has crossover journals like *Harvard Business Review*. The closest the UK comes to that are *Market Leader*, the Marketing Society's thoughtful house journal edited by the eternally youthful Judie Lannon, and *Admap*, an intelligent guide to advertising – but both of those are really practitioner oriented.

My efforts to achieve crossover included giving the equal top prize at the annual UK academic conference to the paper, judged by practitioners, to be of most value to practitioners. It was hard to scrape up any entries amongst the 500 submitted, never mind find a winner worth publishing in *Market Leader*. The awful truth is that British marketing practitioners have as much interest in new knowledge as the academics have in practices. Neither group has any regard for the other and both are essentially followers of fashion.

For example, when someone like Bain's Fred Reichheld comes up with a single marketing metric such as Net Promoter Score, practitioners rush to climb aboard the new bandwagon. Reichheld is not an academic nor even, in my opinion, a responsible researcher and this, like his previous famous suggestions about retaining customers being six times more profitable than gaining customers, is mostly rubbish. Academics publish rebuttals but these are ignored in the practitioner world. Sadly, two separate worlds. To be fair, Reichheld did make some good points and those include get boards to focus on what consumers are saying about your and competitive brands compared with what they are buying. Too many boards do not consider these issues at all.

The Catholic church used to burn heretics because being *nearly* right, they did more damage to the true faith than the pagans did. Indeed, in the course of trying to recruit them, the Catholic church was positively nice to pagans. Burning at the stake has gone out of fashion but the likes of Reichheld and any that promote Return On Investment as a marketing metric should receive the modern equivalent.

In all of this the Director General of the Marketing Society, Hugh Burkitt, has been a tower of strength. We knew each other from the days when Hugh took over some of Winston Fletcher's responsibilities and was CEO of one of IDV's ad agencies. His support was noble but we were both up against forces many times more powerful than us.

That could also be said of the Gods of Golf; we both love playing the game but maybe the game does not love us. In one competition our team won a prize for 'best use of the golf course'. His office diary records these meetings as 'Seminars on Global Projections' whereas my secretary simply had to say that I was on a course. Golf aside he has not only been Director General of the Marketing Society longer than anyone else (in recent times anyway) but done the job better than anyone else. When he arrived it was near bankrupt and staggering; now it is thriving. That may be related to his other great talent: taking the patter song role in Gilbert and Sullivan operas.

Various other areas for research and publication took their place, often in order to cooperate with colleagues. Academia needs collaboration and is far stronger for it both socially and for new discoveries. The truly solo academic researcher is as rare and the truly solo entrepreneur. One usually gets the credit but look a little harder and you will usually find another pair of hands in there somewhere.

The last area that should be mentioned is a series of sallies against the Political Correctness Police. The cause of problems with alcohol, food (obesity) and childhood deprivation (growing up too soon, nine year olds wearing bras etc.) is typically alleged to be advertising.

Most marketing academics regard marketing and advertising as good things that grow consumer well being, choice and the economy. But marketing and advertising are merely tools and any tool can be used for both good and bad purposes. That is the neutral position that almost no one adopts. The main school is that marketing is good except where it can be shown not to be. There is a smaller but vociferous opposition school, known as 'social marketing', who take the view that marketing is bad when it is conducted by profit seeking bodies but good when it is conducted by government. In this perception, advertising cars is bad because the people who buy them will have accidents whereas seat belt advertising by government is good.

So when a government department wishes to intervene with new regulation, it commissions social marketing academics to assess the evidence. In much the same way that I never lost a research battle with Heublein, I have never come across a case where social marketeers failed to provide the government department with the evidence it sought. These are all fine people and I am not alleging any impropriety, just that each of us wears his own spectacles when searching for the truth.

Most of the differences arise from selective use of the literature and faulty analysis and presentation. Papers from social marketeers tend to be polemic, not academic.

Given the social marketeers' disapproval of profit seeking, it is ironic that their line of work is much more profitable than conventional marketing research. Government appears to be generous with our money.

Taking the particular battles:

- Advertising does not, in fact, increase the total sales of alcohol nor under-age sales. The problems mostly arise from a failure to apply existing laws and codes. For example, no alcohol is supposed to be targeted to the under-aged but some manifestly is.
- Obesity is not caused by advertising. The salty/fatty/sweet foods and drinks that get the blame may have a part to play, along with changed parenting and family eating habits and, oddly, central heating. The advertising of the suspect foods has actually been declining as obesity has been growing.
- The case presented for a minimum price of alcohol is speculative at least and highly suspect. At the time of writing, the government has withdrawn its plan for minimum pricing in England and Wales but that is not all that sensible either. There is so little empirical evidence around the world that it would make sense to introduce it is a small region to see the impact, excluding fringe areas which would obviously be distorted.
- Advertising is not robbing children of their childhoods. Digital

communications and family breakdown/health probably are having negative effects.

When I joined in 1991, London Business School was in the upper middle of international rankings if US schools were included and our economics and finance faculties were highly rated but, despite the calibre of Ehrenberg and Simmonds, the marketing area was pretty average. By the time I finally left 20 years later, we were near the top both as a school and as a marketing area. If you have read thus far, you will know that I had little part in that transformation, nothing more than a few papers, a constant irritant and a small hand in some of the recruitment. I just happened to be there at the right time. Lucky again. Part of the reason for the School's success is that it is a magnet for international talent, much of which remains in London. London and the School amplify each other's attraction and the School is surely an important contributor to the UK economy.

The School is lucky currently to have Sir Andrew Likierman as dean. He was the first internal appointment in my time but had proved his worth when holding the fort for a previous incoming dean. Now the School has its own long term veteran but also someone well integrated with both government and the City. He modernised the government's accounting and is Chairman of the National Audit Office. He has been a director both of Barclays Bank and the Bank of England.

Small as my part in the School was, some of my research was pioneering. One can never be entirely sure what one can claim. As soon as one puts a stake in the ground as being first, someone else will pop up with a prior claim. I was the first to introduce the first three topics but just one of the pioneers in the others below:

- Using neuroscience to understand how advertising works (1995).
- Employer branding (with Simon Barrow, 1996). Internal marketing as a vague concept had long been around but not the formal marketing, branding and measurement with employees taking the place of consumers. The original is far the most often requested of my papers.
- Marketing metrics, i.e. formal measures of marketing performance (1997) which led to the dashboard concept.*
- Application of relationship marketing to export markets (with

---

* My first paper on that was a lot earlier: 'Measurement and Control in Marketing', OMEGA, The International Journal of Management Science, 1(3), 1973.

Chris Styles, 1994).
- The Chinese approach to marketing (1995).

Unlike a commercial company, an academic unit, be it a university, school or area, has very little corporate value added from being a unit: reputation is the sum of the individuals. I did a year as Area Chair and can testify that the only parts of the job that need doing well, and perhaps at all, are faculty recruitment and retaining the stars. Plans, committees and reports can all safely be disregarded. Yes, some faculty do need to be eased out but the contract renewal process largely takes care of that. And that is conducted by the Professoriat, not the Area Chair.

Paddy Barwise got the up-scaling going and one of the early recruits, Bruce Hardie, is still there. He is now full professor and has done a number of School roles like improving the PhD programme. He is hugely talented, as are all those mentioned in this section so I will not repeat that point but just mention a few personal matters to bring life to the people. No offence is intended either to them or to those unmentioned only for reasons of space.

Bruce is a quant jock from New Zealand, via Wharton, and distinguished by the most disorderly office (he thinks it is ordered) known to man. If one can get the door open one finds every flat surface covered in piles of books. Visits gladden my heart as the extent of disorder in my own office pales by comparison. Given the exceptionally boring nature of his topics, it is testament to his hard-learned teaching skills that his classes are over-subscribed.

Nirmalya Kumar had a bit of a Simmonds reputation in his early days. His colleagues were very much for or against him but I put that down to jealousy: his output has been and still is amazing. When it mattered for his career, he was gaining top journal acceptances for his papers like a machine gun. His academic reputation built, he turned to the wider business community with books instead of journal articles. One day he would say he was thinking of writing a book on some thought provoking subject and the next day, or so it seemed, the book would be on your desk. He is from Calcutta and is now one of the most famous business academics in his homeland as well as in the US and globally. His energy makes me feel tired just thinking of it. Executives love him and bureaucrats do not. He is not a conformist but he is a fantastic asset for the School.

Naufel Vilcassim is from Sri Lanka but reached us with a big reputation gained in the US primarily as a modeller. His editorial board appointments testify to the width of his interests and readiness to review serious papers: *Marketing Science, Journal of Marketing Research, Quantitative Marketing and Economics, International Journal of Research in Marketing, Asian Journal of Marketing.* I think he joined the School because of its proximity to Lord's.

Nader Tavassoli, the Area Chair for four of the seven years to 2013, has a fine carpet in his office on account of his family being purveyors of oriental carpets. He reached London via Germany, Columbia and MIT and belongs to the psych school of marketing, being particularly expert on brands. The amount of time he gives the School must circumscribe his own interests.

John Roberts is another MIT man but, as a dyed in the sheep Australian, is only prepared to tolerate England in summer. It is hard to believe he is close to retirement as he has taken to climbing mountains. He covers a similar area to Naufel (strategy and models) although John's are not necessarily mathematical. He is also a bon viveur with a fine appreciation of wine and food. His partner, Baljit Sidhu, is an accounting academic, originally from Malaysia. She does her best to keep him in order.

I have already mentioned Kent Grayson, a star in our firmament before returning to Northwestern (Kellogg). Mark Ritson, an Englishman returned via the Carlson School at Minnesota. Kent could do anything, even research, but the playground for them both was the classroom, invariably overfilled. Mark was, and I dare say is still, wonderfully undisciplined except when it mattered, notably being on time for class and hitting magazine deadlines. I don't think he could be serious long enough to write research papers beyond ethnography which is mad anyway and seemed to require camping out with countercultures. When both Kent returned home and Mark went to Melbourne, I lost two good drinking buddies.

Finally, another brief word on Paddy Barwise who, like his mentor Andrew Ehrenberg, is probably the best integrated into British marketing practice be it the Marketing Society, Market Research Society, Which?, broadcast media regulation and the BBC and as an expert witness.

My younger and more recent area colleagues may be grateful not to have appeared above but I should mention a few of the others in the Marketing Area as they were good colleagues: Marco Bertini, Simona Botti, Rajesh Chandy, David Faro, Dan Goldstein, Anja Lambrecht, and John Mullins.

It is probably worth recording two major routes to the same conclusion from all this brain cudgelling. Firstly that metrics are about as important for marketing, or business in general, as keeping score is for cricket. Of course one needs to know the competitive position and the performance when the match is over but both are determined by what happens in the middle, not by the scratchings of the scorer. Important yes, very important no. And the idea that one should predict the outcome from the metrics, i.e. forecast performance, using metrics rather than what the players do in the nets, is plain daft. Modern large firms spend far too much time and money on metrics and accounting matters but not enough on practice, i.e. getting out into the marketplace.

Secondly, firms should think more about how profits arise. I have mentioned before that board time can typically be divided into making, counting and spending money. Making the money is the difficult part; any fool can count it or spend it. Yet boards spend nine times more hours counting and spending the money than they do on making it, i.e. marketing. Business schools should teach nothing but marketing.

But my point is more fundamental than that. Successful firms start with no money but any amount of time and end up with plenty of money but no time. Phone any manager in any large corporation and she will be in a meeting. All of them are run ragged with demands on their time. Banks, on the other hand, are only too happy to lend more money to large, successful corporations.

To become more successful, large firms have to give up their preoccupation not just with metrics but with money itself. Firms do not exist merely to get bank interest on cash surpluses. Added value comes from how they spend their time, not how they count or spend their money. Advertising performance has very little to do with the size of the budget and everything to do with consumer empathy. Money does not breed money but good use of managerial time does.

Cut the market research budget by 80%. Rent office space just one day a week and live the brand the other four. Marketeers will enjoy life more and be more successful that way.

Towards the end of my time at the School, I became more and more involved with political matters, primarily sketching how the costs of government should be reduced and challenging UK and EU regulation. I thought and hoped that this was good for School PR and certainly no one objected. As this chapter has now used its allotted span, these political matters will have to be deferred until the next.

# Chapter 11

# Government: Regulation bad, Marketing good

*This final chapter deals mostly with political matters and in particular tangling with excessive government bureaucracy and red tape. Consumers are not stupid and it is far better to persuade people using market forces than coerce them through regulation and especially regulation that is not enforced and does not work as is mostly the case.*

*I tried, but failed, to sell politicians on the concept of 'Taxpayer value', in other words how marketing and good business practice could give taxpayers better services at less cost. We are all taxpayers, including those who pay no income tax. Writing in 2013 it is encouraging to see all three main political parties moving in that direction, albeit slowly and without the copyline. Tangential is government's failure to engage so many teenage boys or even help the voluntary organisations, such as the Downside Settlement, who do.*

In particular it covers:

- *Politics*
  - *The Tucker dinners*
  - EUtopia
  - Downsizing government
  - Taxpayer value
- *Regulation often does not work, marketing does*
  - The British Chambers of Commerce
  - The Adam Smith Institute
  - Leave regulation to the EU
- *The Downside Settlement in Bermondsey*
- *Wolverhampton and Dudley Breweries*
- *The North Norfolk Conservative Microcosm*

I cannot now recall how the Tucker dinners came about except that Young & Rubicam wanted to entertain clients and prospective clients in a novel way. Probably the idea came from Geoffrey Tucker (1925–2003), a professional networker, who enjoyed good wine and knew that decent wine would lure top politicians to dinner with Y&R and its guests. Geoffrey had been employed by Y&R for many years and was the link man in rescuing the 1987 election for Margaret Thatcher. The driver on the Y&R side was Clive Holland, an old friend. Anyway, the deal was that I would arrange for J&B to provide wine (charged to Y&R) and an expert to talk about the wines and Geoffrey would provide a top politician.

Geoffrey had been amongst the top ranks of Conservative politicians since the 1950s. His *Guardian* obituary put it: 'He helped Macmillan, Heath and Thatcher get into Downing Street.' It also said (waspishly?) that he offered unsolicited advice to John Major. Although he never produced the Prime Minister at our dinners, they did get on well. Geoffrey's star was perhaps beginning to wane by the time I knew him, but he was a pioneer of modern campaigning methods including, shock, horror, the use of advertising agencies. Most of the Cabinet showed up at his annual cocktail parties at Brooks's.

We must have had about eight or nine of these dinners over two years. Our guests included Douglas Hurd (when he was Foreign Secretary), Michael Portillo (when he was Financial Secretary), Lord (Kenneth) Baker (ex Home Secretary and Education Secretary), Willie Whitelaw (when he was Willie Whitelaw) and also, at my instigation, Robin Butler (my Orley Farm friend and then Cabinet Secretary). Butler, unsurprisingly perhaps, has the gift of speaking in such a confidential way that one is convinced one has just heard the innermost secrets of state. Only on reflection later the realisation dawns that one has been entertained but not informed. He was a great guest and created a memorable evening for us all.

The dinners took place in the private dining room of Buck's Club with about eight of us round the table. Whitelaw, true to form, was especially affable. When I was introduced, he grasped my hand warmly and told me how very good it was to see me again so convincingly that I thought I really had met him before. I do not do it as well as he did but the technique works well.

Discussion was frank and Jim Naughtie (later to join the BBC's Today programme) helped ensure it was. Portillo got quite a grilling: for a Financial Secretary, although charming and highly intelligent, he did not seem to know much about financial matters.

The most historically interesting was Douglas Hurd. It was early in the Balkan war and we suggested that peace would only be achieved if the ethnic groups were separated. He did not use the word 'nonsense' but that was the drift of his response. The Foreign Office had, of course, fully considered all options including the mapping of the ethnic populations. A great many lives would have been saved if the separation had taken place although we know from India in 1947 what happens if it is badly done.

The most enjoyable political dinner was my *tête à tête* with Edwina Currie, then Health Minister and one of the few women Margaret Thatcher promoted to ministerial rank. She wanted the lowdown on alcohol and health issues from the industry perspective. The two of us had a convivial dinner in the House of Commons unencumbered by civil servants, something ministers are not supposed to do. Then only 40, she was a very attractive woman but I was not accorded the favours subsequently enjoyed, or so gossip had it, by Prime Minister John Major. Edwina's enthusiasm for speaking her mind cost her the job during the salmonella scare in 1988. It later turned out that she was right but the government was trying to cover it up.

Mike Waterson, the AA's guru and also owner of *Admap*, various statistical records and WARC, the advertising publications database, had earlier introduced me to Keith Boyfield (an independent economist but not a card carrying member of the brotherhood) with whom I worked on a number of papers for the Advertising Association. Boyfield in turn introduced me to the highly effective and genial Director of the Adam Smith Institute (ASI), Eamonn Butler. It has been, for me at least, a most agreeable business relationship in the 10 years or so since. My first paper for them, attacking the methodology of university research grants, was in 2003. ASI kindly titled me 'Senior Fellow' to explain my role as their specialist on regulatory matters, now mostly for the financial sector, although when other matters infuriate me enough, an ASI Blog relieves the stress. They also provide civilised debating shops akin to the Tucker dinners but over lunch.

After some joint work on regulators (see below), Boyfield and I decided to try to make sense of the EU. Irritated, then as now, by ill-informed politicians sounding off about whether we should stay in, or leave, we wrote a 2006 paper for the Adam Smith Institute. The EU is clearly good in principle and, equally clearly, not so good in practice. Neither leaving nor staying in the present EU is optimal but what exactly is the ideal EU in which we should remain?

We researched the costs and issues in the UK and Brussels. We had help and support from many quarters but chief amongst them was Bryan Cassidy, then a member but previously chairman of the EU Economic and Social Committee. He opened doors everywhere in Brussels.

We titled the paper 'EUtopia' and sent it to the usual suspects. It set out a pragmatic ideal, in other words what is the best that can realistically be expected. The fisheries policy for example is daft as it promotes waste not conservation. Some minor improvement has taken place since but not the radical change needed. Sending UK money to Brussels so that they can send it back to UK regions having wasted much of it along the way is equally daft.

In one of my many forays in Portcullis House*, I found myself in a lift with William Hague, then Shadow Foreign Secretary. I asked if he had seen the paper.

'Yes. It is on my desk.'

Soon after, he spoke at a small seminar on the subject at the Adam Smith Institute and pronounced it the best paper on the subject he had ever read. We have tried reminding him of that recently but, sadly, he and his Europe Minister, David Lidington, seem to have been captured by the FCO. Haig did announce, in mid 2013, he would vote to leave the EU if the vote was held today but that was a tactical ploy to take the then heat off Cameron.

An earlier obvious target was government waste. Most civil servants, we considered, could be fired without the country at large even noticing. The front line, namely the spending on schools, National Health Service or anything else of direct benefit to populace was not being challenged, just the bureaucracy behind it. As noted above, I coined the term 'Taxpayer Value' akin to Shareholder Value to indicate this was not a matter of costs but value for money. Taxpayers wanted better services for less cost. Business routinely achieves that even when it looks impossible but public servants do not think that way. The moment someone drops a handkerchief, public servants demand more money to pick it up.

Take nuclear submarines for example. To have one at sea, the engi-

---

* The Westminster MPs' office block.

neers insist on having three others in dock. It's partly because they cannot play with their toys when they are at sea but more because it has always been that way. Initially no doubt, nuclear subs were experimental and needed the time out. After 50 years you might have thought they would have got the hang of them: maintenance should have been routinised and spare parts should be ready to install. Imagine having three Jumbo jets being grounded for every one that was operational. My point was, and is, that the mindset of politicians and public servants needs to be recast to Taxpayer Value.

Keith opted out as an author but provided a number of valuable contacts. Some were supportive but some, such as the Centre for Policy Studies, considered such a study old hat. They were wrong because, although the idea had been much bandied about, it had not been quantified. The guestimation turned out to be quite close to the mark. On the positive side Keith and I found quite a number of knowledgeable informants all of whom were helpful but asked to be anonymous. There was a reluctance to bite the feeding hand.

When Margaret Thatcher did round 1 of this in the 1980s she was surprised to find that first one and then the next private sector heavy she put on the case, failed totally. The union of civil servants yields nothing to the miners when it comes to protecting vested interests. Outsiders simply bounced off the serried ranks. Luckily there was a small group of very bright insiders who saw the need and delivered the first substantial cuts in the civil service since WWII. She and they knew that round 2 was needed but she was gone before she could do it. Luckily, one of these bright civil servants, then retired, was able to brief me extensively and subsequently endorsed my findings.

Given the lack of interest from the Centre for Policy Studies and because I had not then got close to ASI, it was published as a London Business School Working Paper (October 2001) and subsequently in Germany.* No, I don't know why. Without going into details here, the best example is the MoD. By then, the number of staff in the MoD was about the same as the total number of our armed forces. Talking with senior retired military men it became obvious that, apart from a few policy and strategy people, and accountants, in Whitehall, the armed forces could easily fend for themselves and get better equipment sooner and cheaper. Just compare the price of a frigate bought for the Danish navy with that bought for the Royal Navy –

---

* *Withering the State*, 2011, Verlag Dr M_ller, ISBN: 978-3-639-30755-1

the Danes pay about half for ships which do the same job. Yes, the more sophisticated British ship should defeat a similar but less sophisticated foreigner but they do not always fight with the weapons we want them to fight with. The Argentinian navy may not have been up to much but the Exocets bought from the French accounted for HMS *Sheffield*.

*Withering the State* was sent widely. The Permanent Secretary at the Treasury provided a wonderfully courteous civil service reply and Chris Powell, head of the Labour Party's advertising agency, was complimentary but said the ideas would just be stolen without attribution. He was right. A year or so later Gordon Brown produced something very similar, but, being Brown, it was not implemented.

David Laws was interested for the Lib Dems, at least enough to buy me lunch and I think he used it for his 'Orange Book' along similar lines. Not something that was popular in his own party.

But the Tories, for whom it should have been meat and drink, were not interested. Mike Waterson also thought this absurd and arranged for lunch at the Commons with his constituency MP, Theresa May, then Chair of the Conservative Party, now Home Secretary.

I knew it would be a good lunch because, as we sat down, Mrs May said, 'I hope you will be having wine'. I mumbled something equivocal and she continued, 'it is so much easier to order a bottle.'

'None for me thank you,' said the unusually abstemious Waterson.

'Good,' said she, 'then there should be enough for Tim and me.'

She had read, or looked at, the paper and got straight to the point: 'Howard Flight, our Shadow Financial Secretary, is looking at this matter. I suggest you send a copy to him and tell him that was my suggestion.'

Flight had made a ton of money in the City before becoming an MP. His partner was Tim Guinness who had been with me at MIT. Flight had picked up a USA MBA at the same time. He loved the paper and we were off to a good start. He wanted it redone from scratch.

He was right but the original had taken months and it was a daunting prospect. His plan was to send each of the Shadow Cabinet in turn a draft copy of their section and then visit each of them to record comments, agreements and disagreements. I hired, thanks to the Adam Smith Institute, a researcher just down from Cambridge with a good degree, Michael Fry who proved first class. This was an internship before he went on to Sandhurst. I said I hoped my comments on the MoD would not blight his career and asked which branch of the military he intended to join – if he had the choice.

'The Household Cavalry.'

'Can you ride?'

'No.'

'Any family connections?'

'No.'

I explained, as one does to young persons, that being unable to ride, with no connections and no money, he was as likely to be invited to join the Household Cavalry as I was to be invited to join the Royal Ballet. We kept in touch for a few years and the last I heard of him was that he was commanding the Household Cavalry escort for the Queen's opening of Parliament. My invitation to open with the Royal Ballet seems to have been lost in the post.

Howard Flight was wonderful to work with. Despite being so busy, he always had time for the two of us, was supportive and was never knocked back by reverses. Fry re-did what could be done from sourced material and Flight and I traipsed around the Shadow Cabinet. Some were supportive, some were indifferent and some were downright hostile. There were some lovely moments including one when we visited Theresa May in her new very large and pristine corner office in Portcullis House with not an ashtray in sight. Flight was then an enthusiastic smoker and asked permission.

'Well actually, Howard, I'd rather you didn't.'

With which he produced his packet and struck a light.

Mrs May looked at me and raised her eyebrows but said nothing.

She was, of course, one of the supportive ones. The other extreme was David Willetts, then Shadow Work and Pensions Secretary. He was in a towering rage even before I had sat down or said anything bar my extreme pleasure at having the honour to meet him.

'Do you think,' he demanded, 'that an outsider like you could possibly have anything useful to contribute which Oliver and I, with lifetimes in politics, would not have already covered?'

I responded with something about woods and trees but that merely added petrol to the flames. Eventually I was allowed to make my pitch as he sat fulminating. Interesting yes but not an experience I'd care to repeat. Willetts maintained his efforts to undermine our work including several inaccurate, and frankly rather stupid, memos to Flight. I have never understood 'Two Brains' Willetts' reputation. I know he got a First in PPE at Christ Church and was in charge of monetary policy at the Treasury when he was only 26 but I regard that as cleverness rather than intelligence. The truth of the matter is probably that he did not like being challenged by an academic from London Business School.

By contrast, Eric Pickles, who had been given rather a mingy office, was as sensible and straightforward as he always seems on the media.

The best fun was Nicholas Soames, then Shadow Defence Secretary. He should have been given the job when the Coalition got in because Dr Liam Fox had very little grasp of it. Be that as it may, when I explained the proposal was to get rid of 90% of the MoD he made a play of falling off his chair and told me I was talking xxx (fill in your own expletives but they won't be enough). We had four or five meetings and eventually he came round to most of our proposal thanks to discussions he had had with various retired generals all of whom, or so he said, supported our position. He has since been forceful in the House about the MoD bureaucracy and some cuts have indeed been made – but nothing like enough.

Perhaps the most difficult meeting was with Michael Howard, by then Leader of HM Opposition. Flight told me to expect an easy ride as he had softened him up, but I expect Willetts must have got to him as Howard had got completely the wrong end of the stick and did not take kindly to being corrected. The other main source of negativity was Conservative Central Office. This was a Not Invented Here problem in that they were supposed to be in charge of policy initiatives, not Howard Flight. Michael Howard's protégé, a chap called David Cameron, may have had a hand in that.

This stage of the project culminated with a presentation of the final document, which I, wittily I thought if not with any originality, called The Blueprint, to Oliver Letwin, Flight's boss as Shadow Chancellor. Despite Flight's assurances that we had Letwin's support it became clear we didn't. As the meeting closed I asked Letwin what he would like us to do with the report.

'Find the deepest hole you can and bury it for ever.'

Those were, more or less, his exact words and although I got a generous thank you letter from the Party Leader later, it was hardly an appreciation of the work we had done or even the work I had done for Letwin earlier on the immigration figures. Arithmetic is not his strongest suit.

Flight is nothing if not tenacious and he persuaded the Party Leader that the work should be done again, 'properly this time', and he found David James* who had achieved fame by rescuing the Millennium Dome, to lead the new project. A most genial and amiable man, I got on very well with him and he invited me to join his team. As it turned out, he was a formidable spokesman for the findings but was not capable of running the project itself. Conservative Central Office moved in. It was not long before I was moved out but I took satisfaction from Round 3 of this project reaching broadly the same conclusions. The saving was the same £35bn. annual savings as the previous two rounds had found although the calculations were different.

The Party was split on what to do with them. Gordon Brown was very successfully covering the media with allegations that the Tories were the party of cuts and public services would only be safe with him. The Tory response should have been 'Taxpayer Value', i.e. better public services at less cost, but high command, Flight apart, never got it.[†] Central Office claimed that the concept was too complex for ordinary voters so I commissioned some market research which showed that they were wrong. That, of course, simply increased the hostility.

The leadership wanted to get rid of the 'nasty party' image and tried to communicate that the Tories would be just as generous, not least in ring-fencing the NHS, as Labour. At a time when expenditure was running wild and bureaucracy, especially that in the NHS, was killing people off, that strategy was insane. When the Tories came to power in 2010, they had to reverse it and The Blueprint, or its successor, should have been implemented. They did talk the talk but walked little of the walk. Apart from some MoD cuts, Michael Gove has halved the staffing of the Department for Education. Elsewhere the performance is unimpressive.

None of these outcomes were the result of rational analysis but of personalities and emotions, politics in other words, and politics are not my natural habitat. Michael Fry did a grand job and I have no idea if our project had any influence on what later transpired. All I know is that events proved us right.

Howard Flight certainly ruffled a few feathers, as indeed a Financial Secretary should, but, in the run up to the 2005 election, he was

---

* His reward was a life peerage granted in 2006.

† The only other senior politician to buy into the Taxpayer Value label was Boris Johnson, then editor of the *Spectator*. Indeed he was so enthusiastic that he nicked it and based a column on it. He was good enough to invite me to lunch as an apology for the lack of attribution.

unjustly cast aside. Many thought it was unfair and it was a good day for politics when, in November 2010, David Cameron appointed him to the Lords.

In the course of writing *Withering the State*, I met Sally Low, the head of policy at the British Chambers of Commerce. Her primary concern, or that of BCC members, was over-regulation which was costing British business, and ultimately British consumers, a fortune. The Labour government was passing far more regulations than its predecessor did. And it was not just Whitehall, Brussels may create fewer regulations but they were a lot more expensive, bureaucratic and, in many cases, inappropriate. After an initial meeting where lots of people agreed to do lots of things, everyone fell out except Sally, Francis Chittenden* and me.

The BCC had pioneered an annual 'barometer' which showed the extent to which the regulations since Labour came to power had added to the financial burdens on business. Sally wanted us to take over the maintenance of the barometer and expose the incompetence which lay behind the regulations. Over the next eight years Francis and I chronicled, in annual reports published by BCC, the amount of extra burden and how the system supposed to restrict the quantity and increase the quality was failing.

Government took some note and initially we had a fight with the lead department – then Trade and Industry but now known as BIS. That subsided as both they and the National Audit Office discovered that our reports were constructive and even helpful. The Labour government had a series of quangos who were supposed to do what we were doing but they were completely useless until the present one, the Regulatory Policy Committee under Michael Gibbons, finally arrived to bring some commonsense to government regulatory impact assessment.

We also did a similar but EU-wide report for Eurochambres, the EU counterpart of the BCC.[†] The most interesting was on de-regulation.[††] One can slow the additions to the bath, so to speak, of regulation but what about getting rid of the existing bathwater? The Coalition government is now trying to do something about that, such

---

* An accounting professor at Manchester Business School.

[†] Tim Ambler, Francis Chittenden and Asif Bashir, Counting the Cost of EU Regulation to Business, Eurochambres, May 2009.

[††] Deregulation or Déjà Vu? UK Deregulation Initiatives 1987/2006, British Chambers of Commerce, January 2007.

as 'one in and one out' and regulatory budgets. It is too soon to judge if these are working but the previous government only had one shot at it in 2006. We asked those in charge what they had learned from previous de-regulatory studies and efforts. The response was that they knew nothing about them and did not intend to find out as the Minister wanted a paper by the following week.

In other words, it was all for show and had no substance. We were riled by that and agreed with BCC that we should review what had been done before and draw conclusions.

Before 2010, the last serious effort had been by John Major's government. The project was directed by Lord (John) Sainsbury who could not have been more helpful in our effort in the same direction for the BCC. He made all his files available and commented on our work as did Robin (now Lord) Butler, Cabinet Secretary to Thatcher, Major and Blair. They invited business to identify regulations to remove and achieved about 200 unduplicated suggestions. Where the civil servants could kill the suggestions off quickly, they did so. The others they undertook to consider further. So far as we could discover, not a single one resulted in a withdrawn regulation.

As the report's title, Deja Vu, indicated, we knew the then current Labour government review would achieve nothing and so, indeed, it proved. Incredibly, they made the process for annulling a regulation, however trivial, even more difficult than introducing a new one. Something much more radical was needed and only, so far as we knew, New Zealand had done it. Taking one department at a time, the government announced that all business regulation under the charge of that department would be nul and void in a year's time apart from those regulations rescued and justified by that department's civil servants. It worked fine and anything short of that, including what the Coalition is doing, is merely tinkering. Parliament must take much of the blame. MPs have the right to object to new secondary legislation, i.e. regulations, but they do not do so.

Being part of the EU should make that easier. There is a widespread myth that the EU is responsible for our undoubted over-regulation. That is not the case because a single market, as the EU is supposed to be, needs a single set of regulations. Otherwise it is not a single market. Of course they should be fewer but that is not the point: Whitehall produces twice as many business regulations as Brussels and they are all unnecessary. In a single market, if a regulation is required in country A, it is needed in all the other countries. Likewise if it is not needed in country A, the other countries do not need it either. A single market, in short, is defined by having a single set of regulations.

When Britain had ruled half the world 100 years earlier, we had a small fraction of the current British civil service. Governments, whether national or EU, are factories for making rules. Now that Brussels are making our rules, we do not need Whitehall to be doing so too.

Directives are technically different from Regulations and can be implemented differently in different countries and a manifestly a bad idea as it allows politicians to fudge agreements without agreeing common standards.

So the Big Idea would be, for a start, to eliminate any UK business regulation not required in the rest of the EU. Needless to say, we got little traction for this simple concept. The present Minister responsible, Francis Maude, is certainly doing a better job than he did on this same topic as part of Lord Sainsbury team but whether it will have any substance, remains to be seen.

The detail for each of our reports was done, as their final projects, by Manchester Business School MBAs. There were a whole number of reasons why the work was more suitable for them than my School's MBAs and, under Francis's supervision, they did it well. I wrote the higher level stuff, the criticisms and the recommendations. Altogether it was a happy partnership and BCC rewarded Francis, our wives and me with tickets for a Royal Garden party. It was a blistering hot day but otherwise a lot of fun.

In 2010, Sally had left and having done what we could, we said our adieus.

My first ASI paper with Boyfield dealt with regulators, such as Ofwat, rather than regulations. As regulators deal mostly with large companies whereas BCC's members are largely small businesses, BCC was not interested in regulators. My colleague David (now Lord) Currie, an economist, set up a unit at our School to work with regulators, before going on the create Ofcom. There is now a whole school of academics in this area including a department at the University of East Anglia, headed by Professor Catherine Waddams. Winston Fletcher's daughter Amelia is now, after being Chief Economist at the Office of Fair Trading, Professor of Competition Policy there but I do not know where she is personally on regulatory matters. She has an unusual CV for an economics professor: 'Amelia Fletcher is a British singer, songwriter, guitarist, and economist.' (Wikipedia)

Needless to say, whilst Currie and co regard regulators as a good thing and the more we have and the bigger they are, the better, Boyfield, the ASI and I like to remind people that Thatcher only invented them as pathways to competition. They were supposed to achieve competition in each of their markets and then leave the stage. Our paper drew attention to their exponential growth without being accountable to anyone (they are independent of government at least in theory) or under any balancing controls.*

My ASI focus since then has been on the financial services sector and particularly on banks, including the Bank of England, and the Financial Services Authority. To cut a long story short, a large reason, arguably the largest reason, was regulatory – not a failure of the regulations (which were basically fine) but a failure of the regulators to do what they are paid to do. The US ones got it wrong first but the performance by the UK regulators, notably the Bank of England and the FSA was even worse and much later. It seems as if it was only the US regulators that shook them out of their lethargy.

Gordon Brown has to take part of the blame for allowing the credit and housing bubbles and creating the FSA and thereby causing confusion within both FSA and Bank of England.

I suppose HM Treasury is ultimately to blame as they are supposed to be overseeing the regulators. Brown neutralised their effectiveness further by stipulating they should regulate with a light touch, i.e. no one was to do anything beyond ticking boxes.

Sadly, the Coalition is little better on these matters so I have plenty of scope. Before coming to power the Tories announced the FSA would be closed down but then they lost their nerve and, hydra-like, created three new monsters in its place. Their prescriptions for improvement are, mostly, the right medicine at the wrong time and only likely to make things worse. For example telling the banks to build capital, at a time they do not need to do so, aggravates their new-found reluctance to lend precisely at the time that small businesses and the economy most need it. Likewise the silly debate about separating retail and wholesale banks: this is not now the issue.

But enough of all that for here. Producing the reports and blogs

---

* Road Map to Reform: Deregulation, Adam Smith Institute, 18 February 2005

keeps me amused as well as, I hope, followers of the ASI.

The idea that regulation should be left to the EU invariably raises atavistic nationalist emotions however irrational they may be. It is an identity problem: atavists want all England, say, to be exactly the same, with no postcode lotteries, and at the same time utterly different from, say, Calais. Americans, with the possible exception of Texans, identify with the US first and the state second. I do not support the United States of Europe concept nor political integration but I do follow the logic of a single market requiring only, and indeed being defined by, a single set of regulations.

Looking back on my tussles with Whitehall, some conclusions have been thrown into relief. Maybe they are not original but they are important for the economic survival of this country. Civil servants are, usually, bright, nice, well-intentioned and hard working and yet they are every bit as obstructive to the development of this country as the trade unions. The reason is simple: like any other biological organism, their dominant instinct is to perpetuate their existence and, preferably to grow in size. They have no overall performance measure as commerce has with profit. Professor Parkinson studied the civil service *en route* to publicising his famous law: work expands to fill the time available.

As noted at the start of this chapter, civil servants have developed cunning skills in training new ministers to the way things are done, or should, according to their civil servants be done, in government. Ideas developed in opposition are rapidly abandoned.

The large consultancy firms get the vast majority of their new business, year after year, from the same clients. Yes they are professional and well-intentioned and yes, they do try to complete each allocated mission but their over-riding determination is to ensure their geese keep providing golden eggs. They aim to work themselves into the DNA of their clients, not work themselves out.

So it is with civil servants, ever helpful to ministers who come up with new ideas and especially new ideas that distract them from their main goals. As we discovered from the counter-productive attempts to reduce regulation, the long grass is a valuable asset for the civil service. A few projects get terminated in that new laws or regulations are passed but many more are being 'worked on' for eternity.

Oddly, civil servants are missing a trick in the work expansion game by seeing legislation as the end of their responsibility. They are supposed to follow up legislation, after a sensible interval, to see if it achieves the intentions. Regulation reformers have long asked for the inclusion of sunset clauses to ensure this follow up takes place and automatically repeal any ineffective legislation. Civil servants hate sunset clauses and 12 years after the Blair government pronounced that they would be standard practice, few have ever been included, still less acted upon.

The two campaigns in which I have been involved and described in this chapter are cutting regulation and downsizing government.

Creating one set of regulations once in Brussels should be a lot more efficient and consistent than creating 27 inconsistent sets. We need to be a lot clearer on what are 'market' matters that should be left to Brussels and what are political matters, such as national taxes and expenditure, which should be left to member states. So far as the UK is concerned the latter category should be left with Parliament. Take the two together and we do not need a civil service at all.

In particular, we do not need the Foreign and Commonwealth Office*, the MoD†, the Departments for Business, Culture, Education, Health and Local Government. Of course Councils would be required to hand Treasury money over to front line services but that should be a quick and simple allocation procedure, not a round the year way of life for luvvies as the Arts Council is.

Like many other aging executives, I felt I should, to use the ghastly cliché, 'put something back'. Downside has sponsored a boys' boxing club in Bermondsey for over 100 years. The School has limited day-to-day involvement: it offers an annual camp for a number of the boys, one of the monks to be a Trustee, on the management committee and a link in general. Dom James Hood, Gus's housemaster, carried this out as well as he could and as well as the Club could expect given the relative indifference from the rest of the Abbey and School who never seemed to grasp the strategic importance of being seen to contribute to society's less favoured citizens. It was obvious then, and has become more obvious since, that governments will attack private education unless they have a defensive shield of good works. After all, that was what private education was about in the first place: the

---

* That has been made redundant by modern communications not that they were achieving much in the first place.

† In my researches, recently retired service chiefs agreed that the armed forces would be better off taking care of themselves and their own procurement.

wealthy had private tutors but charities provided education for the less fortunate.

The Club was short of a Treasurer, my name was put forward and accepted. Most of the funding came from the local council which first reduced and then eliminated it. One could argue their priorities: keeping boys out of trouble between school and bedtime should have been a high one. We fought hard, with some help from the MP, Simon Hughes, but we failed.

Taking their money away did not inhibit the council in their instructions for the club in the very least. Their main, and my favourite, representative was, in her tight leather outfit, quite an attractive woman of the most extreme left wing, politically correct persuasion. One of the numerous reasons she did not return my ardour was, or so I was told, because she was gay. Another may have been that my youthful good looks had departed, if they ever existed, long since. A third was that she saw me as a stereotypical public school businessman of the type she most disliked. A fourth and possibly critical factor was my pleasure in winding her up. She was wonderfully predictable and it took but little to send her into orbit.

Strangely we acceded to so many of the council's requirements even when they had no sanctions against us. They had already removed the money. But we did need to fit in with the local community – that was what we were for, and my colleagues were probably right.

The first demand was that the Club should teach other gender matters, i.e. the Club should take on the job of explaining lesbianism to the boys. We could see where this was coming from but it made no sense. Ours was a Roman Catholic all male club run under the supervision of a Benedictine monastery. Well at least, the council person said, we should have an active lesbian on the management committee. We said we thought we already had one and the subject went quietly away.

Then we were told the Club should have girl members, not just boys. As it was essentially a boxing club and the local girls preferred to watch rather than participate in boxing, we explained that was a problem. Eventually we started to have girls' nights and peace was restored. They might have enjoyed our insights on lesbianism but they never got the chance to find out.

Then they wanted some club members, i.e. the boys, to be on the management committee so they could understand how the club was run and why decisions were made. That was no problem for us but the boys found it boring and rarely showed up. On one occasion, they didn't and the council person demanded to know why not. Lucky again, the door opened at that moment and two of our oldest, blackest and most massive heavyweight boxers strolled in. In fact they were a couple of lovely lads but you would never have guessed from their demeanour. Menacing was the word.

'This lady says we are not allowing you to participate in the management of this Club. What do you say to that?'

'Well, it's rubbish, innit.' With which they sat down beside her and we never heard another word.

My reports to the committee rarely changed: 'we are about to go broke'. We had a flurry over whether we would be personally accountable for the shortfall but it turned out we weren't. Somehow cash trickled in but not without huge efforts. The annual boxing black tie dinner night in the West End was a big contributor, not that I ever enjoyed boxing or even watching it.

The Club was a huge multi-storey building about halfway between two stations-to-be on the new Jubilee line: London Bridge and Bermondsey. Gentrification was already slowly creeping our way and eventually the building would be worth a fortune. We explored mergers with other Clubs but they were in a worse state. After my ten years were up and by then spending hardly any time in London, I quit the Treasurership although I'm still a Trustee (I think). After my time, the new management team did effect the necessary mergers and, so far as I know, the Club not just survives but is in good shape. Luckily, boxing has become more popular again.

Most of the youth work in the Club is done by volunteers and they all deserve to go to heaven. They are generous people. What used to drive me crazy was that the boys' parents and other relations refused to play any part other than show up to see their boys' performances. Their view was that they were entitled to the Club and its activities without any contribution, financial or otherwise, from them. They could just sit at home. It was OK for strangers, many from far away, to take care of their children without any reward so that they did not have the bother. Television has a lot to answer for. Everyone told me I'd never crack this problem. I tried but they were right.

Perhaps the one part of the job where I can award myself a gold star was keeping our Chairman in order. Robin Gowlland had been a very successful headhunter and since then had had a number of other business interests but the Club was his baby. He had been involved for 30 years and Chairman for about half of that. Robin is a dear friend and a generous man but like a number of us veterans, he does like to get his own way. He is, you might say, stubborn. Always polite, he does not take 'no' for an answer. If he appears to concede, you can bet he will attack from a different angle in 20 minutes time. He was in the Royal Navy and big ships do not turn fast, nor are they impressed by being completely outnumbered.

One consequence was that meetings took far longer than they should have done. We could not blame the boys for not showing up. I think my matching Robin's firepower may have been the main reason my colleagues were sorry to see me go. I did return, some years later, to help Robin rescue the Club from a really dreadful development plan proposed by Robin's successor and supported by the management committee. It would have lost the Club's identity and ownership of the building. The Abbot was reluctant to get involved and many others agreed with both sides. It was a long and bloody battle but Robin won and all is now, so far as I know, as it should be.

Another occupation for aging executives is non-executive board membership. In theory, non execs are buffers, elderly or otherwise, between management and shareholders. The modern infatuation with the word 'governance', the subject of so much wasted board time, spells it out. Non execs are supposed to represent shareholder interests and ensure high business standards. Mostly that does work but sometimes, as with the major banks in 2005/8, it conspicuously does not.

No doubt non execs have many other uses too but one is their specialist expertise. Younger top management, it is thought, should be touching the cloaks of their predecessors so that their strength and wisdom can be passed on; they should be burning to know. This is, of course, mostly rubbish. When I was a young turk, the last thing I wanted was sage advice from my elders.

But there are exceptions. David Miller and David Thompson, Chairman and CEO of Wolverhampton and Dudley Breweries*, recognised that their marketing needed beefing up and thought I could help. Thompson is a hereditary member of the beerage; he hunts, shoots and may well fish. At the same time he is independent

---

* WMTB took over Marston's and then, in 2007, adopted that name for the group.

and very intelligent. Miller is Thompson's uncle and this, though a major public company, was still, in the 1990s, a family business and there was a discernible gap between the two family members and the other executive directors.

Traditional standards have a lot going for them. Matters were decided by consensus, not majority and, if board meetings went into the afternoon, Havanas were on offer. The most important business of the day took place at noon precisely when the Head Brewer would enter with a tray of pints of that morning's bitter. One day it failed to arrive. The increasingly distrait directors looked at one another and Thompson's presentation was losing our attention. The penny dropped:

'I've told the Head Brewer not to intrude on our meetings in future. It is a disruption we really cannot afford.'

The ensuing uproar showed the importance of decision-making by consensus. The Head Brewer returned at the next meeting.

The business was very efficiently run and costs kept down so that, in the early 1990s, Banks's mild could still sell at 99p a pint whereas draught beer was two or three times that price in the south-east.

When I joined, most of the meeting was taken up by the accounts and the details of each new pub or site to be acquired. Whilst the former were of some interest, the latter were of none as we non execs did not know where these dismal parts of the west midlands were, never mind whether they needed more pubs or not. More importantly, there was nothing the non-execs could contribute on these matters.

Ways in old breweries do not change fast but in due course an executive committee was created to give more authority to the executive directors and to keep detail to the level where it can be constructively addressed. And of course the idea was also to make space for strategic and marketing matters on the board's agenda. Company boards get into routines and rarely step back and consider, from a zero base, how best their time could be used. The accounts in particular take up far too much time and drearily report what has happened. Plans rarely present different options for board consideration. As my own experience of the damn things bears out, plans are written to be accepted. Provided they come up with the right bottom line, the more familiar they are the less likely they are to be challenged. Inviting the board themselves to think about the options would be far too perilous.

In particular, boards rarely discuss marketing. Boards are indeed concerned with the company's money but this can be discussed in only three ways: counting it (financial accounts), spending it or wondering where it comes from and how that can be increased, namely marketing. As noted earlier, only 15% of board time is typically on marketing.

Miller and Thompson are exceptions to the general rules above. Thompson is always keen to explore new ideas; strategy and marketing did now come to the board table. The next step was to find an executive marketing director, never an easy job, but eventually achieved to everyone's satisfaction.

After two three-year terms, my job was done. The train up from London was fine but when we moved to Norfolk, the cross-country drive was a nightmare. What I did miss was witnessing the warmth that a local brewery company can have with its community, be they employees, shareholders, publicans or consumers. Loyalty was very real and never more obvious than at the funeral of Teddy Thompson, David's father. And I miss the vintage port too. County brewery boardrooms' loyalty to vintage port may well go back 200 years. Lunch with tankards of bitter followed by 20-year-old port may seem strange but it has much to commend it.

Infighting within the upper echelons of Conservative Party was small beer beside what we could manage in the North Norfolk constituency. Strangely it had been a Labour seat until Ralph Howell chipped away at it and eventually, in 1970, won the seat which he held for 27 years with increasing majorities. North Norfolk, like traditional brewers, is not big on change.

David Prior won in 1997 but, undermined some say by his own HQ in Cromer, the Conservatives were defeated by the Lib Dems under Norman Lamb in 2001. Prior had never really integrated with the constituency and becoming deputy party chairman too soon kept him in London. Some entirely accurate, but nonetheless rude remarks about Cromer did not help either.

The obvious candidate to succeed him was Olga Maitland* who had long weekended in North Norfolk, had been an MP, was well known as a journalist, a big personality, outgoing and feisty. Party HQ said she was too old and Cromer HQ went along with that. That was ridiculous: she was the one person who could have defeated Nor-

---

* Lady Olga Maitland is married to barrister Robin Hay and the daughter of the 17th Earl of Lauderdale.

man Lamb. Whatever her age was, she looked a lot younger.

Next up was Iain Dale, again a big personality but part of the Westminster Village, not North Norfolk. The local chairman, aware he is gay, forgot to mention it to anyone until after Dale was adopted. Many parts of the country have outgrown concern about such matters but North Norfolk is not one of them. Be that as it may, and despite heroic efforts on his part, he had one of the worst results of any Conservative candidate in the 2005 election. Again, some say, he was undermined by his own HQ.

By now, Tory Central Office had declared that North Norfolk was unwinnable. Norman Lamb was well established and was proving to be a good constituency MP. Ambitious Tory candidates stayed away, with one exception. Trevor Ivory lived in Norwich, moved to the constituency and has a delightful wife and son. He is young, enthusiastic and was duly adopted. The local Chairman, Alan Duncan, invited Raymond Monbiot and me to apply our marketing skills to help get him elected.

Monbiot is probably the only other Senior Fellow of the Marketing Society in Norfolk. He learned his marketing from J Lyons & Co (1956-78), Associated Biscuits (1978-82) and Campbell's Soups (1983-88). He was Deputy Chairman of the Conservative Party (2003-06). Thus he brought not only marketing skills but also political know-how and contacts.

Monbiot is a delight to know and work with. Obviously we have a lot in common but while we were doing our best, the in-fighting within Cromer HQ continued merrily and Ivory was left to do his own thing. One way and another, it was mission impossible. The one good thing that has come out of it is friendship with a most congenial neighbour.

Perhaps these memoirs should end here, for this was the end of my life as a marketeer. As Enoch Powell pointed out 'All political lives, unless they are cut off in midstream at a happy juncture, end in failure, because that is the nature of politics and of human affairs.' But I was a marketeer, not a politician. In marketing, failures lead to success whereas in politics, success leads to failure. This last time I was not lucky but that is not a cloud over 40 years of good fortune.

The Afterword shows how this good fortune continued into retired life in Norfolk.

# Afterword

## Is Norfolk the end of the World?

*Our Norfolk home sits 1° East of the Prime Meridian. If you carry on up this line, Norway is to the East and the Faroe Islands to the West. There is no actual land until you start coming down the other side of the planet. So in one sense Norfolk really is the end of the world – but it does have its compensations. This Afterword covers retirement life on this last terra firma and begins with*

- *Gus gets his own family*
- *The move to Norfolk*
- *The CRAFT Club*
- *Debden migrants to Cley next the Sea*
- *Retired US marketeers*
- *Music matters*

Gus's time with DTZ deteriorated with the commercial property slowdown, no fault of either. In 2005, he was seconded to Budapest and dealt with their property interests across Eastern Europe. Budapest was an interesting place to work and for us to visit but not a long-term option so far as Gus was concerned. By then he was engaged to the lovely and delightful Viola (on 16th February 2005). She was from Münster but long resident in London where they decided to remain.

It was a copybook engagement. Viola thought they were going to Bath but it turned out to be the Georges V in Paris with Gus down on one knee offering his grandmother's ring, as is the German custom. (I'd nicked it from Katie's jewel case). A waiter took the photos.

The wedding on 8th October was copybook too. Münster was too distant for their friends and Viola chose the huge medieval Cley church whose curate, Jo Fawcett, would conduct the service assisted by the catholic Fr Michael Simison who would also deliver the sermon. Viola's parents, Professor Helmut and Regina Arntzen, are Lutheran. Getting permission for a service in an Anglican church involving mixed denominations and nationalities, was a nightmare. It turned out they needed certificates of approval from two archbishops – Canterbury and Westminster.

# Afterword

Good at it as he is, I have since learned to be wary of Helmut's speechmaking. No matter how informal the dinner, he is liable to rise to his feet at the end of it and produce a wad of notes from his pocket.

New wife, new life. With the continuing slump in commercial property, Gus decided to leave DTZ and strike out on his own. Their daughter Helena arrived on 25th July 2007 and son Zachary arrived three years and a few hours later in the same room at St Thomas's.

Every grandparent remarks on the pleasure of watching the grandchildren grow up without, usually, any real responsibility. So it is with godchildren. Mark Swabey, now in his 60s, has become a computer whizz with no sign of slowing down. Gregory Stevenson became an accountant like his grandfather. The lovely Felicity Cross became a dentist. Lucky patients. Jonathan Brackenbury more than succeeded in the City. Jonathan Wells was a Westminster Cathedral chorister and still sings well. He developed an amazing business importing weird artefacts from Africa and South America. Strange that there's good money in that but it seems there is. All have married and familied well save Bertie Archer who has now left Exeter and found himself in DEFRA. I suppose someone has to. Marriage looms in 2014.

Life can have a pleasing circularity. People from one's youth, or their children, re-appear after losing touch. The Argonauts at St John's, the Gurkha officer from Singapore insulted by the presence of my platoon, Michael Biscoe and Robin Butler from my prep school and Winston Fletcher's daughter Amelia coming to UEA. In September 2013 I returned to Ardkinglas and caught up with cousin Sarah after 70 years. This circularity is a universal experience; it is, after all what reunions are made of. And we all tell each other that 'you haven't changed a bit'.

One such ongoing reunion is with fellow members of the Lotos Eaters and a few other contemporaries from Downside. We lunch together in London twice a year. Peter Molony began them and when decrepitude set in, Simon Bingham, now Lord Clanmorris, has been in charge. Wine has been of a high standard partly due to Simon's wish to use up the bin ends from his cellar without wasting them on women. The other source of the finest wines, and even vintage cognacs, is Nick Sibley who had the good sense to marry Sally, the older daughter of Keith Stevens, my first IDV employer and MD of Corney and Barrow of which Nick now is the major shareholder.

Other regular attenders include Paul Focke (QC), (Dr) John Keenan, Nick Reynolds and (Sir) Michael Wakeford.

Early in the 1990s, we decided we would be retiring to North Norfolk and found a larger house to replace our cottage. Katie wanted a good sized garden and I wanted a room big enough for a snooker table. We opted for a farmhouse, Swan Lodge, in Cley parish but midway towards Holt.

The garden was not big enough for the tennis court we thought we needed and I approached Tony Blount to buy a corner of his neighbouring field. He was a man of even fewer words then than now and I barely knew him. The appointment was for a Saturday morning in his very small farm office. He sat in one corner and I had the one diagonally opposite with the farm manager working on the books at the desk in between and pretending not to be listening. I was in my sole tweed suit and had been honing my countryside chat about the weather and state of the crops.

Blount said nothing and quite soon my countryside chat ran out. It was time to get to the point and I explained our need for a tennis court and his lack of need for the bottom corner of the field.

'Would, by any chance, you be prepared to sell it to us?'

'No.' That seemed to be his only, and therefore his last, word on the subject and I got up to go muttering something inane about what a pleasure it had all been.

'I would be prepared to sell you the bottom half of the field there. Of course, I would wish to retain shooting rights.'

'Well that's no problem. How big is it?'

'I've no idea.' Silence resumed and I think how we are going to take this further. Blount speaks again: 'You weren't going to talk about price, were you?'

That clearly would have been vulgar and I said of course I would not dream of such a thing. He gave me his lawyer's contacts details and I assured him mine would make contact.

Back home Katie asked how I got on.

'We've bought not the tennis court but the field. I don't know how big it is or what we are paying.'

We inherited the gardener, Count Paul Henriksen von Kleinert. His father was Prussian via a schloss in Bohemia. He didn't like what Hitler was up to and came over in the 1930s. He did valiant service for the Allies in the war but, thereafter, resumed his life as a musician.

# Afterword

Paul's English mother was a singing teacher and it was no surprise that Paul is director of his (catholic) church choir as well as an accomplished pianist and organist. And a senior scoutleader. And can turn his hand to pretty much anything else. Lucky us.

In the twenty years he has been with us, Katie has persuaded him not to stand to attention and click his heels when being given orders and not to trim any vegetation in sight into parade ground squares.

My golf is so bad I am lucky anyone will play with me but three regulars are Tony Pepper (ex textiles), Martin Freeth (previously agent for the Earl of Leicester at Holkham, the largest North Norfolk stately home) and Keith Robinson (who has done everything including selling glass bottles to IDV). Originally, we played for small stakes and fines which were sent annually to charity via the CRAFT* club of which we were all members. The CRAFT club proved such a success that the founders closed it down when they no longer could remember who the members were. We still have the ties, an annual luncheon and monthly golf but donations are no longer accepted.

Whilst the golfing four may be the only local alumni of the CRAFT club, almost all my contemporaries can be considered honorary members. The other three members of our regular bridge four are (in order of first meeting them) Nigel Jenney, Richard Jefferson and Rupert Travis.

Nigel is co-godfather to my one-time flatmate's, Martin Wells's, son Jonathan. Possibly the only time I saw him between then and Norfolk was when Martin and Nigel dropped in for a quick reviver when we were in St John's Wood. In the condition they were in, the last thing they needed was more of the same but they survived the experience. They were colleagues in the oil and chemicals bulk storage business, originally Tar Residuals.

By the time we met up again, Nigel was in course of retiring once he had achieved the sale of the remaining parts of the business to the Mexican part-owners, the huge state fuel business. The Mexicans have no word for manana which conveys quite the same sense of urgency. Periods of dormancy alternated with flurries of activity but, apart from generating fees for professional services, nothing much actually happened. Fifteen years later, closure was finally achieved but I would not be in the least surprised if the phoenix bursts out of

---

* Can't Remember A Fucking Thing.

the ashes.

Nigel read Greats and married young. Perhaps too young, as it did not last. His second wife Kate and he were happily married with three delightful daughters. An unkind fate took her away far too young.

The bridge table is not the only venue for our senior moments. Nigel tells of being at a party in Cambridge when he spotted a very attractive woman across the room and, as one does, sidled across.

'Forgive me,' said Jenney, 'I cannot quite place the name but I'm sure we have met.'

'We certainly have. We were married for two years.'

Richard is the only Cantabrigian at the otherwise dark blue table, the only one with a cricket blue and the only one who has opened the bowling for Surrey. Nigel used to turn his arm over and Rupert occasionally keeps wicket but neither at such an exalted level. The great radio cricket commentator, John Arlott, did not just think he should have played for England but that 'he may well have been the greatest loss to English cricket in the post-war period'.*

His wife Pauline also, very sadly, died young but their four handsome and talented children, two of each sex, are great support. The youngest, Will, was the tallest first class cricketer in the world and also would have played for England if he had not been plagued by injuries. Although a very fine opening bat with a string of centuries, Will has had to retire early and is now a top cadre coach.

One of Richard's claims to fame was, this being the pre-helmet era, removing the front teeth of one Garfield Sobers, the greatest West Indian all-rounder ever.

It is extraordinary how these links come around, but the final member of the bridge four, Rupert Travis, is a great friend and long-time colleague of Denis Cross, member of Crombleford at Downside. Both worked at Hambros and lived beside Wandsworth Common. Rupert is not a man who does things by half. In addition to the above, he skis, plays tennis, and is a lay preacher and a founder director of Victory Housing Trust, the company that acquired all the Council houses in North Norfolk. He also gives time to the Tallow Chandlers Company where he was Master, to the Norfolk Churches Trust and I'd not be surprised by any other activity I may have overlooked. Importantly, he is a noted driver – a driver of cars, of golf balls and of sailing boats where he maintains an unrivalled record.

---

* 'Richard Jefferson' from CricketArchive

# Afterword

Michael Biscoe re-emerged into my life in Debden by which time he was married to Kari and had two children, Guy and Henrietta. Both tall and handsome Kari and Michael made an imposing couple but they were not alike in all respects. Michael is an architect, and therefore a man of elegant taste and refinement, including in his wines, and an arbitrator in building and property matters. A past Master of the Leathersellers company, he is immensely respectable.

Kari, however, made even me blush. 50% Norwegian she had an open approach to matters sexual and considered that they should be freely discussed. Thank goodness they both had a strong sense of humour. Otherwise their 40 years of marriage would not have survived the first. Katie reckons such things go in threes and Kari was the third wife in our small group to be lost to cancer. All three were incredibly brave.

The Biscoes had been drawn to North Norfolk by Mary Norwak who was originally with us all in Debden but moved in the 1970s to Cley in order to educate her children at Greshams.* Mary was formidable. Her husband died young leaving her penniless with three small children. A journalist by training, she turned to cookery writing and had the good fortune to write the definitive book on the best use of home freezers just as they were becoming popular. Although sylph-like as a girl, and probably when she worked for Vogue, by the time we met her, she had the shape and firepower of a Sherman tank. She was not a woman to cross.

She bought Cley Old Hall from the Blount family when Tony's father died and became, de facto, queen of Cley. She took charge of the Village Hall, the WI, the church, Cley Amateur Dramatic Society, the Cley branch of the Conservative Party and the Parish Council, not to mention the Saturday stalls on the village green. The Rector and the villagers, mostly immigrants to North Norfolk, got their orders and mostly complied, albeit not without the occasional grumble.

Amongst many disgraceful evenings with the Biscoes were a couple of New Year's Eve fancy dress parties at the Chelsea Arts Club. It is, or was, notoriously louche and no matter how badly one normally behaves, for the Arts Club it should be worse.

A capital investment in a bishop's outfit would see me through all future fancy dress parties, so I sent IDV's head driver down, with my credit card, to buy one from J Wippell and Company, the posh cleri-

---

* The public school in Holt, two or three miles away.

cal outfitters.

'Tell them,' I said, 'that a bishop is staying with me and we are giving a dance but he left his evening wear at home. These are his measurements. And if they press you on who the bishop is then say he's the Bishop of...(casting around for a distant spot)...Mauritius.'

The driver was muttering darkly when he returned with the goods and informed me that he would not be undertaking any such missions in future. The gentlemen of Wippell had given him a hard time. Apparently the then Bishop of Mauritius was Trevor Huddlestone who was well known to them as being eight inches taller and eight inches thinner than the measures I had provided.

At the Chelsea Arts Club, everyone dances with everyone (and you can read that how you like). One exceptionally pretty girl, and fine dancer, seemed strangely drawn to me. The reason arrived all too soon. She wanted my advice, or so she said. This is a fancy dress party and I assume she is playing along with my bishopric, so to speak. By the time I discovered she was deadly serious, I was in too deep. Her large and muscular boyfriend looked threatening.

This was a Bertie Wooster moment. There was only one thing for it: be a real bishop. After all, Anglican bishops customarily wrap things up in cotton wool and I made my advice as arcane as I could. She wanted to know how to get her local clergyman to marry them when she had been married already. Thanks to Jason, I had some experience in this matter.

'Now, you mustn't mention my name, my dear, but here's what you should do...'

Of course it was all in confidence and I cannot therefore share it with you. She went off happy enough and I sometimes wonder what happened next. Katie banned me from any further appearances at the Chelsea Arts Club New Year's Eve Ball.

One could list the other Debden migrants to North Norfolk but I will just mention Tony and Cherry Vernon with whom we have shared many holidays and opera evenings. As personnel director in a City merchant bank, Tony spotted a niche market providing reliable data to the boards of public companies to help them establish directors' pay and perks. He set up shop in the 1970s and by the end of the 1980s had published half a dozen books on the subject and become the leading expert, or at least one of them.

It is an important specialist consultancy role but also a neat way to make money. Which kind of pay advice does a PLC board admire? The 11th Lord Vernon, when not attending sheep and grandchildren, now pedals his bicycle madly from Land's End to John O' Groats. Cherry meanwhile is an acclaimed textile artist specialising in quilting.

Old marketeers certainly die but, until then, they tend not to fade away. This section recounts a little about three anglophile American booze marketeers: Bill Elliott, Bill Seawright and Jack Keenan.

You may recall that Elliott was Marketing Vice President of Heublein. According to an obituary: 'Recognized as 'Man of the Year' by Advertising Age in 1982, he was widely regarded as one of the most creative minds in the industry and developed numerous marketing opportunities for products such as Smirnoff Vodka, Black Velvet, Yukon Jack and others.' But he proved too eccentric for the corporation and went off to do his own thing, mostly inventing and launching new brands. His son, Bill Jr, was a sales manager with a wholesaler and that helped. Rumpleminze peppermint schnapps was his big success and we acquired that for sale by Paddington.

Bill died on 4th February 2009, aged 78. We remember especially the lovely lazy days boating with him on the Connecticut River in late summer.

Bill Seawright worked with Bill Elliott for 20 years or so but on the international side of Heublein, in Brazil and travelling the world for Smirnoff. Both were keen on, and experts in, wine and cooking, both had small boats and loved shooting, both were creative and good at launching new brands and each with a Bill Jr. who was a sales manager in a large wholesaler, although the Seawright one switched later to imports. Inevitably the two did not get on and we had to be careful not to mention either in front of the other.

The aftermath of the Heublein acquisition was rocky but one bright spot was the appointment of Bill Seawright to succeed Peter Thompson as CEO of Paddington. Peter had never really adapted to the pressures of IDV or the thuggery of the US liquor trade. He was as nice as nice people go and, as nice people go, he went.* Seawright, always an IDVophile, fitted Paddington like a well worn glove. Among his many successes there was the introduction of Goldschläger but this came about in a curious way.

---

* Sorry, Saki.

Paddington had the number two brand of Sambuca, Sambuca Romana, but it was being challenged by a black version launched by Allied. Paddington wanted a black version too.

'No,' said I, 'we don't copy others, we lead.'

After some toing and froing, I suggested we countered with a premium Black Sambuca, the premium being justified by including real gold leaf in the manner of Goldwasser*, which had no competitor at the time. That was agreed.

A few days later, I was wandering around the R&D labs and was attracted, as one is, by a blonde in a white coat wielding a razor blade.

'That looks interesting. What are you doing?'

'I'm cutting up gold leaf to put in Black Sambuca which some idiot at HQ thinks is a good idea. Any fool would realise that you cannot see gold leaf in a black liquid.'

I beat a hasty retreat and our me-too Black Romana was duly launched without the gold leaf. It may have slowed the Allied one but no more.

Coincidentally or otherwise this gold leaf idea struck home. Paddington came up with a 'schnapps' partner for Rumpleminze, same strength, sweetness, usage and target market, namely Goldschläger, with fragments of gold leaf in a sweet cinnamon 'schnapps'. The liquid looked like Goldwasser but the bottle had a handsome bell shape, based on the hammer used to beat out the gold. It proved a winner.

The third American booze brand warrior is Jack Keenan. To quote from the Stock Spirits Group[†] which he joined as Chairman in 2008: 'After retiring as Chairman of Kraft International in early 1996, he joined the board of Grand Metropolitan PLC., becoming CEO of their global wine and spirits business. There he led the consolidation of global drinks by merging the businesses of Grand Met and Guinness in 1997 (to form Diageo) and leading the acquisition of Seagrams.'

'Jack received his MBA from Harvard Business School and is now the Patron of the Centre for International Business and Management and chairman of the Harry Hansen Research Fellowship Trust, both

---

* The authentic (400 year old, supposedly) gold leaf liqueur from Danzig.

[†] http://www.stockspirits.com/en/executives/7-Jack-Keenan-

at Cambridge University.'

In effect, Keenan was my successor's successor, albeit in a more senior capacity. We met in passing once or twice after his appointment but he showed no interest in learning from my wisdom. David Gluckman and Chris Nadin chipped away at that and, eventually, Gluckman, Keenan and I had a series of dinners together. Keenan, surprisingly given his background, is a great wine buff and gourmet. He has the finest cellar in Suffolk and maybe in East Anglia. His wife Lynda's culinary expertise played a part in bringing them together. Her other great love is dressage. She keeps a fine stable of, in a good year, international level horses and has a professional dressage trainer.

After rubbishing ex-colleagues about whom we had remarkably similar views, discussions turned to Gluckman's favourite topic, cricket – which turned out to be Keenan's too. The Keenans are not only anglophile; Jack is the world's greatest amateur expert on the rules of cricket. These days we meet mostly at Lord's and the Oval and it is a continuing pleasure to watch the amazement of the cricket fans around us when this American corrects them on the finer points.

Katie had told me to find something new to do in retirement and writing music was it. Step 1 was becoming deputy organist at our little Catholic church in Blakeney. When the organist, well, keyboardist, was away, hymn singing was even more cacophonous than usual. I cannot play any musical instrument but my computer could download hymns from cyberspace.

Choirs also provided an outlet for an untalented singer. Angela Dugdale directs the Kelling Singers. Trained at the Royal College, despite being deaf for much of that time, she ran the Broadland Singers, one of the top East Anglian choirs, before being persuaded by John Arkell, the talented incoming headmaster at Greshams, to sort out the music department. She refused the permanent job but agreed to give him two years to transform the situation. Job done she recruited the talented Mark Jones to do the job and the school has produced outstanding singers ever since.

The Kelling Singers were expanded to include men when Angela started giving one of Bach's major choral works each Good Friday. The Matthew and John Passions rotated with the B Minor Mass. The choir became popular, too popular, and, when she and husband Keith downsized, so did the choir. Somehow I survived the cut.

At the same time she trained to become a vicar. When the health of the parish priest failed, she conducted the services in the three church-es of the parish, running between altar, organ and pulpit. Her MBE was richly deserved.

Nigel Jenney and Mark Jones run the Christmas Iceni Choir, a small group founded partly so that Nigel's three daughters, all excel-lent singers, could display their talents at two Nine Lessons and Car-ols services. Nigel, Robin Waters and I provide most of the bass department in the rehearsals until, fortunately, we are reinforced for the main events by some of Mark's ex pupils who do not seem to need rehearsals.

Playing with my new computer-linked keyboard, music composition did not look that difficult. Matthew Martin, then the organist at Westminster Cathedral, allowed himself to be talked into giving les-sons. Katie thought this was a bit of a cheek and she was, of course, right. Angela recommended an elementary text book. I also attempt-ed the wonderfully named Gradus Ad Parnassum by Johann Fux, the famous 1725 elementary (supposedly) textbook on counterpoint which Mozart had used as a child. Mozart being rather better at this than me was no surprise and I soon gave that up.

At that time, Julian Cotton, my old flatmate, was dallying with another newly nubile American girlfriend. Her older sister, Gabriele, had died in a car crash and the family were desolated. I volunteered to write a short anthem in her honour for her memorial service. Mad-ness of course but Matthew and some stanzas from Tennyson's In Memoriam came to my assistance. It worked and the family was gra-cious.

Martin Baker, the Cathedral's Master of Music, was minded to be helpful due to my sponsoring Peter Maxwell Davies to write a Mass as a memorial for my parents. Stretching a point or two, he agreed to have his choir perform my Ave Verum. The professional lay clerks discovered that, even with Matthew's help, a few errors (parallel fifths in particular) had slipped past (later corrected) but they were more amused than annoyed. They later sang my Gate of the Year anthem.

Martin Baker has also been immensely supportive and helpful. I had no idea that being a cathedral director of music was such a com-plex job. These lessons seemed to inspire Matthew to do more com-position himself. He is quite a musician with a string of awards from the Royal Academy where he studied and I'm delighted that his music is being commissioned at the highest levels.

I was now on a roll. Angela had engaged a recently arrived professional soprano, the lovely Jayne May-Sysum, for an Advent Sunday service at Binham. When we all repaired to the pub afterwards, I approached her with a proposition. If she nominated her favourite poem, I would put it to music for her to sing. Not many professional singers, I know now, would agree to that but Jayne is an enthusiast and we had been in the pub quite a while. Angela told me later that Jayne had called her for the phone number of rather a strange man who had approached her in the pub.

'That can only be Tim Ambler.'

So 'The Heart that Flutters' was born and Jayne gave it a stunning performance at her next concert in Letheringsett, her home village.

I was lucky in my composition training. Matthew got me off to a great start but London was too far to go. John Mason, the occasional organist at St Botolph's in nearby Trunch and previously a director of music in several schools of note, became my next mentor. A great choice as he was used to dealing with primitive musicians. He deserves most of any credit my efforts have elicited.

I am not listing all the ups and downs of my compositions as that would be wearisome. There were many more downs than ups. One such 'up' was, thanks to Ed Armitage, a trumpet, organ and choir piece on a published CD. Another was the acceptance of choral works, five years in a row, by the London Festival of Contemporary Church Music. Its Director, Chris Batchelor, is now my hero.

Norfolk has not proved to be end of the world any more than was Chelsea's 'World's End', where I lived as a child. The latter area took its name, of course, from its pub. For someone lucky enough to have spent much of my life marketing the products of public houses, that too has a pleasing circularity.

As Shakespeare pointed out, music is the food of love but liquor was quicker.

# Index

# Index

# Index